1001 BIZARRE ROCK 'N' ROLL STORIES

First published in 2013 by
Carlton Books
An imprint of the Carlton Publishing Group
20 Mortimer Street
London W1T 3JW

ISBN 978-1-78097-279-4

Printed and bound by CPI Group (UK) Ltd, Croydon, CR0 4YY

1001 BIZARRE ROCK 'N' ROLL STORIES

Robert Lodge

CARLTON BOOKS

"Rock 'n' roll is all about looking good, living fast and dying young."

Joe Jackson

Introduction

Who hasn't dreamed of becoming a rock 'n' roll star? The limos, world tours, pampered lifestyles and adoring fans have an enduring appeal that continues to capture our imaginations. With every whim catered for it is a job like no other but there's an extra special talent truly to living a rock 'n' roll lifestyle of excess, more excess and excessive excess. That's when rock stars do the stuff we only dream of – and then much more.

Loyal to the holy trinity of sex, drugs and rock 'n' roll, this book delves deep into the often murky world of rock and pop, the highs, the lows, the triumphs and the tragedies.

We have thrust adulation on rock stars, given them wealth beyond their wildest dreams and carte blanche to be way out, spaced out, bizarre, mad and bad. As you will find here, rock stars and musicians live life to the limit then push life and living to the extreme.

As a fully paid-up member of the 'Rock 'n' Roll Generation' I was there when much of what is between these covers happened. I cried when Buddy Holly, Elvis and John Lennon died; roared when Keith Moon drove a limousine into a swimming pool; and shook my head in disbelief at the many other rock headlines.

As the lusty infant that was rock 'n' roll screamed its way into being so did I and I have trailed along the rock and pop road ever since as record buyer, journalist, record reviewer, DJ and bedroom guitarist.

Researching this book crystallized for me that there must be a special rock gene making its exponents talented, obsessive and maybe just a little bit mad. I am convinced that their hearts pound to a totally different beat.

But I'll let a line from the Who's 1965 'My Generation' sum up the rock 'n' roll philosophy – "I hope I die before I get old".

As for me, if there's a rock 'n' roll heaven, roll over Beethoven, I want to go there.

Robert Lodge, 2013

The King dies on the throne

As one of the greatest names in rock 'n' roll the manner of Elvis Presley's demise was so ignominious. After years of addiction to prescription drugs and faced with a fast-fading career, a bloated Presley died after falling off the toilet at his Graceland home on 16 August 1977. It is alleged that Presley was found with his trousers around his ankles and had 14 different drugs in his system, 10 in significant quantity. Stunned fans the world over couldn't believe such a humiliating end had befallen the King.

The not-so-Fab Four

For four years in the early 1960s appearances by the Beatles brought fans around the world to the edge of hysteria. But an early performance by the band left one record label's artist and repertoire (A&R) man unimpressed. They emerged rejected and crestfallen from an audition for Decca Records in London in 1962. Despite a 15-song set that included some of their own compositions, their manager Brian Epstein was told: "Guitar groups are on the way out." With those words Decca executive Dick Rowe famously became 'the man who turned down the Beatles'. Rowe's judgement was not that flawed, however, as he later signed the Rolling Stones for Decca, ironically on the recommendation of Beatle lead guitarist George Harrison.

Tugged to his death

Death by tugboat has to be one of the most uncommon demises – even in rock 'n' roll circles. But a Mississippi river tug was involved in the death of Jeff Buckley aged just 30 in 1997. The singer-songwriter had gone swimming fully clothed and wearing boots at a favourite spot in Wolf River Harbor near Memphis, Tennessee. A roadie from Buckley's band was watching him swim but had momentarily looked away as a tugboat passed and, by then, Buckley had disappeared. It took four days before the body was found and a post-mortem found no trace of drink or drugs in Buckley's system. A verdict of accidental drowning was handed down by the coroner on Buckley.

Wilson's paternal lawsuit

One-time leader of the Beach Boys, Brian Wilson, sued his own father. The Californian group which rose to fame on the surfing sounds of the early 1960s was famous for being a family affair with Brian, his brothers, Dennis and Carl Wilson and cousin Mike Love forming the backbone of the band. But in the 1990s Brian went to court to regain his rights to the publishing company, Sea of Tunes, which owned the copyrights to most of the Beach Boys' hit songs, some of them money-spinning million sellers. The suit stemmed from Wilson's allegedly forced decision to sign over his publishing rights to his father Murry Wilson in 1969. A court found that the contract Brian Wilson had signed was not valid because of the mental problems he was suffering at the time and although Wilson junior failed to regain the copyrights, he won a $25 million settlement.

Seat switch saves Jennings

Country singer and guitarist Waylon Jennings had an extra 43 years of life because he gave up a seat on a doomed air flight to a friend – and was haunted by the experience for the rest of his days. Jennings was in Buddy Holly's backing group the Crickets on tour in 1959 when he gave up a seat on the fatal flight that killed Holly and support acts Ritchie Valens and J.P. 'The Big Bopper' Richardson. Jennings, who instead endured the trip in a freezing cold tour bus through the snowy northern states of the USA, lived until 2002 but was haunted by comments made on the day Holly died. When Jennings agreed to go by road, Holly joked that he hoped the bus would freeze up. Equally jokingly and without malice, Jennings responded that he hoped the plane crashed – and regretted the comment for the rest of his days.

Daniel's a long player

Irish singer Daniel O'Donnell created a record in his homeland in 2012 by having an album in the Republic of Ireland national charts for 25 years in succession.

High pilot kills rocker Rhoads

The burgeoning career of heavy metal guitarist Randy Rhoads was cut short when his aeroplane crashed into his own tour bus. In 1982, while touring with former Black Sabbath frontman Ozzy Osbourne, Rhoads was in Florida with his new band mates. Rhoads was talked into taking a joyride in a light aircraft owned by tour bus driver Andrew Aycock. But once in the air, Aycock at the controls decided to 'buzz' the tour bus where other band members were sleeping. The plane's wing clipped the bus and crashed in a huge fireball. Rhoads, 25, Aycock and another passenger all died and Aycock was later found to have had cocaine in his system.

Patsy's prophecy?

The last song country star Patsy Cline sang on stage was 'I Fall to Pieces' on 3 March 1963 – two days later Patsy's mangled remains were found in the wreckage of a light aircraft at Camden, Tennessee. As a standard part of her repertoire Patsy had sung the song at the end of a benefit gig in Kansas City before flying home on her last fateful trip.

Alice chickens out

American rocker Alice Cooper took some time to deny that he killed a chicken on stage. The chicken incident during a Toronto gig in 1969 caused a worldwide media furore but was great publicity for Cooper's emerging career. It put Cooper, real name Vincent Damon Furnier, into the top echelons of 'shock rock'. After basking in the notoriety for several decades, however, he later denied media claims that he either killed the chicken or drank its blood on stage. He said he threw it into the front row of the hysterical audience thinking it would fly away but, he said, it was killed by fans in front of the stage, including several in wheelchairs.

No closure for the Doors' Jim

At the time of his death on 3 July 1971, the Doors frontman Jim Morrison had been living in Paris for months escaping the suffocation of fame and detoxing from his alcohol and drugs habits. Though his longtime girlfriend Pamela Courson told French police that Morrison hadn't been using drugs, she confessed to friends that they had snorted heroin after a night of drinking. According to her, she got Morrison into a bath before she fell into a drug-induced sleep. She awoke to found him unresponsive. Incredibly Morrison's body was never autopsied and after a limited investigation, the Paris authorities ruled his death due to heart failure. In the ensuing years many fans have cast doubt on Courson's story but she was not around for much longer after Morrison's death to answer any questions. She died of a heroin overdose in 1974. Inevitably urban myth grew up around Morrison with claims he never died at all but merely disappeared from the intense pressures of the rock world.

A lie starts a pop career

Rick Nelson's music career started with a fib to a girlfriend. Irked in 1956 that the girl he wanted to impress thought Elvis Presley was fabulous, the 16-year-old Nelson boasted that he was also going to cut a record. At that time it wasn't true but, within a year, he had a record deal and a chart-topping debut album and, within two years, a number-one single in the US charts. Nelson's hits during the 1960s and 1970s included 'Poor Little Fool' and 'Hello Mary Lou'.

Drink-dive kills Beach Boy

Beach Boy Dennis Wilson drowned diving for items he had thrown overboard from his yacht – three years previously. A notoriously heavy drinker, he died in 1983, shortly after his 39th birthday, at Marina Del Rey near Los Angeles. After drinking all day he decided to recover items he had thrown overboard at the marina in 1980. The drummer, keyboard player and singer with the Beach Boys was buried at sea off the California coast in the ocean that killed him.

Parsons' body goes missing

Loyal friends tried to fulfil Gram Parsons' burial wishes – by stealing his body. Parsons, who abused a variety of drugs and alcohol, had made his name as a guitarist, pianist and songwriter with US west coast bands the Byrds and Flying Burrito Brothers. He was fascinated with California's Joshua Tree National Monument and spent days at a time there searching for UFOs. On his death – ironically at the Joshua Tree Inn – aged just 26 in 1973 from a drugs and alcohol overdose his family wanted Parsons buried in Louisiana. But friends stole his body from Los Angeles Airport in a borrowed hearse and drove it to the national park where they tried unsuccessfully to cremate it. Caught by police, they were fined for stealing a coffin as, incredibly, there was no law about stealing a body or leaving 35lbs of charred human remains lying around a popular tourist spot.

Lesley comes out

Forty years after her first big hit single Lesley Gore came out as a lesbian in 2005. Not that it was much of a surprise because she had been hosting an American TV show of lesbian, gay, bisexual and transsexual issues for a year and had been living with a same-sex partner for 23 years. A 1964 album by Gore was appropriately called *Girl Talk*.

Armstrong meltdown

Six months after an amazing on-stage meltdown Green Day frontman Billie Joe Armstrong admitted to his booze and prescription drug abuse that led him to rehab. In 2012 during a performance at the iHeartRadio festival he smashed his guitar and shouted: "I'm not f***ing Justin Bieber, you mother***rs!" In 2013 a contrite Armstrong said that because of his addiction: "I couldn't predict where I was going to end up at the end of the night."

Manics' star disappears

Manic Street Preachers' lyricist and rhythm guitarist Richey Edwards mysteriously vanished during a period of depression on 1 February 1995. Two weeks later Edwards' car was found at a service station near the Severn Bridge, a renowned suicide location in western England. It was widely believed that he took his own life by jumping from the bridge and in November 2008, 13 years after his disappearance, he was officially presumed dead. Later, bones on the banks of the Bristol Channel, near the bridge, were thought to be Richey's but tests proved otherwise.

Smith's death mystery

Mystery will probably forever surround the death of former Heatmiser front man Elliott Smith. Girlfriend Jennifer Chiba emerged from a shower in October 2003 to find singer-songwriter Smith, 34, with two stabs to the chest and a note alluding to suicide. The note read: "I'm so sorry–love, Elliott. God forgive me," but the authorities investigating the death were not totally convinced of the suicide scenario. A police chief said: "Several aspects of the circumstances are atypical of suicide and raise the possibility of homicide." Added to that an autopsy questioned the absence of hesitation wounds; the fact that Smith stabbed himself through his clothing; and the presence of "possible defensive wounds" on his right arm and left hand. A long-term drug addiction had made Smith unstable to a point where he struggled to remember lyrics and stay conscious on stage but by the time of his death he had managed to sober up and no alcohol or illegal substances were discovered in Smith's body. Chiba said she heard Smith scream and found him still standing with a kitchen knife in his chest.

Sound fishy?

Incredibly reggae master Bob Marley had a parasitic crustacean named after him. *Gnathia marleyi* infests and feeds on the blood of certain species of Caribbean fish.

Brown is pissed off

Singer Bobby Brown's reaction to being arrested after a high-speed car chase in Florida in 1996 was to urinate in the back of a police squad car.

Chucking money Berry's way

Chuck Berry was known to be watchful of any infringements of his songwriting royalties – even if he was behind bars. Berry was in jail in 1964 when new band the Beach Boys appropriated Berry's 'Sweet Little Sixteen' music, added new lyrics and launched it as 'Surfin' USA'. Berry sued and won back royalties and sole songwriter credit.

Thunders' death leaves questions

The death of former New York Dolls member and frontman of the Heartbreakers Johnny Thunders left behind a cluster of possibilities as to the cause. Thunders, 38, could have been murdered in a New Orleans hotel room in April 1991. Or he could have died from a methadone overdose. Or from advanced leukaemia. There was morbid interest in the punk songwriter's death because it was some time before the body was discovered and his remains were described as 'U-shaped' and shaped like a 'pretzel' such was the extent of rigor mortis. After his death a syringe was found floating in his toilet and there were several vials of methadone lying around. However, his autopsy stated that the amount of drugs in his system wasn't lethal; instead his death is suspected to have been caused by leukaemia. A murder theory surfaced later when, in his autobiography, Dee Dee Ramone of the American punk band the Ramones said Johnny was mixed up with "some bastards" – presumably drug dealers – claiming they had ripped him off for his methadone, then murdered him.

Picketed Pistols

Carol singers and Christian ministers picketed the venue for a Sex Pistols concert in south Wales in 1976.

Mum 'helped' Sid Vicious die?

It was alleged that the mother of the Sex Pistols' Sid Vicious helped her son overdose on heroin to escape prison. Anne Beverly, herself a long-term heroin abuser, reportedly admitted supplying the drug and administering a lethal dose to her son in February 1979. Vicious, real name John Ritchie, was due to stand trial for the murder in New York of his girlfriend Nancy Spungen in October 1978. Vicious had been granted bail and his new girlfriend Michele Robinson threw him a party to celebrate. It is claimed that Beverly brought her son a package of heroin and watched him inject it. The next morning Vicious was dead. The admission is said to have come prior to her own death, also of a heroin overdose in 1996, because she wanted to spare him from life in prison. In denying Nancy's murder, Vicious claimed to have awoken from a drugged stupor to find Nancy with a single stab wound to her abdomen and she appeared to have bled to death. The knife used had been bought by Vicious.

Battling Brian

The Beatles' manager Brian Epstein was so convinced of his band's potential that he was prepared to put up his own money after the Decca record label failed to offer John, Paul, George and Ringo a contract. Refusing to give up, Epstein travelled back to London for further meetings with Decca, even promising the label's sales team that he would buy 3,000 copies of any single they released.

Howzat brother?

The Gallagher brothers who headed up the Britpop band Oasis were notoriously short tempered even with each other. There are many stories circulated about Noel and Liam coming to blows but it has been reported that in the 1990s Noel once famously broke Liam's foot with – a cricket bat. It seems Liam had brought drinking pals from a pub to a studio where Noel was working. This irritated Noel who was said to have taken a cricket swing at Liam.

Sex clash ends in death

Stumbling across a couple having sex led to the death of folk singer Tim Buckley in June 1975. Buckley, who was into experimental rock, funk and soul, was drinking heavily with his band when he walked in on long-time friend Richard Keeling having sex, which led to an argument. In order to placate him, Buckley was handed a large dose of heroin and, according to reports, challenged to "take it all". He did, and was later taken home in a bad condition. Buckley's wife Judy put him to bed and later found him dead.

Crossing lives

Associations with rival Elvis Presley were eerily close for 1950–60s American singer Rick Nelson. The two heartthrob singers vied for places in late-1950s pop charts and Nelson worked with Presley's backing singers the Jordanaires and guitarist Scotty Moore. When Presley died in 1977 Nelson, who was trying to revive his flagging career, was signed up by Elvis' former manager Colonel Tom Parker and dubbed by the media the 'New Elvis'. Sadly, like Elvis, he died young. Aged just 45, he perished in a plane crash in 1985.

Flaming Jacko

Michael Jackson was badly burned when his hair caught fire during the filming of a Pepsi Cola advert in 1984. The cause of the blaze was not known but the gel on his hair was well alight causing second-degree neck and scalp burns.

Kelly acquitted

After years of pre-trial delays and a three-week hearing a Chicago jury in 2008 took just a day to acquit singer R Kelly of 14 charges of involvement with child pornography.

Fan flare for Frank

The Mothers of Invention took a gamble when they played at a Swiss casino in September 1971. While appearing at the Casino Montreux with frontman Frank Zappa in fine form, a fan let off a flare which burned down the building and destroyed all the Mothers' equipment.

Great Korea move

South Korean rapper Psy earned the dance hit of 2012 with sleepless nights. Psy, whose real name is Park Jae-sang, claimed he stayed up for 30 nights developing the horse-riding dance for his high-energy worldwide hit 'Gangnam Style'. He said he tried unsuccessfully basing the dance on elephants, monkeys, kangaroos, snakes, falling leaves and even the moon. 'Gangnam Style' became the most watched and 'liked' video in YouTube history.

Punk suicides

The British punk scene lost the frontmen of two emerging bands within weeks of each other in 1980. Both Ian Curtis, 24, of Joy Division and Malcolm Owen, 26, of the Ruts were touted as heading for the top before they both died by their own hand. Curtis, an epileptic and a depressive, hanged himself in his kitchen in May while Owen, in poor health and a heroin addict, overdosed on the drug and died in his parents' bathroom in July. Ironically for Malcolm, 'H-eyes', the B-side of their first single 'In a Rut', was a song against heroin use. Two other Ruts' songs, 'Dope for Guns' from the album *The Crack* and the reggae-styled 'Love in Vein', had an anti-drug message.

Selena honoured

One of the top Latin music artists of the 1990s, Selena Quintanilla-Pérez, was honoured in 2011 by being on a US Postal Service stamp. She was shot dead in 1995 aged just 23.

Flying was tricky for Ricky

1950s hit-making vocalist Ricky Nelson dreaded flying – ultimately with good reason. The added problem was that he also refused to travel the hard way by bus with his band back and forth across the USA on their many tours. So, despite his fears and 30 years into his career in 1985, he leased a luxurious but ageing, 14-seat Douglas DC-3 that once belonged to pianist rocker Jerry Lee Lewis. It is not known if Nelson was made aware of the 1944-built Dakota's troubled mechanical history. The plane crashed into trees near De Kalb, Texas less than two miles from the safety of a runway, killing seven, including Nelson and all the members of his band.

'Twat' gets respectable

A spoken song called 'Twat' shocked Britain in the late 1970s because of its reference to female genitalia but two decades later it achieved respectability in education. Written by John Cooper Clarke, known as the Bard of Salford (a town near Manchester, England), 'Twat' was eventually put on Britain's GCSE examination syllabus for 16–17-year-olds. Cooper Clarke, also known as the 'Punk Poet', worked with many of the top bands of the British punk era including the Buzzcocks and Joy Division, which also hailed from the musically fertile punk scene of the north-west of England.

'Oh Well' did well

A single that band members didn't rate went on to huge success for the early incarnation of British band Fleetwood Mac. Drummer Mick Fleetwood reckoned 'Oh Well Part One' was so innovative for 1969 that it wasn't worth releasing. But composer, guitarist and singer Peter Green, stood by his brainchild. It was at number two in the UK charts for two weeks, went to number one in the Netherlands, top 10 in Germany and top 100 in the USA.

Pussies pay for their riot

Few musicians go to jail for their art but members of a political punk band ended up incarcerated in Russia in 2012. The Moscow-based feminist punk rock collective Pussy Riot comprised approximately 12 members, who wore brightly coloured balaclavas and used only nicknames during interviews. They had a reputation for staging unauthorized provocative guerrilla performances in unusual public locations, which were edited into music videos and posted on the Internet. Their lyrical themes included feminism, lesbian, gay, bisexual and transsexual rights. On 21 February 2012, five members of the group staged a performance in Moscow's Cathedral of Christ the Saviour and the women said their protest was directed at the Orthodox Church leaders' support for President Putin during his election campaign. But they were criticizing the most powerful man in Russia and the authorities pounced. Three group members, Nadezhda Tolokonnikova, Maria Alyokhina and Yekaterina Samutsevich, were jailed for up to two years for hooliganism by religious hatred although Samutsevich was later freed on probation and her sentence suspended.

The wonders of YouTube

Elvis Presley duetted with his daughter 35 years after his death – thanks to the wonders of 21st-century technology. Computer graphics artists put a seamless 2012 video on YouTube in which Lisa Marie, who was 11 when her father died in 1977, walks as a woman into her father's famous live 1968 performance of 'Blue Christmas'. Lisa Marie's recording of the song was made in 1986 but the electronic union between father and daughter was unique.

Tracks of tears

Canadian punk guitarist Alex Soria died when he was run over by a train in 2004 at St Henri near Montreal. He was songwriter for a number of bands including The Nils.

Unlucky 13 for Jerry Lee

A controversial marriage reduced piano rock 'n' roller Jerry Lee Lewis from $10,000-a-night concerts to $250 spots in beer joints and small clubs – because his bride was just 13 – and his first cousin twice removed. Lewis, 22 at the time, married his third wife Myra Gale Brown in 1957 but it was later revealed that she wasn't 15 years old as the couple claimed. In the uproar concerts were cancelled and Lewis songs, such as 'Great Balls of Fire', 'Whole Lotta Shakin' Goin On', 'Breathless' and 'High School Confidential', were blacklisted by radio stations and TV hosts. The marriage to Myra lasted 13 years.

Gaye's long suicide bid

Soul and R&B singer Marvin Gaye spent almost two decades trying to take his own life but ironically when he did die it was at the hands of his own father. Marvin, whose hits included 'I Heard It Through the Grapevine', died on 1 April 1984 from two shots fired by his father, also called Marvin, after a day of bitter rows at the family home. Marvin Jr had battled depression and drug problems throughout his life yet recorded some of the most iconic songs of his era. He had first tried to end his life with a gun in the late 1960s while on a bad LSD trip. In 1979, Gaye attempted suicide a second time by ingesting an ounce of cocaine while in Hawaii and four days before he was shot by his father in his Los Angeles home he threw himself out of a speeding car only to suffer bruises. Friends said later that even his ultimate death was a "premeditated suicide" because the handgun that killed him was bought by Gaye and given to his father – ostensibly for his protection. Marvin Sr served five years' probation after pleading guilty to involuntary manslaughter.

Janis' shame

Plagued by acne and constantly battling weight gain Janis Joplin suffered the horror in the early 1960s of being voted 'Ugliest Man on Campus' in a college poll at Port Arthur Texas. Small wonder a nervous breakdown and heroin addiction followed.

Lynott's back in town

Few rock musicians get a statue dedicated to them in their home town but Thin Lizzy frontman Phil Lynott is in some illustrious company in Dublin. The capital of the Irish Republic has honoured the late singer and bass guitarist with a statue in Harry Street. Other creative greats forged in bronze include James Joyce, Oscar Wilde and the fictitious Molly Malone of the 'Cockles and Mussels' traditional song. Lynott died aged 36 in 1986, 11 days after collapsing from a drink and drug binge.

Roy was a spectacle

Roy Orbison's trademark dark glasses were not the result of an eye disorder, it seems. The affectation came about because the clear Buddy Holly-style specs he usually wore were lost before a concert in the mid-1960s. So Orbison, whose hits included 'Oh, Pretty Woman', 'Only the Lonely' and 'Running Scared', put on a pair of dark glasses and the idea stuck. Orbison died of a heart attack aged 52 in 1988.

Peter's a strapping lad

New Order's Peter Hook had the reputation of wearing his bass guitar the lowest in the rock and pop business. Hook, who started his chart success with the ill-fated Manchester band Joy Division, said in a 2012 interview that he actually liked his strap as long as possible and achieved it by strapping together two normal-length ones. He said the inspiration for his trademark was his mother, who once told him: "You need a gimmick."

Sandy keeps drumming

Losing his right foot and part of the leg didn't stop drummer Sandy Nelson. He was severely injured on a motorcycle in 1963 at the height of his fame but he fought his disability and continued to release albums into the 1970s. He even learned to play keyboards.

Long story of a band name

A hatred of long hair won a place in pop history for American physical education teacher Leonard Skinner. In 1970 a bunch of ex-pupils of Robert E. Lee High School in Jacksonville, Florida were brainstorming for a name for the rock band they had formed and decided on 'Leonard Skinner' as a mocking tribute to the teacher who was notorious for his strict enforcement of the school's policy against boys having long hair. With a later adjustment to the spelling of the name the band became Lynyrd Skynyrd and went on to notch up three double platinum plus platinum and gold albums as well as hit singles 'Sweet Home Alabama' and 'Free Bird'. Despite their high-school acrimony, the band developed a friendlier relationship with Skinner in later years, and even invited him to introduce them at a concert at the Jacksonville Memorial Coliseum.

One-armed drummer wonder

Drummer Rick Allen was not going to let a little thing like losing an arm interfere with riding the wave of success with British rock band Def Leppard. Allen lost his arm in a car crash in England on 31 December 1984 and was lucky not to be killed when his high-powered Chevrolet Corvette smashed through a wall near the city of Sheffield. The drummer realized that he could use his legs to do some of the drumming work previously done with his arm and had a customized drum kit made to suit his needs.

Fatal cut of the cards

An ill-fated gamble led to the death of Metallica's bass player Cliff Burton in bizarre circumstances in 1986. While on a tour, band members drew cards to see which bunk of the tour bus they would sleep in. Burton won and chose to sleep in lead guitarist Kirk Hammett's bunk. Around dawn on 27 September near Dörarp, Sweden, the bus driver lost control and skidded, which caused the bus to roll over several times. Drummer Lars Ulrich, Hammett, and lead vocalist and rhythm guitarist James Hetfield sustained no serious injuries but Burton was crushed to death under the bus.

Oh, pretty vehicle

Singer Roy Orbison, who started his music career alongside Elvis Presley, was fascinated with machines – especially motorcycles and cars. He was famous for following a car that he liked and making the driver an offer for it on the spot.

Grunge life takes toll on Cobain

Mystery still surrounds the death of Nirvana frontman Kurt Cobain in 1994. The body of Cobain, the grunge band's principal songwriter, was discovered at his Seattle home three days after he apparently committed suicide on 8 April with a shotgun blast to the head. A note was found nearby. The Seattle authorities officially concluded it was suicide but this has since been disputed by a private detective working for the Cobain family. At the time of writing no further proof has been established.

Gaye's baby fix

A complex arrangement of surrogacy led to the birth of soul singer Marvin Gaye's son Marvin Gaye III in 1965. At the time Marvin II, whose hits have included 'Let's Get It On' and 'Sexual Healing', was married to Anna Gordy, the sister of Motown label founder Berry, but she could not have children. A deal was struck with Anna's niece Denise to be the biological mother of Marvin III.

Orbison tragedies

Singer Roy Orbison suffered many personal tragedies in his life – losing a wife and two sons. He was just repairing his faltering marriage to wife Claudette when she was killed in a motorcycle accident on 6 June 1966. They were riding home near Bristol, Tennessee when Claudette was struck by a truck and died instantly. Just two years later on 16 September 1968 and during a tour of England, he received the news that his home in Hendersonville, Tennessee, had burned down and his two eldest sons had died. His youngest son, Wesley, survived.

Zappa zapped by fan

Frank Zappa's life was devastated by an overzealous fan at a concert in 1971. An audience member pushed the multi-instrumentalist frontman of the Mothers of Invention off the stage down into the concrete-floored orchestra pit during an encore at London's Rainbow Theatre in December. The injuries he received were devastating. It was feared Zappa was dead as he had serious fractures, head trauma and injuries to his back, leg and neck. Worst of all was the fractured larynx which made his voice drop by a third. It was September 1972 before Zappa performed again wearing a leg brace, sporting a noticeable limp and unable to stand for very long because of constant back pain. With Zappa confined to a wheelchair for six months, the Mothers were left in limbo and eventually set out on their own.

Chapin death mystery

The world will never know for certain what killed folk-rock singer Harry Chapin in the USA in 1981. Chapin was dragged from the burning wreckage of a car crash on the Long Island Expressway near New York. Despite attempts to resuscitate him he died from a heart attack. But the mystery is whether he had a cardiac arrest before the crash or as a result. He was, seconds before the crash, seen to activate the hazard flashers on his Volkswagen before veering towards the centre lane, swerving left, then right again before ending up directly in the path of an articulated truck. Chapin's car burst into flames but the truck driver and a passer-by pulled Chapin out of the burning car through a window. Acknowledged workaholic Chapin's chart hits included 'W.O.L.D.' and 'The Cat's in the Cradle'. His widow Sandy won a $12 million pay-out in a negligence lawsuit from the owners of the truck.

Rod rings the changes

Despite his past reputation as a hard-drinking, hard-living rocker, Rod Stewart has always had a famously un-rock 'n' roll hobby. He loves making model railways.

Iggy pops out

Iggy Pop was exposed – quite literally – to controversy with his 'Kiss My Blood' video in 1991 because his penis was almost the star of the show. Directed by top music video director Tim Pope and filmed at Pop's much raved about Olympia concert in Paris, his exposed penis became a major talking point.

Green Day bash Bush

American punk band Green Day got into politics in 2004 with a musical attack on George W. Bush, who had been US President for four years. The band released *American Idiot* two months before Bush was re-elected. The album contained many protest songs, like 'Holiday' which was against George Bush's decision to invade Iraq.

Drumming the same beat

Jason Bonham took over the drums of Led Zeppelin, 32 years after the death of his father John who was the previous percussion incumbent. The son joined Jimmy Page, Robert Plant and John Paul Jones from the original Zeppelin line-up for a one-off reunion in 2012. John died in 1980 aged 32.

Pioneer Buddy is first to die

Rock 'n' roll lost one of its greatest pioneers – after a career of just 18 months. Buddy Holly died in a plane crash on 23 January 1959 as he was being ferried from a gig in Iowa to another in Minnesota. The pilot took off in a snowstorm when he was not qualified to fly on instruments only. Holly, from Texas, had made a huge impact on the rock 'n' roll scene in a short time with hits such as 'Raining in My Heart' and 'Peggy Sue'. The pilot plus fellow rockers Ritchie Valens and the Big Bopper also died in the snow that day. A few weeks later the crash that killed Buddy at just 22 years of age claimed another victim when Maria Elena, Holly's wife, miscarried their first child following the trauma of the tragedy.

Rap kidnap

A battle of Russian political rappers ended with one of them staring down the barrel of a gun. Miron Fyodorov, whose stage name is Oxxxymiron, was kidnapped in 2010 by a gang of supporters of another rapper and, at gunpoint, forced him to apologize for insulting the rival who had nationalist views that Miron didn't share. Roma Zhigan had eulogized President Vladimir Putin in his lyrics – a political stance Oxxxymiron found objectionable. Miron was unhurt in the incident but went on to take the Russian rap scene by storm in 2012 by winning top awards, amassing a huge following and getting more than a million hits for his music video 'Lie Detector'. He was later nonchalant about the kidnap and said in an interview: "No one got killed."

Alcoholic haze

Guns N' Roses bass player Duff McKagan confessed to the extent of his hard-living ways in the 1980s and 1990s. While touring during the period when the aptly titled *Appetite for Destruction* was a global hit Duff admitted taking cocaine and drinking four pints of vodka per day and later switching his daily tipple to 10 bottles of red wine. By 1994 he was in hospital with a ruptured pancreas and a doctor telling him never to drink alcohol again. He heeded the warning and adopted a healthy lifestyle.

Mourning Moon

Rod Stewart says he will never forget the last words he exchanged with the Who's late drummer Keith Moon. Back in the 1970s Faces singer Stewart shared a hard-drinking lifestyle with his contemporaries in the pop industry. Having had enough after an all-night session with Moon and others he tried to sneak away only to be spotted by Moon who shouted: "You fucking ponce, Stewart, come back and finish what you started!" Later in 1978 Moon was dead from a drug overdose.

Ozzy puts the bite on

Winged animals may have good reason to take flight when former Black Sabbath frontman Ozzy Osbourne is around. He is alleged to have bitten the head off a live bat during a concert in Des Moines, Iowa in January 1982. In his memoirs Osbourne backtracked on the notoriety by claiming he thought the bat was a rubber toy, while the fan who claimed to have thrown the bat on stage said he thought the animal was dead.

Pete's porn ordeal

The Who guitarist Pete Townshend was cautioned by the British police as part of a crackdown on child pornography. Townshend claimed it was research for his campaign against the widespread availability of child pornography on the Internet and he had not downloaded any images. A four-month police investigation confirmed that Townshend was not in possession of any illegal downloaded images but the police elected to caution him, stating that 'research' or 'curiosity' were not valid reasons to break the law.

Spector's a big shot

The gun obsession of celebrated record producer Phil Spector led to some scary moments for some of the artists he worked with, or so it is claimed. The temperamental genius of the pop world was alleged to often have a gun with him and to have produced it in the presence of Leonard Cohen and the Ramones. It was also alleged he actually fired a shot in the studio where he was working with John Lennon.

Iggy boldly goes into space

Iggy Pop was truly spaced out in 1998 when he made a guest appearance on *Star Trek: Deep Space Nine*. Pop played the alien Vorta in a New Year's Day episode based on the film *The Magnificent Seven* but entitled *The Magnificent Ferengi*.

Nugent confusion

Pro-military and Republican voter Ted Nugent has left the world confused over the real reason he didn't get drafted during the Vietnam War period in the 1970s. The former Amboy Dukes guitarist, who has had a long solo career, once claimed he avoided the draft by not brushing his teeth, bathing or combing his long hair and beard 30 days prior to his appearance before the draft board. He also claimed in an interview that in order to ensure getting an unfit for military service classification he ate nothing but high-fat junk food and drank nothing but cola and beer. Then, a week before his physical, he said only peed and defecated in his pants. Nugent has since claimed recently that he made this whole messy story up and actually had a student deferment. However, a copy of Nugent's Selective Service Record shows that he had at separate times both a 1-Y medical deferment and 2-S student deferment but that his last examination designated him 4-F (unfit for service).

Izzy sensible?

Guns N' Roses guitarist Izzy Stradlin is said to have hit on a cunning, if not quite sensible, plan when his manager told him to get rid of any drugs he might have before going into Japan, where customs officers were notoriously hot on searching rock stars. Stradlin put them where he knew he wouldn't lose them – he swallowed them. But apparently something went wrong inside and he is said to have woken up from a coma more than 96 hours later.

Crosby, Stills and Hash?

There seems to be rock credibility in claiming that you have smoked dope in the home of a US president – and it always seems to be in the time of hapless one-term President Jimmy Carter. There were claims that Crosby, Stills and Nash had performed at the White House in 1977 and, during a moment alone, smoked a joint in the Oval Office. Some years later, legendary country music singer Willie Nelson revealed in his biography that, while visiting Carter in the late 1970s, he also smoked marijuana there, but on the White House roof.

Mama Cass

A legend surrounding Cass Elliot may have come about as a result of a cruel and hurtful snub to the Mamas and the Papas' star. A bizarre story was built up that founder John Phillips wouldn't let her join the band because she couldn't hit the high notes their songs required. Then, the story goes, in 1965 Cass was hit on the head by a falling pipe, and when she recovered from the concussion she was miraculously able to sing the requisite notes. She joined the group and the rest is history with a string of hits including 'Monday, Monday'. Many have come to disbelieve the 'pipe-on-the-head' story as a cover to save the blushes of Phillips, whose real objection was that he thought she was 'too fat'.

Holiday Inn says "out"

British band the Who earned a worldwide bar from the Holiday Inn hotel chain after a momentous and unforgettable day of rock mayhem in September 1967. The Who were in the unsuspecting town of Flint, Michigan on the first of their US tours and on the 20th birthday of drummer Keith Moon a party started of epic proportions around which rock legends are built. More and more drink flowed, more and more people turned up at the party beside the hotel pool. People jumped fully dressed into the pool, and dozens of bottles of various alcoholic beverages were dumped in the waters. A giant cake presented to Moon by the Premier drum company was soon the ammunition for a massive bun fight. Ultimately, after more than a day of wild excess the hotel management wanted to call a halt to the revelry and rang the police. Apparently by this time a very drunk Moon was naked and ran to a luxury car which rolled back into the swimming pool when Keith released the handbrake. Moon might have been drunk but his survival instinct was intact and he managed to swim free of the fast sinking limousine. His further attempt to escape the police was, ironically, thwarted by slipping on a piece of birthday cake. The hotel bill for damages was reputed to be $24,000 (£15,000) and a ban for the Who from all Holiday Inn hotels as well as the town of Flint.

Man, that's loud!

American heavy metal band Manowar like to break records as well as ear drums. At the Magic Circle Fest in 2009 the rockers achieved a sound pressure level of 139 decibels during the sound check to become the loudest band EVER. In 1984 the band, which hails from Auburn, New York, was included in the *Guinness Book of World Records* for delivering the loudest performance, a record which they have since broken on two occasions. At the time of writing Manowar also hold the world record for the longest heavy metal concert after playing for five hours and a minute in Bulgaria in 2008.

Lost for ever

A huge part of rock history went up in flames in 1979. One of the biggest rock archives and memorabilia collections was in the house of blues guitarist John Mayall when it was destroyed by a brush fire in Laurel Canyon, California. Mayall was famous for his band the Bluesbreakers through which some of the greatest rock legends passed including Eric Clapton, Mick Fleetwood, Mick Taylor and Jack Bruce.

Chubby feeling cocky?

Chubby Checker went to great lengths to file a lawsuit over penises in 2013. The singer, who started the twist dance craze with a hit song of the same name, filed against a smartphone app called Chubby Checker which measures penis sizes. Seventy-one-year-old Checker, whose real name is Ernest Evans, was suing Hewlett Packard and a subsidiary for $500 million (£320 million) claiming the app associates his name with obscene, sexual connotation and images without giving compensation for the Chubby Checker name and trademark. In the USA a "chubby" is urban slang for an erection.

Beatle in a box

Although a world-famous rock star, Paul McCartney became an anonymous prisoner in a Tokyo jail cell for nine days in 1980. The Japanese customs service caused a global media frenzy when the ex-Beatle, then with his new band Wings, entered the country with a fist-sized bag of marijuana in his luggage. Unaware that the Japanese had a less liberal attitude towards drugs than other countries he had toured, McCartney got off lightly because after spending nine days in a cell he was put on a flight out of Japan where the maximum penalty at the time for drug smuggling was eight years.

Jerry Lee's a survivor

Rocker Jerry Lee Lewis had to wait until he was 77 before he achieved million-selling success with an album. The poignantly named *Last Man Standing* sold a million copies because Lewis was the last of the Sun Records 'Million Dollar Quartet' alive by 2012. The other artists on the iconic Memphis-based record label of the 1950s – Elvis Presley, Roy Orbison and Johnny Cash – had all passed away before him.

Off air

Memos that were circulated around radio stations after the 9/11 terror attack removed the Barenaked Ladies' 'Falling for the First Time' and Buddy Holly's 'That'll Be the Day' from DJ's playlists in 2001.

Members only club

Self-confessed groupie Cynthia Allbriton caused a sensation in the late 1960s by taking casts of rock stars' penises and testicles. With zany Frank Zappa as her mentor she became know as the 'Plaster Caster' and among her willing subjects were said to be members of the Monkees and Jimi Hendrix.

Elvis wasn't always top

Elvis Presley made his first public performance aged 10 at the Mississippi-Alabama Fair and Dairy Show in October 1945. Showing little sign of the legendary performance skills that made him 'The King of Rock 'n' Roll', the young Elvis was dressed as a cowboy and had to stand on a chair to reach the microphone and sing 'Old Shep'. He came only fifth in the kids' talent competition but years later he reprised the song into a hit with his fans.

Sounds like a family firm

Three brothers in the same band is rare in rock and pop circles and the most notable are the Gibb brothers of the enduring Bee Gees. But in the mid-1960s Simon Dupree and the Big Sound was a British psychedelic band formed by a trio of brothers – Derek, Phil and Ray Shulman on vocals; saxophone, trumpet; and guitar, violin, trumpet respectively.

David's a man of few words

Former the Byrds member David Crosby had a bizarre explanation for a car crash in 1982. Crosby had lost control of his car and crashed into a divider on a California freeway but when police asked him why cocaine and a gun had been found in his car, Crosby replied, "John Lennon". Lennon had been assassinated in New York in December 1980.

Skynyrd tragedy

The title of the album *Street Survivors*, released just three days before, was tragically ironic for rock band Lynyrd Skynyrd. On 20 October 1977 and five shows into their most successful headlining tour to date, Lynyrd Skynyrd's chartered aircraft crashed in a forest in Gillsburg, Mississippi after running out of fuel. Band members Ronnie Van Zant, Steve Gaines and Cassie Gaines were among six killed on impact and those who survived, including musicians Allen Collins, Gary Rossington, Leon Wilkeson, Billy Powell, Artimus Pyle and Leslie Hawkins, suffered serious injuries.

Guitar is a defining moment

Elvis Presley may owe his success to an 11th birthday present that he didn't want. The young Elvis, living in Tupelo, Mississippi, was disappointed to be given a guitar by parents Vernon and Gladys when he really wanted a rifle or a bicycle. But it was an inspirational gift as just a year later a classmate described him as "crazy about music". By 12 Elvis had made a live appearance on Tupelo local radio station WELO.

Voice problem is a Killer

The case of the disappearing voice meant one of the shortest rock concerts on record in 2012. The Killers' gig at the Manchester Arena in England was just 25 minutes old when the voice of lead singer Brandon Flowers seized up. No frontman means no gig so the US band apologized to the 21,000 fans and cancelled the performance.

Justin loses his roots?

The intellect of teen pop sensation Justin Bieber came under the spotlight in 2010 when he failed to understand what the word German meant. Canadian-born Bieber was asked in a New Zealand TV interview what his name meant in German. Whether it was the interviewer's strong Kiwi accent which threw him or not, the 16-year-old failed to grasp the word 'German'. Further ridicule was heaped on the young star, whose great grandfather was German, when he had to look at the interviewer's crib card to see what the word was and then blurted out: "We don't use that word in American." The interviewer claimed Bieber was German for 'basketball', but most dictionaries translate it as 'beaver'.

Batty cat

Singer Lesley Gore, who had a pop number one in many countries with 'It's My Party' in 1963, played Pussycat in two consecutive episodes of the 1960s TV adaptation of *Batman*.

Social hatred

Jealous teenage girls sent online death threats to 22-year-old American singer-songwriter Taylor Swift because she was dating one of their idols. The threats exploded after the media revealed that Swift was dating 18-year-old One Direction singer Harry Styles. The band's popularity with their – predominantly female – fans has been likened to 'Beatlemania'.

Trauma changes the law

The death of Buddy Holly in 1959 had the posthumous effect of changing the law in the USA. The shock death of Holly and others in a plane crash was announced to the media before Holly's bride of six months had been told. The trauma of finding out in this way led to Maria Elena miscarrying their first child. This prompted American authorities to change regulations so that no names are announced to the media until families have been informed first – something that is still in place today.

Unimpressed by Elvis

Fourteen years before the Beatles were rejected by Decca Records, Elvis Presley, who was to be dubbed 'The King of Rock 'n' Roll', was spectacularly failing to impress his music teacher at Humes High School in Memphis, Tennessee. In 1948, at the age of 13, Presley received only a C grade in music from a teacher who told him he had no aptitude for singing. The unique voice of Elvis went on to sell more than one billion records worldwide in a recording career that spanned 21 years.

Madonna and no child

Few music legends can have found themselves being blamed for causing a country's birth rate to fall. But it happened to raunchy rock star Madonna in 2012. Protesters launched a lawsuit claiming that Madonna's support for gay rights in Russia would affect the birth rate. It claimed Madonna's words at a St Petersburg concert would traumatize children but Russian judges threw out the action.

Woman-beater shamed

Rapper and singer Chris Brown became vilified as a woman-beater when pictures of his battered girlfriend were released across the world. Fellow singer Rihanna's face was shown severely battered and bruised in 2009 after a row with Virginia-born Brown developed into violence. He later pleaded guilty to felony assault and a plea bargain led to him accepting five years' probation and domestic violence counselling. The deal enraged organizations against domestic violence as not severe enough for the crime and three years later, despite his apologies to Rihanna and a 2013 reconciliation with her, Brown's career was still suffering.

Gang theory of Tupac death

The drive-by death of rapper Tupac Shakur remains a mystery 17 years on. A falling out between gangs is thought to have been the explanation for the shooting in a Las Vegas street in 1996. Tupac, who performed under the names of 2Pac and Makaveli, was gunned down in his car by attackers who pulled alongside and let loose a hail of automatic gun fire. Shakur, who had five million-selling albums released during his short career between 1991 and 1996, was hit in the chest, pelvis, lung, right hand and thigh and died in hospital six days later. Various theories about who was behind the assassination of Tupac included rival rappers and gangs but no one was charged with his murder and many of the people peripheral to the situation have since died in violent situations.

Flaming mistake

A whole US airport went into lockdown when a rock star landed – with a grenade in his luggage. The Flaming Lips' frontman Wayne Coyne had forgotten that the gold-painted, harmless gift was in his luggage but he soon had security staff at Will Rogers Airport in Oklahoma City hitting the panic button when his bags were scanned. Coyne was released without charge when he explained he had been given the grenade at a party and that it had no explosive parts.

Roy's dark secret

The trademark black hair of singer Roy Orbison, whose worldwide hits included 'Oh, Pretty Woman' and 'In Dreams', was not his own colour. He dyed his almost-white hair from his teenage years before he went on to cultivate his slightly sinister 'Man in Black' stage persona.

Feeling Blue about name

In 2012 American singer and songwriter Beyoncé Knowles failed in her attempt to trademark her daughter's name. Blue Ivy was born to Beyoncé and her rapper husband Jay-Z in January 2012 and the couple planned a range of baby clothing with the name Blue Ivy. The couple had the attempt rejected because a wedding planner in Boston had had the name since 2009.

Mistress gets pay-out

Bee Gee Robin Gibb is said to have paid his housekeeper an estimated £5m prior to his death in May 2012. The third of the four Gibb brothers to die had a son with Claire Yang and is said to have settled an inheritance on her in advance of his death from cancer, including a house in England. Manchester-born but Australia-bred, Robin left a £93m fortune to his wife and children.

Scotch on the rock

A special Scotch whisky was created to celebrate the 50th anniversary of the Rolling Stones in 2012. Fans, already used to splashing out hundreds of pounds for tickets to rare Stones concerts, forked out £400 a bottle for the commemorative tipple.

The J Factor

The loss of the lead singer Jay Traynor of Jay and the Americans in 1962 might have meant a band name change but they recruited another Jay, Jay Black, to counter that. Traynor led on the hit 'She Cried ' and Black took them on to even greater success.

Murder at Jessie gig

Singer Jessie J missed witnessing a horrific murder by minutes in 2012. BlackBerry executive Phillip Sherriff, 37, was viciously slashed with a bottle soon after Jessie had walked off stage from a performance at a London nightclub. He died in hospital four days later from a cut to his carotid artery and jugular vein during the attack on 4 April. Later Ashley Charles, 26, was jailed for a minimum of 14 years after he was found guilty of murder.

Childhood horror for guitar ace

The Who guitarist Pete Townshend revealed for the first time in 2012 that he was abused as a child. At the age of six he was sent to live with a grandmother in London and during his two-year stay he claims some of her male acquaintances abused him. He said the effects of these dark times have come through in many of the songs he has written over 40-plus years with The Who.

Fatal decision for Buddy Holly

But for one fateful decision, Buddy Holly might have lived a longer life and influenced rock music even more. Instead he died aged just 22. His new bride Maria Elena was usually his companion on his rock 'n' roll tours but for the fateful one in February 1959 Maria Elena stayed at home because she had just discovered she was pregnant and was not feeling well. Had she accompanied Buddy they would not have flown but as she wasn't there he took the plane which crashed in snowy Iowa killing Holly, the Big Bopper and Richie Valens. Traumatized Maria poured her heart out in a rare interview saying: "In a way, I blame myself. I was not feeling well when he left. I was pregnant and I wanted Buddy to stay with me, but he had scheduled that tour. It was the only time I wasn't with him. And I blame myself because I know that, if only I had gone along, Buddy never would have gotten into that airplane."

The Simpsons fame for bassist

The Duff beer much loved by cartoon buffoon Homer Simpson was named after the legendary alcohol intake of Guns N' Roses band member Duff McKagan. Bass player Duff said he was pleased the makers of the hit animated series wanted to use his name. "I thought it was cool," he said.

Gunning for Rod

Rod Stewart's enduring friendship with fellow British star Elton John meant they enjoyed some wild times together and shared many jokes. Stewart claims Elton once hired a sniper to shoot down giant footballs which were promoting Rod's shows at London's Earls Court venue.

The long and short of Mick

The size of Mick Jagger's manhood might have been something female fans have fantasized about over 50 years but if they consult two of the Rolling Stones frontman's mates they will be none the wiser. Keith Richards, the Stones' guitarist and Jagger's song-writing companion, famously claimed in his memoir *Life* that Mick was "tiny" in the trouser department. But Jagger must have been relieved to hear the Who guitarist Pete Townshend add quite a different description in his 2012 book *Who I Am*. Townshend describes Jagger as "very well-endowed" after clocking him in loose pyjama-style trousers without any underwear in 1969.

Don't you think I'm stretchy

Rod Stewart's association with yoga was short lived – because he hurt himself the first time of trying. Stewart, whose numerous hits have included 'Don't You Think I'm Sexy' and 'Sailing', tried the stretching regime when it became a popular fitness fad in the 1990s but fell into a fireplace – fortunately unlit – when he tried the basic moves.

Lyrical trouble for Ozzy

Heavy metal rocker Ozzy Osbourne has ended in legal trouble over song lyrics, twice. In 1985 and 1991 bereaved families blamed Ozzy's songs for suicides of loved ones. After California teenager John McCollum committed suicide while listening to Osbourne's anti-alcohol 'Suicide Solution' his parents, despite knowing McCollum suffered clinical depression, blamed lyrics in the song that spoke of "suicide being the only way out". Six years later Osbourne was sued for $9m for the same reason by the parents of Michael Wallerbut. On both occasions the courts ruled in Osbourne's favour.

Madonna's video fear

Madonna has never been one to back down from controversy as her raunchy stage persona and books, such as *Sex*, have proved. But in 2012 she stepped back from one of her more dangerous proposed stunts that could have upset Muslims. She planned a video singing her song 'Terror Bride' while wearing a combination of a traditional Iraqi bridal veil and dressed in a US military uniform. According to advisers she had even got to the stage of trying on the outfit before agreeing that her life might be in danger from Muslim fanatics who would be offended by the costume. The song was a comment on war and women's oppression. Some radical Muslims already despised the singer for her dedication to the Jewish Kabbalah sect.

Bum performance for Jay-Z

Working with a wife as beautiful as Beyoncé Knowles can affect your performance as rapper Jay-Z discovered in 2012. During a joint gig in New York he was so fascinated watching Beyoncé's leather-clad 'booty' from an off-stage monitor that he fluffed his cue. He also had left his microphone on, and the audience heard him say: "Oh shit, I should probably rap here."

Slow hand wash

Eric Clapton has admitted that he does his own laundry when touring. Unhappy with hotel service for "putting too much starch in the wash" the guitarist, nicknamed Slow Hand, finds local launderettes and does it himself.

The Bible rocks

Given his wild lifestyle over many decades, the idea of Keith Richards reading the Bible seems a little strange but the Rolling Stones guitarist maintains it contains "some very good phrases". He said the New Testament book Thessalonians chapter 5, verse 2 inspired the title of the 'Thief in the Night' track from the 1997 *Bridges to Babylon* album.

Hotbed of music

Freddie Mercury at one time was so afraid he would forget a tune that came to him in the night that he used a piano as a headboard for his bed. If a composition came to the Queen singer he was only a step away from playing it and getting it down on paper. The flamboyant performer, who died in 1991, claimed it was how he got started on 'Bohemian Rhapsody' in 1974, which became a multi-million-selling worldwide hit for Queen.

His number's up

Engelbert Humperdinck may have lost out on one of the most lucrative pay-days of his life because he misplaced a piece of paper. The British singer, whose hits included 'The Last Waltz' and 'Please Release Me', was approached in a London street in 2012 by a man who wanted to pay £2 million for the personalized number plate EH1 which was on Hump's Rolls-Royce. The singer agreed to sell to the man, who said his name was Hussein, but lost the contact details to carry the deal through with what was thought to be a wealthy Arab.

Audience member to the rescue

When Alex Bampton went to a Mika gig in 2012, the last thing he expected was to end up on stage with the artist. The problem was that Mika, who had a 2007 British number one with 'Grace Kelly', asked the audience in Sheffield, England for requests and one was called out that his band did not know. However Alex, 18, did and Mika invited him on stage to play keyboards for the number. Fearless Alex went down a storm with the 250-strong audience, who cheered his composure and courage in steeping into the breach for Mika.

Name in vain?

The BBC banned Bob Dylan's 'Baby, Let Me Follow you Down' because it contained the lyric "God-almighty world".

Thieving fans

Fans had a very different way of showing their affection for Canadian singer Alanis Morissette – they robbed her. Normally stars such as Tom Jones are showered by underwear but Morissette followers stole hers from her. Alanis said her hotel room was never secure enough and fans stole underwear and other items. She said fans would pounce on her and take cuttings from her hair.

Starship crash

Jefferson Starship's 1978 European tour got off to a wobbly start as self-confessed alcoholic front woman Grace Slick's drinking got the better of her. The first night in West Germany was cancelled because she was too drunk to perform and this sparked a riot by disgruntled fans. She made it on stage the following night but was so inebriated she could not sing properly. Slick made matters worse by mocking the German audience for their country losing World War II and then she groped female audience members and band mates.

Zealous or jealous?

Jackie Wilson was shot twice in the back in 1961 but the real mystery is what really happened? Wilson's management's official story about the incident that cost him a kidney was an overzealous fan but rumour said otherwise – that it was a jealous lover. Juanita Jones was alleged to have wounded him in a jealous rage when he returned to his Manhattan apartment with fashion model Harlean Harris. One bullet lodged too close to the 'Reet Petit' singer's spine to be operated on but otherwise Wilson recovered and Jones was never charged.

Hammer-ed by legal case

The appropriately named Christian recording artist, Kevin Christian, filed a lawsuit in 1992 against MC Hammer alleging copyright infringement for the rapper's song 'Here Comes the Hammer'. Christian filed a $16 million (£10 million) claim alleging his song entitled 'Oh-Oh, You Got The Shing' was plagiarized. Hammer's label Capitol settled but the details remained sealed. The artist settled with Christian the following year.

Neighbourly conflict

Very private rocker Van Morrison took legal action against two neighbours after making his home in the Irish seaside village of Dalkey near Dublin. Disputes, centred on safety and privacy issues, erupted in 2001 and in 2010 with one of them going as high as the Irish Supreme Court.

Eagle predator?

Eagles drummer Don Henley was fined $2,500 (£1,650) and put on two years' probation in 1980 after a 16-year-old girl was found naked and claiming she had overdosed on Quaaludes and cocaine at Henley's California home. She was arrested for prostitution and a 15-year-old girl, also found in the house, was arrested for being under the influence of drugs. Henley pleaded no contest.

No sweet outcome

A plagiarism case brought in 1971 against George Harrison over his song 'My Sweet Lord' actually took 18 years to settle. A US court found against the ex-Beatle in the claim that his song was too much like the Chiffons' 'He's So Fine' and originally ordered him to pay almost $1.6 million (£1 million) in damages. This was later halved when it later transpired that Harrison's manager Alan Klein had been duplicitous in his efforts to purchase for himself the ailing Bright Tunes company which was the plaintiff. It emerged he was hoping to sell the rights for 'He's So Fine' on to Harrison and, to that end, was supplying to the opposition insider details regarding the sales figures and copyright value of 'My Sweet Lord'.

Drifting through troubles

The Drifters had persistent personnel changes from the early 1950s but it was nothing compared to the upheaval of 1958 when the whole band was sacked. Manager George Treadwell owned the band name and wielded the axe, replacing the Drifters with a group called the Five Crowns with star singer Ben E. King. By the time the year's advance bookings were completed original Drifters fans were getting hostile.

Running for her life

ABBA's Anna-Frid Synni was less than two when she had to flee for her life. Frida, as she came to be known in the Swedish supergroup of the 1970s and 1980s, was the product of an affair between her Norwegian mother and a soldier of the German occupation army in 1945. They were forced to flee to Sweden because of reprisals in Norway against people who co-operated with Germans. Frida thought her father was dead but later tracked him down to Germany and was reunited.

All day and all of the fight

Members of the Kinks had a very public – and bloody – fight before a packed audience. In front of shocked fans, drummer Mick Avory and guitarist Dave Davies battled it out at the Capitol Theatre, Cardiff on 19 May 1965 – just one song into their set. After finishing the first song 'You Really Got Me', Davies had angry words with Avory and kicked over his drum set. Avory responded by hitting Davies with his foot pedal (although other pieces of drum equipment have been alleged), rendering him unconscious, before fleeing from the scene. Davies was taken to hospital where he needed 16 stitches to a bad head wound. To avoid prosecution Avory told police that it was a new part of the stage act in which band members would hurl their instruments at each other. However all must have been forgiven because Avory remained a Kink until 1984, when he left amid creative friction with – guess who? – Dave Davies.

Geographical error?

Some US radio stations stopped playing The Bangles' 1986 hit 'Walk Like an Egyptian' during the 1991 Gulf War. Even though Egypt was not among the combatants.

Sixx of the best punishment

Controversy surrounded Mötley Crüe's guitarist Nikki Sixx in 1997 when he goaded the audience at a concert in Greensboro, North Carolina to attack a security guard for repeatedly punching a female fan. In 2001 Sixx claimed he had apologized for his part in the débâcle.

Del's suicide

Sixties singer and guitarist Del Shannon committed suicide on 8 February 1990 after several failures at reviving the hit-making career he enjoyed in the 1960s. Del, real name Charles Weedon Westover, was found dead at his California home with a self-inflicted head wound from a .22-calibre rifle. Shannon had been a regular in the early 1960s pop charts of Britain and the USA with 'Runaway', 'Swiss Maid', 'Little Town Flirt' and 'Hats Off to Larry'.

Drink kills Winehouse

The meteoric music career of British singer Amy Winehouse was tragically short. After a rapid rise to fame in the early years of the 21st century in which she became the first British female singer to win five Grammys including Best New Artist, Record of the Year and Song of the Year, she died aged 27 in 2011 at her London home. An inquest ruled that the cause of death was alcohol poisoning but Amy, who had a tempestuous and chaotic personal life, also had a history of drug abuse and once had to be treated for an overdose of a cocktail of heroin, ketamine, ecstasy and alcohol. She suffered from eating disorders, depression, self-harming and, later, early-stage emphysema. Her death, alone in her bed on 23 July 2011, came after a three-day drinking session.

Hear me better

Neil Young was so adamant that his fans were not getting the true quality of his songs on their MP3 players that he launched a rival device in 2012. Young, whose *Harvest* album was fêted as one of the greatest ever, had been a critic of digital music, claiming the sound quality was lower than on vinyl. He and some major record labels invested in the Pono, an iPod rival which he claimed had better sound quality than any other similar mobile listening device.

Robbie Willy-ams

Singer Robbie Williams was so proud of his penis that he wrote a song about it in 2012. The song called '*I.L.M.P.* (*I Love My Penis*)' appeared on a spoof album compiled by former BBC radio disc jockey Chris Moyles. Some of the lyrics include "I love lying on the beach and playing in the sand. I love walking in the park with the wind in the trees but most of all I love my penis. I take mine everywhere."

Tragic McCartney fan

The jailing of Paul McCartney in Japan in 1980 had an inadvertent tragic sequel. While the ex-Beatle languished on drugs charges in a Tokyo cell for nine days a man believed to have been a fan named Kenneth Lambert turned up at the airport in Miami, Florida demanding a ticket to fly to Japan to "free Paul". He had no money or identification and in the resulting confrontation with reservation staff and police 29-year-old Lambert pulled a realistic-looking toy gun from his pocket. A policeman shot the young man dead.

Calculated move

Guns N' Roses bass guitarist Duff McKagan started a new venture in 2012, looking after the financial affairs of fellow rockers. Although still touring with bands Walking Papers and Loaded, McKagan went to business school after quitting Guns N' Roses and launched a company offering bands advice on financial matters and the pitfalls and rip-offs in the industry that prevent artists getting the full benefit of their earnings.

Things that go bump in the night

Elvis Presley fans who have listened closely to their idol's work may have noticed a strange sound on his 1960 recording of 'Are You Lonesome Tonight?' The sound of a microphone being knocked can be heard because Presley insisted on total darkness in the studio to ensure the right mood for the ballad, which topped the pop charts in both the USA and the UK. Unfortunately he did not completely get his bearings before the lights went out.

Great sex-pectations

Rapper Kanye West was holding his breath for a while in 2012 when a sex tape he had made with an ex-partner was stolen from his computer. Despite the musician, film director and fashion designer issuing threats of lawsuits against anyone airing the steamy 20-minute video, adult industry experts said if such a movie hit the Internet it could be worth millions. At the time of writing in 2013 the video had not surfaced in the public arena.

Making a point

Bobby Darin's 1959 single 'Mack the Knife' was banned by many radio stations in Britain and the USA because it was thought to promote gang violence.

Bobby shuns funeral

Multi-million-selling singer Bobby Darin had no funeral as his last wish was that his body be donated to medical research. He died in 1973 after heart surgery but for a while before he died he had to have oxygen after each concert performance.

Girls fall out

Multi-million-selling singer Mariah Carey had a very public spat with *American Idol* co-judge Nicky Minaj leading to a gun threat and a lot of unladylike language. The problem arose soon after rapper Nicky joined the talent contest's panel and during North Carolina auditions in 2012 the fur flew. During the heated row Nicky, who had a hit with 'Stupid Hoe', said of Mariah: "If I had a gun I would shoot her, I am not going to sit here every fucking minute to have her harass me every minute, every day. Don't tell me I'm a gangster. Every time you patronize me." Referring to the mouthy rapper as a "crazy bitch", big-voiced Mariah added: "Why do I have a three-year-old sitting around me?"

50 Cent survives hit

Rapper 50 Cent incredibly escaped with his life after being shot nine times. In 2000 a gunman struck as he sat in a car outside his grandmother's home in Queens, New York. 50 Cent, real name Curtis Jackson, was hit in the hand, arm, hip, both legs, chest and cheek, but survived. Incredibly 13 days saw him out of hospital although he needed five months of physical therapy. The shot to his face left him with a slight slur in his voice because a bullet shaved off part of his gums and left a hole between the bottom and top rows of his teeth. The alleged gunman was killed just a week after 50 Cent left hospital.

Fab four wheels

A car owned by Beatle Paul McCartney sold in 2012 for a massive £307,500. The James Bond-style Aston Martin DB5 was bought by Macca in 1964 and unusual extras included a record player. The Beatles' bass player, who penned such songs as 'Baby, You Can Drive My Car', had sold the DB5 in 1970. The sale price at the 2012 auction beat the £288,000 paid for a similar car which belonged to late Beatle guitarist George Harrison when it was auctioned in 2007.

Rolling into a trap?

A transatlantic conspiracy was hatched to try to smash the 'anti-establishment' Rolling Stones at the zenith of their 1960s success. It is claimed that the American FBI and Britain's MI5 were keen to wreck the band because of what was regarded as their 'unhealthy influence' on the potentially rebellious youth on both sides of the Atlantic. Author Philip Norman claimed in a 2012 biography of Stones frontman Mick Jagger that the FBI was keen not to have the band in America as had been planned and hoped a drug conviction in Britain would stop them touring there. It is alleged that a drug dealer was enlisted to inform on the Stones when they had a party at Keith Richards' Sussex home in 1967. Right on cue the police raided the West Wittering property, found drugs, and Jagger and Richards were arrested and initially jailed for possession. But the alleged MI5/FBI plot was foiled when they were freed on appeal, including Richards' convictions being quashed, and the US tour went ahead to great success. The 'Establishment' had lost and the Stones went on to chalk up 50 years in the rock business.

Arty Rod

Rod Stewart has been a keen art collector throughout his rock career and had by 2012 built up an impressive portfolio spread among his four homes. His first artwork was bought for a mere £18 when he was struggling for recognition as a singer. Stewart has been quoted as saying that when he is struggling to sleep he counts the paintings in his mind.

Tulisa causes quite a buzz

The incident of the shivering British pop star's suitcase will be remembered by US Customs officers for many years. Staff at Miami Airport were alarmed by buzzing luggage and on checking found a sex toy belonging to N-Dubz star Tulisa Contostavlos had started vibrating all by itself. Tulisa was quick to say that the sex aid had been purchased as a joke for a friend but the star's tweets on Twitter suggested she was quite a fan of the 'wabbit' (sic).

George defies death

George Michael survived a near-death experience that left him needing therapy for post-traumatic stress in 2012. The former Wham! singer was said to have been close to death in 2011 when he collapsed with pneumonia before a concert in Vienna, Austria. Several times during the next month in hospital he was close to death, according to doctors, but with intensive care he survived. A concert tour in Australia was cancelled in late 2012 while the star, whose hits include 'Careless Whisper', was treated for what was described as on-going anxiety brought on by his brush with death.

Fate's hand in Cochran death

A late change of plan and a strange twist of fate featured in the death of Eddie Cochran in 1960. The rock 'n' roller died from injuries sustained in a car accident in England's West Country. Cochran, whose hits include 'Summertime Blues' and 'C'mon Everybody', was wowing British fans while performing in Bristol but planned to go back to the USA via London. The car which had brought him with support act Johnny Gentle was full so Cochran and fellow rocker Gene Vincent ordered a taxi. After having got temporarily lost, the driver was driving fast to make up for lost time when he crashed into a concrete lamp-post in Chippenham, Wiltshire. Eddie, who was 22, died the following morning. Vincent was seriously injured but survived.

Bashful Amy

Wife-beating has been prevalent enough among the scandals of rock and pop over many decades but Amy Winehouse shocked the world with boasts about beating up her husband. In a frank 2007 interview she admitted that if she had been drinking and hubby Blake Fielder-Civil said the wrong thing she would "chin him". She was criticized by men's campaigners for 'bragging' about abusing her husband. One said that "a male abuser would have been locked up, stigmatized, and vilified". Winehouse and Fielder-Civil, ever stalked by the British paparazzi during their stormy marriage, were often photographed bloodied and bruised after alleged punch-ups. In 2009 the couple divorced.

They're Gaga for the Lady

Lady Gaga became the first Twitter user to register 20 million followers. As of 2013 rock and pop stars were the world leaders in Twitter followings. After Lady Gaga, real name Stefani Joanne Angelina Germanotta, came Justin Bieber with around 18 million, Katie Perry with some 15 million. At the same time newly elected President Barack Obama could only muster 13 million.

Jessie's mirror image

British pop sensation Jessie J had a shock when she looked at a figure in the audience. In front of her was a fan looking like the singer's twin sister. Jessie was so amazed she invited lookalike Melissa Frayne on stage with her. Coincidentally the two, though not related in any way, had more than looks in common. They both were 23 at the time of their meeting; they both suffered from panic attacks after being bullied at school and both had life-threatening heart defects discovered at the age of 11. There the resemblances end because Melissa, a model who claims she had the Jessie J signature look years before the singer did, admitted she can't sing a note.

Plug pulled on Paul and Bruce

Bureaucrats managed to silence aristocrats of the pop world Bruce Springsteen and Sir Paul McCartney who had got together for a rare gig. In 2012 council officials pulled the plug and left the duo singing into dead microphones because a deadline for loud music in London's Hyde Park had been breached. Springsteen, who has a reputation for long performances, was supposed to stop at 10.30pm when McCartney joined him on stage but at 11pm council officers warned organizers of the Hard Rock Calling event that they were in breach of noise regulations, leaving Sir Paul, Bruce and his E Street band fuming. Even London's Mayor Boris Johnson said the Westminster Council officials had been high-handed and should have allowed the set, which included 'I Saw Her Standing There', to finish so that the audience could be thanked.

50 Cent escapes again

50 Cent survived another threat to his life in 2012 when his car was hit by a lorry in New York. The rapper's Sports Utility Vehicle (SUV) was hit from behind by the truck, almost flipping it over on the Long Island Expressway. 50 Cent recovered from back and neck injuries, 12 years after he survived an assassination attempt in which he was hit by nine bullets.

Dead singer's home raided

Heartless thieves raided the home of tragic singer Amy Winehouse a year after her drink-related death in 2011 and thus robbed a charity of a fundraising bonanza. The raiders stole two of Amy's most iconic dresses, together worth £130,000, which were due to be auctioned to raise money for a charity foundation set up in the singing star's name. One of the dresses was worn by Amy when she married husband Blake Fielder-Civil and the other, a newsprint pattern, was famous from one of her TV appearances in Britain. The foundation created in Amy's name supported children's hospices and drug counselling services and lost vital funds through the theft from the London house in which Winehouse died, aged 27.

Cochran's cop becomes a star

A rookie policeman who was first on the death crash scene of American rock 'n' roller Eddie Cochran eventually became a pop star in his own right. A young Wiltshire Constabulary cadet called Dave Harman was there when a fatally injured Cochran was rushed to hospital on 17 April 1960 but inside five years with his name change to Dave Dee he was part of the million-selling British band David Dee, Dozy, Beaky, Mick and Tich. Dee, who had taken Cochran's guitar from the crash scene and held it until it could be returned to his family, charted with hits such as 'Hold Tight', 'Bend It', 'Save Me', 'Zabadak' and 'Last Night in Soho', the band had nine top-selling hits in Britain including a number one with 'The Legend of Xanadu' in a two-year hot streak between 1966 and 1968.

Sexy Claire

A member of a British boy/girl band admitted to having sex in a car, on a train and backstage as her pop career blossomed. Claire Richards had revealed in her 2012 biography that as Steps soared in the late 1990s she had an insatiable appetite for sex, especially with a member of the group's management team. She said she had a long-running affair which started with the loss of her virginity and then sex in some bizarre and public places. The three-women, two-men group split in 2001 and re-formed in 2011.

Coma girl saved by song

A song by British singer Adele was credited with inspiring a miracle recovery for a girl who had been in a coma for a week. Doctors had warned the parents of seven-year-old Charlotte Neve to prepare for the worst when the girl suffered major brain damage after a haemorrhage and slipped into a coma in 2012. Charlotte's mother sang Adele hit 'Rolling in the Deep' to her and Charlotte responded after seven days in a coma with a smile. Within two months Charlotte confounded all medical opinion by learning to walk again and returning to school.

Alarming tour

A fire alarm heralded the opportunity for singer Rihanna to take a middle-of-the-night tour of London. The Barbados-born star was awakened in her hotel by the alarm and grabbed her laptop and jewellery and instead of waiting around for the all clear she grabbed a black cab in August 2012. After seeing Downing Street, Big Ben, Westminster Abbey and Buckingham Palace by the light of dawn and downing a McDonald's breakfast she returned to the hotel and her bed.

Elton's blessing

Elton John turned back the clock in 2012 to his days as a pianist struggling for recognition by becoming a wedding singer again. Elton agreed to perform at the wedding reception in Canada of an anonymous man and his new wife after the groom made a huge donation to Elton's AIDS Foundation.

Venomous towards wrinkles

N-Dubz singer Tulisa Contostavlos announced in 2013 that she uses a synthetic snake poison to smooth out wrinkles. Even though she was only 24 at the time she was using the £135 potion that mimics the effect of viper venom.

Off the menu

Meat was off at a Morrissey concert in the US in 2013. Vegan Morrissey convinced the Staples Center arena in Los Angeles not to sell meat at concessions during his performance. The long-time animal rights' activist and former singer for 1980s band the Smiths got organizers to shutter the concession stands of fast food chain McDonald's and halt the sale of meat by other outlets at the venue. Instead fans had vegan Sloppy Joes, sushi and hummus and pitta bread to satisfy their hunger.

Tragedy strikes Stuart

Less than a year after leaving the Beatles on the verge of success, the so-called 'Fifth Beatle' Stuart Sutcliffe was dead. As the band's original bass player Sutcliffe realized he was a better visual artist than a musical one he quit the band in July 1961. In April 1962 he died from a brain haemorrhage in Germany, where he was studying art.

Frank knows best

The management of Frankie Avalon, who first hit the charts in the 1950s, tried to thwart his plans to marry beauty pageant winner Kathryn Diebel. They said his teen idol mystique would be damaged but Avalon, who charted with songs such as 'Venus', defied them and married in January 1963. At the time of writing in 2013 the couple were still together and had eight children and even more grandchildren.

Kirsty the heroine

Singer Kirsty MacColl died a heroine saving the life of one of her sons in 2000. On 18 December 2000, she and her sons Louis and Jamie were diving in a national marine park off Cozumel, Mexico when a speeding powerboat came at them as they were surfacing. Kirsty, 41, who was also a talented songwriter, saw that Jamie was in the boat's path but in pushing him out of danger she was killed instantly. Jamie sustained minor head and rib injuries.

Gately mystery

There was no mystery about the cause of the death of boy band member Stephen Gately in 2010 but there was about how his body was discovered. Bulgarian Georgi Dochev, whom Gately had met the night before and had slept in the spare bedroom, said he found the body on a sofa. But the long-term partner of openly gay Gately said he discovered the body. Boyzone singer Gately died of a congenital heart problem aged 33 but had been addicted to prescription drugs a few years before.

Commercial change of heart

Followers of Chumbawamba were outraged in 1997 when the alternative rockers signed for the EMI record label in Europe. It came eight years after the politically motivated band issued a compilation album called *F*** EMI* and had criticized the label in earlier songs.

Command performance

Bee Gee Robin Gibb was a man with a mission despite dying from cancer. The singer dedicated his final years to having a memorial in Britain for the members of RAF Bomber Command who died in World War II. He tirelessly helped with fundraising for the memorial in London's Green Park but died before the memorial was dedicated in 2012. However Robin, who was the third of the four Gibb brothers to die, dedicated royalties from his last single 'Don't Cry Alone' to go towards the upkeep of the memorial.

Michael's big cat

Michael Jackson kept a tiger at his Neverland Ranch in California. The beast, called Thriller after Jackson's biggest hit, went to an animal sanctuary when the cash-strapped singer left the ranch and eventually died in 2012 aged 13, outliving its owner by three years.

That's a Gaga price

Lady Gaga is said to have paid £85,250 for a dress designed by her late friend Alexander McQueen. The ivory silk empire-line gown was auctioned in London in 2012. McQueen hanged himself in a 2010 suicide.

Cougar hunt

A female DJ, aged 31, was forced into hiding after admitting bedding One Direction heart-throb Harry Styles when he was just 17. In 2012 Lucy Horobin spent months fearing attacks from 1D's army of British fans. Twitter threats were so bitter and threatening she was forced to close her social networking account.

Royal death lyrics

Lady Gaga struck yet another controversial note in 2012 when she performed a song about the death of Britain's Princess Diana which included the lyrics "So bob your head for another dead blonde". During the concert in Melbourne, Australia Lady Gaga, who claimed the princess had been an inspiration to her, resurrected the memory of the princess who died in a car crash with boyfriend Dodi Fayed in 1997 with her song 'Princess Die'.

Dance death

The 2012 dance craze Gangnam Style claimed its first victim as the year's Christmas party season arrived. Father of three Eamonn Kilbride collapsed and died aged 46 at a works party as he performed the fast-paced routine made famous by Korean rapper Psy. The video of the Psy dance likened to horse riding became the most watched ever on YouTube.

Michael Jackson death shock

One of the biggest shocks in pop history was the death of Michael Jackson on 25 June 2009 at the age of 51 but the aftermath did not end there. In November 2011, a California jury found the singer's personal physician, Conrad Murray, guilty of involuntary manslaughter after about eight hours of deliberation and he was sentenced to four years in prison. Propofol, a surgical anaesthetic that put the singer to sleep when other powerful sedatives could not, was self-administered by Michael. Lorazepam and midazolam were also said to have created a 'perfect storm' of a drug combination that killed Jacko instantly.

Miles of potential for Miley

At the tender age of 17 in 2009 pop and country singer Miley Cyrus had notched up 29 US Hot 100 chart entries. It put the daughter of country rocker Billy Ray Cyrus into the *Guinness Book of Records* as the most charted teenager.

Sweet writing man

Mick Jagger is not only a dab hand with words in his famous compositions for the Rolling Stones but at love letters, too. Ten passionate letters written to a girlfriend in 1969 sold for a massive £187,250 at auction in 2012. Jagger, who has written many of the Stones' iconic songs with Keith Richards, penned the letters to then girlfriend and singer Marsha Hunt while on location in Australia filming *Ned Kelly*. Jagger's loving words obviously worked on Hunt because the couple later had a child, Karis, together.

Stone in love with the Roses

A band which had been defunct for 16 years sold out 220,000 tickets in just 68 minutes when they re-formed. Fans had waited since 1996 for the Stone Roses to get back together so when a three-day reunion was announced for June 2012 tickets for the gigs at Manchester's Heaton Park went in record time at a rate of 3,235 per minute. The Stone Roses split in acrimony in 1996 after recording such iconic tunes as 'Fools Gold' in 1989.

Just like Eddie

For many years George Harrison cherished a rare piece of memorabilia from the late Eddie Cochran – one of the rocker's shirts. The ex-Beatle had seen Eddie when his ill-fated UK tour played in Liverpool prior to Cochran's death in a car crash in 1960. Later the then-unknown Beatles were touring Scotland backing Johnny Gentle who had supported Cochran before the tragedy. Eddie had given Gentle his stage shirt after his final show in Bristol hours before his death and following a week of pestering by the young Beatle, Johnny eventually passed it to George, a gift he treasured for many years.

Going for reality

50 Cent went for realism when he landed a film role in 2010 and was prepared to put his health at risk for his art. The rapper cum entrepreneur deliberately lost 50lbs (22.6kgs) to play a cancer-stricken football player for the film *Things Fall Apart*. Consuming only liquids and working out in a gym for three hours a day, he lost the weight in just nine weeks.

Pat begs a boon from fans

1950s heartthrob Pat Boone later apologized for his music choice over the years. Often rated as bland and saccharine, Boone's version of rock songs such as 'Tutti Frutti' sold in massive numbers but lacked the bite of the originator Little Richard's version. Years later Boone, who maintained a clean-cut, all-American preacher image, said producers sought out songs during his heyday and he just sang them. He admitted: "I have as much chance as getting into the Rock 'n' Roll Hall of Fame as getting on Mount Rushmore."

Loo ordeal for Jessie

Security staff employed by rapper Jay-Z needed to be beefy for the task of rescuing a damsel in distress – Jessie J stuck in a toilet. The singer was doing her make-up when the toilet door got stuck and it was 15 minutes before Jay-Z's staff shouldered it down at a BBC concert in Hackney, London in 2012.

Burma bar

'Walk On' by Irish rockers U2 has not been heard in Myanmar (Burma) because of a government ban. The song was about pro-democracy activist Aung San Suu Kyi, who was sentenced to house arrest in 1989 but has since been freed.

Tragic similarities

In an uncanny series of coincidences and associations the little-known name of rock musician David Box was tragically entwined with that of Buddy Holly. Both were from the Lubbock area of Texas and Box fronted Holly's band, the Crickets, after Buddy's death in 1959. Box sang on 'Peggy Sue Got Married', the follow-up to the Holly hit 'Peggy Sue', then, just like Buddy, he died on tour in his early 20s in a plane crash.

Stage death

An outdoor stage weighing many tons collapsed just an hour before 40,000 people were due at a Radiohead concert in Canada. But one of the band's roadies Scott Johnson was crushed to death and three others seriously injured. The 2012 tragedy was at Downsview Park, Toronto just before a gig by the British band. Scott was a drum technician making adjustments to Phil Selway's kit when the structure, which was rigged with lighting, collapsed. The concert was scrapped.

Spector jailed

Legendary record producer Phil Spector was jailed for murder in 2009. He was convicted of second-degree murder in the 2003 shooting of actress Lana Clarkson in Spector's California home. He was serving a prison sentence of 19 years to life and would be 88 before being eligible for parole. Spector developed the famous and influential 'Wall of Sound' which resulted in many global hit records including the Ronettes' 'Be My Baby'.

Heil Keith

Keith Moon was reported to begin his daily drinking early with a bottle of brandy at breakfast. The Who drummer, who died in September 1978 of a combined drink and drug overdose, also delighted in dressing as a Nazi to annoy mainstream opinion.

Ozzy pisses off Texas

Ozzy Osbourne made an enemy of the gun-toting state of Texas in the 1980s – because he needed to take a leak. While on tour in the US in the early 1980s, he found himself with a full bladder and nowhere near a lavatory. Relieving himself against a nearby building, he was arrested by an irate cop, who told him he had been urinating on the Alamo, the icon of Texan independence. "Son, when you piss on the Alamo, you piss on the state of Texas," he was apparently told. The Alamo, near San Antonio, was the scene of American resistance against superior Mexican forces in 1836 in a last stand which cost the lives of famous frontiersmen Davy Crockett and Jim Bowie and contributed to Texans winning independence from Mexico.

King-sized appetite

Elvis Presley had a huge appetite – as proven by the weight he carried later in his life. Born in America's Deep South, where the propensity for frying has often been a source of concern to doctors, a Presley favourite was a sandwich consisting of bacon, peanut butter and mashed banana – all fried in a pan. And Presley often had several at a sitting.

Sparks flying

All-girl punk band L7 never shied away from shocking their audiences. Singer/guitarist Donita Sparks once reacted to a boisterous Reading Festival crowd in 1992 by removing a tampon from herself and yelling "Eat my used tampon, fuckers!" before throwing it into the audience. The audience had been restless after an equipment failure had stalled the L7 set and retaliated by pelting the stage with mud.

Iron will

Led Zeppelin frontman Robert Plant was said to relax and get in the mood for gigs by ironing his shirts.

Love to bare all

Courtney Love put a whole new slant on magazine interviews. In 2002, the ex-wife of Kurt Cobain and former Hole frontwoman, during her chat with Q music monthly, had a bikini wax, poured a bottle of champagne over her head and stripped naked.

Whitney drug death

One of the biggest-selling female artists, Whitney Houston, was found dead in her hotel room bath in February 2012. Whitney, 49, had admitted a history of drug use and an autopsy found that she had used cocaine shortly before her death in the California hotel. The local coroner reported the cause of Houston's death as drowning and the "effects of atherosclerotic heart disease and cocaine use".

Fired up

Guitar genius Jimi Hendrix was not a great respecter of good guitars and he was not one to reverently pack his instrument back in its case after every gig. In March 1967, at a Jimi Hendrix Experience gig at London's famous Astoria venue, he set fire to a Fender Stratocaster at the end to create one of the 1960s most iconic rock images. The broken guitar in question was rescued by the band's press officer – and later sold for £280,000.

Slim chances

Country singer Slim Whitman, whose voice was famously used to repel invading aliens in the film *Mars Attacks!*, also repelled numerous premature announcements of his death. At the grand old age of 89 in 2013 the yodeller, whose hit 'Rose Marie' was a sales record breaker in the 1950s, said premature news of his demise seemed to happen to him every 10 years or so. The last time was in January 2008 by a radio DJ.

'F' for fired

The Sex Pistols cost popular British TV presenter Bill Grundy his career. The punk movement's flag bearers were a last-minute addition to the early-evening current affairs show *Today* after Queen pulled out in the summer of 1976. Led by guitarist Steve Jones, the Pistols got out of hand by the standards of the era's TV audiences and proceeded to sprinkle their chat with the 'F-word'. Apparently blamed for goading the band into being outrageous, the career of programme host Grundy went into meltdown. The band, although short lived, went on to play a legendary part in modern music history.

Bonding metal

Life on the road is not greatly conducive to band members getting along well. Metallica, arguably one of the world's biggest heavy metal acts, were barely speaking to each other by the time they came to record what would become their 2003 album *St Anger*. Needing to bring a new unity the band spent tens of thousands of dollars on performance coach Phil Towell's group therapy sessions. The process was recorded in the 2004 documentary film *Some Kind of Monster*.

Sixx times lucky

Mötley Crüe's founder Nikki Sixx has admitted that he took a long time to learn his lesson about drug taking and had overdosed on heroin "about half a dozen times". The band's bassist said about his addiction: "When I met heroin it was true love." In 1987, Sixx was revived by a paramedic who plunged an adrenaline injection direct into his heart after he overdosed. Clearly a slow learner, Sixx suffered another overdose the very next day, which he also survived, but used the experience as a basis for the song 'Jumpstart My Heart'.

Music on high

Beach Boy Brian Wilson once described the inspiration for his ground-breaking music from the surfing sound period onwards as making "teenage symphonies to God".

Zeppelin flight pioneers

A particularly bad bout of turbulence led to Led Zeppelin pioneering a new type of rock 'n' roll band transport. After being badly shaken about in a leased Falcon private jet during an early-1970s US tour, Led Zeppelin band members – Robert Plant, Jimmy Page, John Bonham and John Paul Jones – vowed to travel in something bigger. The mega-band was wealthy enough to lease a Boeing 707 airliner christened 'The Starship' which flew the band and its big entourage around the US.

Elton confessions

Elton John used a 1995 *New Musical Express* (*NME*) interview to bare all about the wild lifestyle behind his eccentrically dressed 'Mr Nice Guy' stage persona. Despite counting many mums and grandmothers among his vast fan club, Elton revealed he once had an out-of-control booze and cocaine addiction. He also talked about his bulimia eating disorder in which he said he would gorge himself on cocaine, jars of cockles and then ice cream, before making himself throw up.

Ranch of desire

Pop's most famous eccentric, Michael Jackson, set himself up for life with the 1982 album *Thriller*, which enabled him to buy the Neverland ranch in California, a 2,800-acre spread with its own funfair and zoo. However, it was later to leave him with hundreds of millions of dollars of debt.

That's a lot of sound

The Flaming Lips frontman Wayne Coyne was always one for innovation, hence the band's incredible live shows, and was experimenting even before they broke through. In the early 1980s his ideas included the Parking Lot Experiments, where tracks were played simultaneously on up to 40 car audio systems in an attempt to produce symphonic music.

Managed release

The late-1990s hysteria around Britpop band Oasis became so massive that their third album *Be Here Now* was in danger of being over-hyped. Brothers Noel and Liam Gallagher and co had earlier released *Definitely Maybe* and *(What's the Story) Morning Glory?* to almost universal acclaim. In an attempt to stop the band becoming over-hyped, journalists were told they could only listen to the third album in the band's management offices and were forced to sign gagging orders promising they would not discuss the album before its release. The 1997 album broke sales records.

Diva tales

Media stories about Mariah Carey's diva demands have become legendary. The multi-million-selling American soul singer was once said to have insisted that a £50,000 antique table be used for a signing session in a department store and that her dog be ferried around in the luxury of a private jet or a chauffeur-driven car. It was also claimed she once booked a floor of rooms at a top London hotel costing £20,000 a night.

Iconic gig scrapped

A matter of principle led to the Stone Roses refusing to play a sold-out gig at the famous Madison Square Gardens in 1989. Band members Ian Brown and co. were miffed that the concert was booked without consulting them.

Feeling sheepish

British acid house leaders the KLF – formed by Jimmy Cauty and Bill Drummond – shocked Britain's music industry when they left a dead sheep outside the venue of the BRIT Awards in 1992. Drummond, who had come on stage wearing a kilt and shooting blanks from a tommy gun over the crowd, explained that the dead sheep gesture was a compromise, replacing his earlier intention to cut off his hand at the ceremony.

Live Aid life saver

The world of rock and pop music came together in a massive effort to save millions of Ethiopians from famine in the early 1980s. Some of the biggest names of the time put their rivalries aside to support *Live Aid*, a massive televised charity concert that moved with the sun from its start in London, across to the USA. The idea came from Boomtown Rats frontman Bob Geldof, who whipped and cajoled the music industry into taking part in the greatest concert on earth. The live audiences alone numbered 72,000 in London's Wembley Stadium and across the Atlantic 100,000 at the John F. Kennedy Stadium in Philadelphia; and there were simultaneous concerts in Germany and Australia for the same cause. The global TV audience was around 1.9 billion and it is estimated that £150 million ($240 million) was raised as a direct result of the concert. Acts who appeared included Queen, Status Quo, Paul McCartney, Mick Jagger, David Bowie and Black Sabbath complete with Ozzy Osbourne.

Paint attack revenge

Members of the Stone Roses ended up in court after a paint attack on the owner of their former record company. The band had moved labels from FM Revolver around 1990 but the former label had rights to release the 'Sally Cinnamon' recordings it owned and did so with the blessing of Ian Brown and other band members. Problems arose when the band refused to co-operate with a supporting video but FM Revolver went ahead with their own anyway. Infuriated by the video the band members launched a paint attack on the company's premises in revenge and were later fined for criminal damage.

Different strokes

Rolling Stone Ronnie Wood revealed that he rejected the chance to join a newly formed band which turned out to be rock giants Led Zeppelin. Wood, who replaced Mick Taylor in the Rolling Stones line-up in 1975, had an offer to get together with a project called the New Yardbirds but scoffed at the idea. He admits saying: "I can't join that bunch of farmers". The embryo band, with ace guitarist Jimmy Page in the line-up and Robert Plant as frontman, went on to become Led Zeppelin, one of the biggest bands in the world with multi-million global sales.

An unhappy Monday

Outspoken Happy Mondays band member Bez went to jail for assaulting a woman. In August 2010, Bez, real name Mark Berry, was convicted of assaulting his ex-girlfriend, Monica Ward with whom Berry had a son, by throttling and threatening to kill her. He first received a community service sentence despite calling Manchester magistrates hearing the case a "kangaroo court". But he refused to co-operate and received an alternative sentence of four weeks in jail.

Commando cock-up

Bulgarian singer Krassimir Avramov had a rude awakening with armed troops smashing his apartment door down in the middle of the night. A commando unit was searching for a crime boss in Sofia in 2012 but got the wrong apartment and dragged Avramov, who had competed in the 2009 Eurovision Song Contest, out of his bed. As soon as the mistake was realized all was forgiven and the singer was soon signing autographs for the troops.

Hands off

Vocalist of Texas-based band Giant Princess, Collin Hedrick, said in 2012 that he refrained from masturbating before a gig because he needed to retain his nervous energy to perform.

Suitably convinced

Blues star Sonny Boy Williamson, who was born in rural Arkansas, was unable to convince the folks back home that he had successfully toured Britain and Europe in the 1960s blues boom. So he went to a Savile Row tailor in London and had a harlequin-style suit made from a dozen kinds of fabric on the basis that it was something one could not get in the USA.

Hair-raising threat

Members of the British band, the Stone Roses, threatened to disrupt a prime-time chat show in the 1990s by ripping the wig off its host. But the prank against former BBC radio presenter Terry Wogan was foiled when the controversial Manchester-based band members discovered the show was to be pre-recorded. So they pulled out of appearing.

Unlucky 27

A legend which has grown up about the bad luck surrounding the number 27 in the music industry was sparked by the death of so many performers at that age. By 2012 with the death of Amy Winehouse the previous year the '27 Club' boasted such names as blues pioneer Robert Johnson, Rolling Stone Brian Jones, Jimi Hendrix, Canned Heat frontman Alan Wilson, Nirvana's Kurt Cobain, Jim Morrison and Janis Joplin. The deaths of Morrison, Wilson, Joplin and Hendrix were drug-related while mystery still surrounds the deaths of Johnson and Jones. Cobain committed suicide by shooting himself.

Bad sports

The Sex Pistols may have broken up many years previously but when the four original members plus Sid Vicious were inducted in the Rock and Roll Hall of Fame in 2006 none of them attended. Sneeringly they said they regarded the Hall of Fame as a "piss stain."

Rape sparks Connie lawsuit

American singer Connie Francis made history from being a rape victim. The ballad star who had a string of hits in the late 1950s and early 1960s was raped in her hotel room near New York in 1974 and despite the trauma she sued the Howard Johnson hotel chain and won a historic victory. A court ruled that the sex assault on the star at the Jericho Turnpike hotel by a man who has never been found occurred because adequate security had not been provided and reportedly awarded Francis, whose hits included 'Lipstick on Your Collar', 'Carolina Moon' and 'Stupid Cupid' a record $2.5 million in damages. At the time the award to Francis was one of the largest such judgments in history and led to a reform in hotel security.

Upsetting Texas

Heroin addict Sid Vicious was always one to shock. When he was bass guitarist with the Sex Pistols in the late 1970s, he appeared in stage in Dallas, Texas with the words "Gimme a fix" scrawled across his bare chest. Texas was one of the less liberal-leaning American states at the time.

Open-air performance

The basis of the Small Faces' British hit 'Lazy Sunday' was singer Steve Marriott recording his acoustic guitar musings on a home cassette recorder in his garden. The hit single retained his dogs barking in the background.

Freaky death

House of Freaks frontman Bryan Harvey was slaughtered by a mystery gang, along with his whole family in 2006. The bodies of Harvey, 48, wife Kathryn and their two daughters Stella (nine) and Ruby (four) were found when a friend arrived for a party and instead found the house in Richmond, Virginia ablaze and the bodies of the slain in a basement.

Bieber castration plot

An obsessed killer put a $2,500 bounty on each of Justin Bieber's testicles, a court was told in 2012. It was alleged that Dana Martin, who sported a Bieber tattoo on his leg, conspired to arrange for two men to abduct and kill the teenage singer. Pruning shears had been bought to carry out the gruesome castration. Mark Staarke and his nephew Tanner Ruane were accused of being involved in the plot to be enacted while Bieber was in New York for concerts in November 2012. Martin was already serving two life sentences in New Mexico for rape and murder. It was alleged Martin devised the conspiracy because he was upset the Canadian-born singer had ignored Martin's attempts to contact him.

Meek freaked

1960s British record producer Joe Meek was so crippled with paranoia he was convinced the record label EMI was bugging his studio. He 'retaliated' by bugging it himself. Meek, who was terrified his mother would discover he was gay, produced hits such as the Tornados' 'Telstar' in 1962.

Voice blow for sob singer Connie

After 22 years of recording and 35 top 50 hit records Connie Francis had to learn how to sing. The effects of a nasal operation in 1977 left her completely without her distinctive ballad voice and its famous 'sob'. She went through several more operations and even when she got her voice back, was forced to take vocal lessons, something she had never needed before in a singing career which began with talent contests when she was just four.

Lee has a burn up

Reggae and dub music producer Lee 'Scratch' Perry claimed to have burned down his Jamaica-based Black Ark studios to drive away evil spirits. Black Ark and Perry were responsible for some of the world's most innovative sounds and recording techniques in the latter half of the 1970s.

Shocking time for Roky

An on-stage breakdown for 13th Floor Elevators' leader Roky Erickson led to three years in mental hospitals. After suddenly speaking gibberish at the HemisFair festival in San Antonio, Texas in 1968, he was diagnosed with paranoid schizophrenia and was admitted to a mental hospital where he was involuntarily given electroconvulsive treatment.

Frank plays the Grinch

Not everyone was enthusiastic about the rock stars' *Live Aid* charity concert in 1985. Frank Zappa, who was invited to perform but refused, was quoted as saying at the time: "I think *Live Aid* was the biggest cocaine money-laundering scheme of all time." He questioned the legitimacy of *Live Aid* and said he believed that money raised by it did not address the core problems facing the developing world.

Jaz changes

Jaz Coleman of Killing Joke was not just a member of a post-punk band – his musical experience was far more extensive. He studied piano and violin under the head of music for Cheltenham College in England until the age of 17 and was a member of several cathedral choirs. In 1973, Jaz was awarded the Rex Watson Cup at the Cheltenham International Festival of Music. Coleman also studied classical music in Leipzig, Germany in 1987 and at the Cairo Conservatoire in 1979 where he made an extensive study of Arabic quarter tones. In 1982 he temporarily quit Killing Joke and moved to Iceland. Reports of his reasons for leaving ranged from "escaping the apocalypse in Britain" to "leaving to become a classical composer".

Dexy's go running

Dexy's Midnight Runners might as well have been called 'Dexy's Morning Runners' when they formed in the 1980s as their leader Kevin Rowland is said to have insisted band members went jogging at dawn. He was also said to have banned alcohol in order to keep the hit makers of 'Come on Eileen' and 'Geno' in shape.

Pre-minstrel tension

Ritchie Blackmore, arguably a founding father of heavy metal, reinvented himself as a medieval minstrel in 1997 with a band that played Renaissance music. Blackmore, who was singer and guitarist in the 1970s with heavy metal bands Deep Purple and Rainbow, formed Rainbow Nights with his lover Candice Nights in which Blackmore eschewed his electric guitar for mandolin and acoustic guitar. The band released a number of acclaimed albums and also performed at festivals in the 21st century.

Views from the Bush

British singer Kate Bush, who had hits with 'Wuthering Heights' and 'The Man with the Child in His Eyes' in the 1970s, turned to protest songs later in her career. Her 'Never for Ever' railed against the possibility of nuclear holocaust and 'The Dreaming' was pro-Australian Aboriginal rights.

On borrowed time

A drummer drafted in at the last minute to back a new duo at a 1976 music festival in Kent, England would become world-famous for all the wrong reasons. His name was John Ritchie and he graduated to Sid Vicious, bass player of the infamous punk band the Sex Pistols. The duo he backed didn't do badly either – they developed into Siouxsie and the Banshees with a career spanning two decades.

Bastard's a hero

Rapper Russell Jones, better known as Ol' Dirty Bastard of the Wu-Tang Clan, saved a little girl from a blazing car. In February 1998, Jones witnessed a car accident from the window of his recording studio in Brooklyn, New York and surged into heroic action. With a friend he ran to the accident scene and organized a dozen onlookers who assisted in lifting the 1996 Ford Mustang enabling the four-year-old girl to be rescued from the wreckage. She was taken to a hospital with first- and second-degree burns and Jones visited the girl in hospital frequently until he was recognized by members of the media. Heroism was an unusual role for the bad-boy rapper who was jailed many times for a range of crimes including assault, crack cocaine possession and traffic offences.

Dress for Kevin

Singer Kevin Rowland appeared on stage at the 1999 Reading Festival in England dressed in a white dress, panties and stockings. The look didn't go down well and the crowd threw bottles and booed him off.

Record record

Jack Hill became the world's youngest record producer in December 2012. At the tender age of just 12, the young DJ from Weston-super-Mare in England released his first track called 'Club DJ'.

Taking it lying down

Guitarist Eric Clapton recently recounted how outrageous rock star behaviour became almost the norm for fans. He gave the example of how during the 1970s being drunk was almost part of the act. He said: "You were almost expected to be drunk. I remember doing one entire show lying down on the stage with the microphone stand lying beside me and nobody batted an eyelid."

Calling up record spirits

Producer Lee 'Scratch' Perry had various bizarre ways of trying to enhance the spiritual properties of his recordings. He would blow cannabis smoke on to his tapes while recording, bury unprotected tapes in the soil outside of his studio and surround himself with burning candles and incense, whose wax and dust were allowed to infest his recording equipment. He would also spray tapes with a variety of fluids, including urine, blood and whisky.

Freaky life

Addictions to cocaine and crack not only hampered the career of funk star Rick James – his health suffered, too. James, whose hits included 'Super Freak' in 1981, died from heart failure in 2004 at the relatively young age of 56. He had earlier recovered from a stroke suffered on stage in 1998.

Cursed BBC

Lee 'Scratch' Perry, who produced reggae hits such as 'Return of Django', put a curse on the British Broadcasting Corporation in the 1970s. The producer, known for his heavy cannabis use, said the hex would only be lifted if the BBC agreed to play his music around the clock.

Bosom of Love

Courtney Love, the musician widow of Nirvana's Kurt Cobain, seems to have a penchant for revealing her body. In 2004 she was photographed apparently allowing a homeless man to suck one of her breasts in public.

Coping with acid

Singer and bass guitarist Julian Cope, who had a well-documented affair with the mind-bending drug LSD, said he once took so much that he lay on his kitchen table thinking he was a city centre.

Ozzy hears voices

Former Black Sabbath frontman Ozzy Osbourne's attempt to strangle his wife Sharon in 1989 ended with him being committed to rehab. He was arrested in California after trying to throttle Sharon while he was under the influence of illicit substances washed down with copious amounts of vodka. It was reported even in Sharon's autobiography that Ozzy was obeying voices in his head. It was also said that his first request when admitted to the Betty Ford clinic for rehab was "where's the bar?"

Vibrating on

The Beach Boys' million-selling 'Good Vibrations' was a breakthrough in a new method of recording. Departing from the standard live-taped performances typical of studio recordings at that time, 'Good Vibrations' was a modular format with separately written sections individually taped and linked together. The driving force behind the project, Beach Boys leader Brian Wilson, was said to have taped 90 hours of material for the recording issued as a 1966 single of barely three minutes' duration but which was a number-one seller in the USA, UK and Australia.

James jailed

Funk wild man Rick James was jailed for three years in 1994 for assaulting two women. It was alleged he imprisoned and tortured them while under the influence of crack cocaine, one of the substances to which James had been addicted. He did not help his case by falling asleep during the court case and enraging the judge.

La la land?

Lee Mavers, the songwriter behind the Liverpool one-hit wonders The La's, was said to have carried a pouch of 'original 1960s dust' to sprinkle on guitars and amplifiers in order to achieve an authentic sound.

Connie is committed

American singer Connie Francis was committed to a mental hospital by her family in the early 1980s. After years of tragedy in which Francis was raped, she lost her voice and her brother was assassinated, the singer, who had two US number ones, was diagnosed with manic depression which brought her resurrected career to a halt for a further four years. She was committed to 17 different hospitals and in her autobiography *Who's Sorry Now?* she admitted that she was close to committing suicide because the hospitals were extremely depressing.

Pretend marriage for Pretender

Chrissie Hynde was rejected as a bride by two of the Sex Pistols. Johnny Rotten claimed in his autobiography that in 1976 he was due to marry the woman who was later to lead the Pretenders. It would have been a marriage of convenience, he contended, to allow Ohio-born Hynde to stay in Britain. Rotten chickened out as did hastily assembled alternative Sid Vicious. Hynde eventually had two failed rock 'n' roll marriages to Kink Ray Davies and Jim Kerr of Simple Minds.

Love overdose

Courtney Love was taken to hospital and treated for a drug overdose that she was said to have taken in front of her 11-year-old daughter Frances. The incident in 2003 was said to have involved the painkiller OxyContin and Love, whose band Hole had broken up the previous year, recovered. The rock star and actress, then 39, is understood to have taken the overdose less than an hour after being arrested for smashing windows at a friend's house.

On yer bike

Perfectionist producer of Meat Loaf albums, Jim Steinman, was said to have tested the skills of a sound engineer with a very special request. Witnesses said he asked for a guitar solo to be made to sound "like a Harley-Davidson morphing into a gargoyle-like beast who is mad at his parents".

Key to success?

Music experimentalist Don Van Vliet, alias Captain Beefheart, was reputed to have written all 28 songs for the *Trout Mask Replica* album during an eight-and-a-half-hour session on the piano. Not bad, given it was said to be an instrument the multi-genre fusion artist hadn't played before.

Syd disappears for life

Pink Floyd founder Syd Barrett abandoned the band's success in 1969 and never returned. Although allegedly having drug and mental problems, Barrett tried a brief solo career before disappearing from public view completely and living as a recluse gardening and painting in Cambridge, England. He died in 2006, aged 60.

Door slammed

The doors to the *Ed Sullivan Show* in America were firmly slammed on the Doors in 1965 in a row over suggestive lyrics. The band headed by Jim Morrison had agreed to remove the line "We couldn't get much higher" from the song 'Light My Fire' because the Sullivan show producers felt it had drug connotations. But Morrison and company reneged and left the line in. Needless to say, the Doors were not invited back by Sullivan, who had a reputation for being dictatorial about what visiting artists could perform.

Prince Charming turns nasty

British glam rocker Adam Ant escaped jail in 2002 after pulling a gun in a London street. The singer, who sold 16 million records and had 15 hits in three years of the 1980s as Adam and the Ants, was charged with affray under his birth name of Stuart Goddard. He pleaded guilty, was fined £500 and ordered to undertake psychiatric treatment. Following a row in a pub he had thrown a discarded car alternator through a window and, when chased through the back streets of Camden by pub security and others, drove them back by brandishing a World War II starting pistol, once the property of his father. Adam, whose number ones included 'Prince Charming' and 'Stand and Deliver', was spotted by a police patrol, gun still in hand. Earlier he had been mocked in the pub about the flamboyant way he was dressed. A year later Goddard was back in court again charged with affray plus criminal damage and spent time in psychiatric treatment. In September 2003 he was sectioned under the Mental Health Act.

High-flying trouble

Kurt Cobain's wife Courtney Love was arrested by police at London's Heathrow Airport in early 2002 after a fracas on a Virgin Atlantic flight from Los Angeles. She was accused of attacking and shouting abuse at a member of the airline's cabin crew during the 10-hour flight.

Passing off

The Happy Mondays included a laminating machine in their gear for their 1990 performance at the UK Glastonbury Festival. They annoyed festival management and security by issuing their own backstage passes.

Getting the point

The Kinks slashed their way to early success in the mid-1960s by vandalizing an amplifier. Guitarist Dave Davies was experimenting with getting a meaner and more distorted sound and got it by slashing the amp speaker. The iconic Kinks sound resulted in a string of hits such as 'You Really Got Me', 'All Day and All of the Night', 'Till the End of the Day' and 'I Need You'.

Wilson's private beach

Beach Boy Brian Wilson created a songwriting area in his California home by having a sandpit built around his grand piano.

Gas blast

A long-lost Sex Pistols track was discovered after 35 years in 2012. The 1977 studio demo track called 'Belsen was a Gas' turned up when the band's archive was moved. The song was not unknown as it had been recorded live and with Great Train Robber Ronnie Biggs but as this was the first known studio version it was immediately released on the reissued Pistols' album *Never Mind the Bollocks*.

All fired up

For the recording of the Brian Wilson track 'Fire' the composer went for authenticity by making the session musicians wear toy plastic firemen's helmets while a small fire burned in a bucket. The track appeared on the 2004 *Smile* album.

Jay murderers escape

Hi-hop musician Jam Master Jay was gunned down in a New York recording studio on 30 October 2002. Jay, real name Jason Mizell, was 37 and had been a member of the groundbreaking rap band Run-DMC. Although several people were investigated no one was ever convicted on his murder.

Accentuate the accent

George Michael claimed that he awoke from a coma in 2012 speaking with a different accent. Michael, who was taken ill with pneumonia while on tour in Austria, had a bizarre English West Country accent for several days. Doctors thought it was a variation of the rare, but not unknown, phenomenon of Foreign Accent Syndrome which can occur in cases of brain injury. Michael, from north London but of Greek descent, soon lost his 'new' accent and puts it down to the fact that before his critical illness he had been following a TV programme starring a Somerset-born actress.

Long player

A record concept conceived in the 1960s eventually made it to the buying public's ears in the 21st century. Brian Wilson was the driving force behind the Beach Boys' *Smile* album planned for the late 1960s. Hundreds of hours of recorded work then lay dormant after Wilson's mental health deteriorated and it was 37 years later in 2004 that Wilson released it as a solo album.

Raid list

A 1973 police raid on the then London home of Rolling Stone guitarist Keith Richards revealed a massive haul of 'dangerous' items. Drugs taken away by the armful included marijuana, heroin, methadone and Mandrax. Drug paraphernalia snatched included brass scales and water pipes, while firearms and other weapons included a .38 Special revolver, a miniature antique French blunderbuss, two shotguns, eight boxes of bullets and a collection of ratchet knives. Also taken by police and deemed 'suspicious' was a plaster bust of guitarist Jimi Hendrix. Given that judges of the time came down hard on any 'wrongdoing' by the anti-authority Rolling Stones, Richards was treated leniently. He was only fined and his girlfriend of the time, Anita Pallenberg, received a year's conditional discharge.

Facing the crunch

Paul McCartney literally had a 'bit' part at a 1967 recording session. The Beach Boys song 'Vegetables', released on the *Smiley Smile* album, featured the novel use of raw vegetable chewing as percussion. Sir Paul was on celery.

Nanker Phelge?

Careful observers of early Rolling Stones records may have noticed several songwriting credits for the oddly named Nanker Phelge. The composer of B-sides such as 'Stoned' was actually five very famous people – Mick Jagger, Brian Jones, Charlie Watts, Bill Wyman and Keith Richards. The name – Nanker a revolting face that band members, Brian in particular, would jokingly pull – and Phelge – the surname of a former flat mate – was a vehicle for the whole of the band to share composing royalties when they collaborated on songs between 1963 and 1965. Since then Jagger and Richards have been behind the bulk of Stones' compositions.

Meaty problem

A Meat Loaf tribute act ran into legal trouble with the 'Bat out of Hell' singer himself in 2012. Briton Dean Torkington was Meat Loaf's build, dressed like his hero and even had a van decorated with Meat Loaf artwork – much to the original Meat Loaf's annoyance. The two met and clashed in Liverpool in 2006 before the genuine Meat Loaf, real name Michael Aday, won £18,412 in a court case over a website domain name. By 2013 fake Meat Loaf Torkington was broke and claimed to have lost his home and was living in the van. He also claimed to have lost his living as a Meat Loaf impersonator because the strain and pressure of the legal row meant he lost 168lbs (76kg) and he no longer looked like his idol.

Dual use

The Pyramid stage at the famous Glastonbury Festival in England was only a performance area while the annual festival was on. The rest of the year it was a cattle barn. It burned down in 1994 and was replaced by a structure that could be stripped down between festivals.

What's in a name?

British band Duran Duran got its name, albeit misspelled, from Dr Durand Durand, a character in the 1970s science-fiction film *Barbarella*.

Have drumsticks will travel

Mick Avory made history – albeit briefly – by being the drummer at the first Rolling Stones gig on 12 July 1962. Sitting in at London's Marquee club he drummed for Jagger and co. for 50 minutes but later found fame in his own right as the backbeat to the highly successful British band the Kinks.

Three-year-old saves Richards

Rolling Stone Keith Richards may not have been around to have become one of the 'pop pensioners' of the 21st century but for having his life saved by his son aged three. In 1973 young Marlon needed to throw a glass of wine over his deeply sleeping father to alert him to the fact their 300-year-old thatched cottage in West Sussex, England was on fire. Richards and his lover Anita Pallenberg managed to get Marlon, his year-old sister Angela and some antique guitars and furniture to safety before the blaze took a real hold. Despite the valiant efforts of the fire service, Richards' timbered cottage at West Wittering was gutted. No cause of the fire was ever revealed but Richards postulated at the time that he thought that a mouse might have chewed through electrical wiring.

Beck backs paper

Sheet music made a comeback in the 21st-century digital age thanks to multi-instrumentalist Beck Hansen. In 2012 the American-born singer-songwriter, whose stage name is just Beck, rejuvenated the concept of sheet music to fans more used to MP3 digital files when his 20-track album *Song Reader* was published as individual hard paper copies only, with full-colour art for each song and in a hard cover carrying case. The individual song booklets of previously unreleased works came complete with lyrics and musical notation for instruments as unusual as the ukulele. Sheet music was popular in the 19th century until the arrival of gramophone records in the 1920s. Beck, real name Bek Campbell, previously had hit albums through the 1990s and the Noughties with such works as 'Mellow Gold', 'Odelay' and 'Sea Change'.

Brock 'n' roll

Animal-loving rock legend Brian May turned his 70-acre English home into a wildlife sanctuary. By 2012 the guitarist had a host of injured animals including 36 hedgehogs, seven badger cubs and two owls at his estate in Surrey.

Drumming DNA

Zak Starkey got minimal encouragement from his father Ringo Starr to take up the drums – just one lesson. Ringo, who found fame as the Beatles' drummer, wanted his son to be a lawyer or a doctor but young Zak, born in 1965 at the height of his father's fame, wanted to follow in the paternal footsteps. At eight, Starkey became interested in music and by 10 he had begun teaching himself to play the drums. One of Ringo's best friends in the rock music industry was the Who drummer Keith Moon and he bought Zak his first professional drum kit. Starr later praised his son's drumming abilities as Zak went on to work with the Who, Oasis and members of Iron Maiden.

Jacko gets refund from the grave

Michael Jackson got a refund on a carpet – three years after his death. The eccentric singer, recognized as the most successful entertainer of all time with such hits as 'Billie Jean', 'Beat It' and 'Thriller', died in 2009 when he was planning a series of concerts at London's O2 Arena. He had ordered a £15,000 luxury silk and wool carpet for his dressing room from an exclusive London shop, but died before he could use it. In December 2012 staff responsible for Jackson's estate returned the carpet unused and still rolled and received a full refund.

Job under threat

Three members of the Beach Boys knew they were to be sacked as they played their 50th anniversary reunion tour in London in 2012. Frontman Mike Love owned the band name so the specific anniversary tour meant founders Al Jardine and Brian Wilson plus guitarist Dave Marks were to get their cards at the end.

Pete lashed Moon

The Who's guitarist Pete Townshend attacked Keith Moon 34 years after the group's drummer's death. Writing candidly in his autobiography *Who I Am* Townshend said wild man Moon was "such a twat sometimes" and also reckoned appearing at Woodstock was "a crock of shit".

Riled Rihanna

Singer Rihanna launched a foul-mouthed attack on her French fans' calling them "fucking insane" for besieging her at a Paris station in 2012. Hundreds swamped security at the Gare du Nord station and caused a public danger. But they wouldn't have known the singer, who took 'Diamonds' to the top of the Hot 100 in the USA, was taking the Eurostar train if she hadn't posted the number of her train and its arrival time on Twitter. She later tweeted: "The French are fucking insane. I just had to fight my way out of the damn train station."

The Doors slammed again

It takes something to silence a rock crowd but Jim Morrison did it in 1966 when singing 'The End'. The Doors frontman went into a vocal rant stunning the Whisky a Go Go crowd in Los Angeles by singing about killing his father and "fucking" his mother. The Doors were fired as the house band as a result but soon landed a contract with Elektra Records and within a year had gone global.

Religiously against Akon

Rapper Akon was barred from performing in Sri Lanka in 2007 because of his legal track record and the island's National Monks' Association protesting that his music video for 'Sexy Chick' insulted Buddhism. A Buddha statue could be seen several times in the background.

Missing missus

In the 1970s, conservative Canadians criticized their Prime Minister's wife Margaret Trudeau because she missed state occasions to go to rock concerts. Margaret, in her 20s at the time, was married to Premier Pierre, who was in his 50s. She was particularly associated with some members of the Rolling Stones.

FBI too slick for Grace

A rock star's outrageous plot to drug former US President Richard Nixon was thwarted by eagle-eyed security men. Jefferson Airplane's Grace Slick was invited for tea at the White House in 1969 because she had been to the same college as the President's daughter, Tricia, but it was alleged Slick meant to pour more than tea. The plan of Slick and her political activist escort Abbie Hoffman was said to be to spike Nixon's tea with LSD but they were thwarted because Slick, who was on an FBI blacklist, was recognized and prevented from entering.

Stitched up?

Two heavy metal bands engaged in a 30-year feud – over some sewing. Cross-dressing Americans Twisted Sister were in a war of words with Swiss counterparts Krokus from the 1980s when Krokus hired the wife of Sister's Dee Snider to make their stage costumes but never paid her. Snider was not long ago quoted as calling the Swiss outfit "Crapus" and saying to them: "You have no idea how close you came to landing on the bottom of a lake." Krokus said recently they did not like the creations of, ironically Swiss-born, Suzette Snider and burned them. But at the time of writing peace may have been about to break out as Krokus' Chris von Rohr was quoted as saying: "If we have not treated his wife with due respect, we are sorry." He was said to have proposed the two bands bury the hatchet– by headlining a festival set together.

What's the story – spider furore

Former Oasis guitarist Noel Gallagher found a fan who was so attached to him it followed him halfway around the world. Out popped a green fanged spider as his gear was being unpacked for a 2012 festival gig on the Channel Island of Jersey and a 20-minute quarantine cordon was placed around the set where he was due to play with his High Flying Birds band. Noel, who had the number-one album (*What's the Story*) *Morning Glory?* with Oasis, had been touring in Argentina and Japan previously and it is believed the rare tube web spider, *Segestria florentina*, hitched a lift. For the spider, whose non-lethal bite is likened to a deep injection, the travelling days with a rock band were over and it went to a new home at an island wildlife refuge.

Voodoo hoodoo

A woman who dated One Direction star Harry Styles when she was almost twice his age became the subject for a voodoo doll. DJ Caroline Flack, who was 32 when she was seen out with the 17-year-old Harry, was vilified by 1D's teenybopper fan base and an unofficial fanzine printed a cut-out voodoo doll of her in 2012.

Coffin shocker

If there was one person that Screamin' Jay Hawkins would have liked to put a spell on for real, it was who locked him in a coffin. Hawkins, whose only major hit was 'I Put a Spell on You', emerged from the coffin as part of his stage act in the 1950s, but one night at the Apollo Theatre in New York someone locked him in the coffin as a 'joke'. Hawkins admitted panicking and 'soiling' himself in the claustrophobic box and, although the finger of suspicion pointed at one of the Drifters who were on the same bill, no one ever owned up.

Fiery Keith

1973 was not a good year for Rolling Stone Keith Richards when it came to fire. He escaped a fire in his Munich hotel room before a concert in Germany only weeks after he, his girlfriend and two children fled a blaze which destroyed their thatched cottage in the English countryside. The Stone found himself barred by several hotel chains as a result of the Munich incident.

Snoop Dog becomes a cat

Snoop Dog underwent a transformation when he announced a change of music style and name. Rapper Snoop Dog became reggae star Snoop Lion as he reinvented himself after embracing the religion of Rastafarianism while visiting Jamaica. He had already eschewed his real name Calvin Cordozar Broadus to become a big hit in gangsta rap but said in 2012: "I want to bury Snoop Dog and become Snoop Lion."

Flight death

Guitarist Paul Kossoff was already halfway to the angels when he died on an aircraft in 1976. Kossoff was 26 and in poor health when he died on 19 March from drug-related heart problems on a flight from Los Angeles to New York. He was cremated and interred near his London birthplace, where his epitaph reads 'All Right Now' after Kossoff's first major hit single with the band Free in 1970.

Adam loses battle

Beastie Boy Adam Yauch died at the age of 47 on 4 May 4 2012, after a three-year battle with salivary gland cancer that he had claimed was "very treatable". After surgery and radiation therapy Yauch, a Buddhist, also became a vegan on the recommendation of Tibetan doctors.

Bloody hell for Keith

Press stories of Keith Richards turning into the vampire Dracula abounded in the 1970s after it was revealed that the guitarist had undergone haemodialysis. In reality Richard flew a specialist from the USA to a Swiss villa to have his blood filtered and waste toxins removed on a kidney machine, but the story went further into myth that he had excised his big drug habit by this method. Richard himself later agreed he had told journalists that because he was sick of being asked how he had cleaned up his drug habit.

Jackson's moon walk for real?

Michael Jackson certainly reached for the moon during his lifetime and was one of the largest owners of lunar land. In 2005 he bought a 1,200-acre plot in the Lake of Dreams and owned a smaller parcel in the Sea of Vapours. After his death, a crater on the moon was renamed Michael Joseph Jackson by the Lunar Republic Society in Jackson's honour.

Bianca's marriage confession

Bianca Jagger admitted that her marriage to Rolling Stone singer Mick lasted only hours. On 12 May 1971 the couple married in a French chapel in front of half the world's entertainment press. But the shine of the sunny day in St Tropez had already been taken off by Jagger presenting her with a 28-page pre-nuptial contract. She left the wedding party after just one dance with her new father-in-law and later admitted the marriage had ended on her wedding day.

Hot Christmas

One of the greatest Christmas chart songs 'The Christmas Song (Chestnuts roasting on an open fire)' was written in a California heatwave in July 1946. Lyricist Bob Wells and music composer Mel Tormé earned more than $12 million from the song that still endures and entered the pop charts with Nat King Cole three times over several decades.

Gunplay death

With the final words "gun's not loaded" American rhythm and blues singer Johnny Ace's fascination with firearms led to his downfall. In an attempt to prove it to a group of friends, he pointed the .22 calibre revolver at himself and fired, killing himself instantly in 1954. Ace, born John Alexander, had in two years eight hits in a row, including 'Cross My Heart', 'Please Forgive Me', 'The Clock', 'Yes, Baby', 'Saving My Heart for You' and 'Never Let Me Go'. There had been hints that his death at the age of 25 in Houston, Texas was a result of playing Russian roulette but this has been denied by witnesses to the shooting. Ace, who had been drinking on the day of his death, was known to tote a gun, often took it out to play with and even blasted holes in road signs.

No 001 for 007

While the James Bond film franchise has been a box-office number one for over 50 years, there has been a curse on Bond title songs topping the British charts. Despite such musical luminaries as Paul McCartney and Wings, Shirley Bassey, Duran Duran, Tina Turner, Nancy Sinatra and Adele recording Bond themes none of them has yet made number one in Britain.

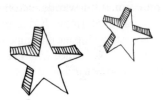

Shape of things to come

The Rolling Stones debuted to a sober-suited audience of 80 on 12 July 1962. Featuring only Keith Richards, Brian Jones and Mick Jagger of the line-up that was later to conquer the world, the gig at the Marquee basement club in London's Soho was mainly attended by jazz fans. Mick Jagger and the Rollin' Stones, as they were named at the time, served up a 50-minute set of American rhythm and blues. Later in their prime the Stones would play to audiences of hundreds of thousands.

Death crashed websites

The global outpouring of grief over the death of Michael Jackson led to chaos on the Internet in 2009. So many fans wanted news that Twitter reported a crash, as did the websites of Wikipedia, the *Los Angeles Times* and AOL. So many people hit the net that Google, fearing it was targeted by a Distributed Denial of Service attack (DDoS) when multiple systems flood the bandwidth, blocked searches related to Michael Jackson for 30 minutes. Later in July 2009, 31.1 million people made Jacko's memorial service one of the most watched events in online streaming history.

Bruce sings the blues

Bruce Springsteen admitted in a magazine interview that he had suffered from depression for 30 years – even to the point of being suicidal. The rock legend who fronts the E Street Band said the condition struck as he found fame and success in the 1980s with hit singles such as 'Born To Run' and multi-million-selling albums. He also revealed in 2012 that his father's life was blighted by depression. Of his legendary epic three-hour live performances he said: "They are the product of pure fear, self-loathing and self-hatred."

Solos can be so low

Solo rock and pop stars are twice as likely to die early as those in a band, a study in 2012 found. Researchers and psychologists at a university in Liverpool, England studied 1,500 performers over 50 years and reckoned singers who go it alone miss the support and company of band mates. Cases in point include Amy Winehouse dead at 27 in 2011 and Dickie Valentine killed aged 41 in 1971.

Brown behind bars

Whitney Houston's widower Bobby Brown was sentenced to 55 days in jail in 2013 after being caught drink-driving twice in a year. Brown had a long history of drink and drug abuse and was also ordered by a Los Angeles court to undergo alcohol counselling.

Coyote attack kills singer

Folk singer Taylor Mitchell died on the brink of stardom when she was killed by coyotes in 2009. Toronto-born Taylor, 19, was hiking alone in an eastern Canada national park when the coyotes struck, fatally injuring her before she died in hospital. Taylor was a promising young musician promoting her new album *For Your Consideration* when the attack came in Nova Scotia. Tragically she achieved greater fame as the only adult person, and second person overall, known to be fatally attacked by coyotes.

Help rolls in for Stones

'Not Fade Away' in 1964 was the first time that the Rolling Stones brought in outside talent for a recording – and some big names were among the helpers. Legendary producer Phil Spector played maracas while Graham Nash, eventually of Crosby, Stills and Nash, and Tony Hicks of the Hollies added their vocals and guitar work. Also drafted in was regular American hit maker Gene Pitney. Pitney and Spector were also on 'Little by Little' which was recorded at the same Regent Sound Studios session in London. 'Not Fade Away' charted at number three in the UK and saw the Stones break through into the American charts at 48.

Missed chances

In the early 1960s Decca Records in Britain decided not to sign up the Yardbirds and Manfred Mann on recording contracts yet both bands went on to multi-million sales with other labels, Columbia and HMV respectively.

Having a pop at pop world

Performers have never been averse to biting the hand that feeds them and in 1964 the record industry was under fire from some of the era's biggest names. The song 'Andrew's Blues', by Gene Pitney with the Rolling Stones was a satire on the then chairman of the Stones' record label Decca and was a swipe at the industry as a whole. The Andrew in the title was Stones' producer/manager Andrew Loog Oldham.

Missed millions

Britain's Decca Records' senior executives were so against the Ray Peterson recording of teenage tragedy song 'Tell Laura I Love Her' that they not only refused to release it but also ordered the destruction of several thousand copies of the record. It left the way open for rival label Columbia to release the same song covered by Ricky Valance, which shot to number one in the UK, stayed there for three weeks in 1960 and made Valance the first Welshman to hit the top of the UK pop charts. Peterson's version on the RCA Victor label made the US top 10 and the song has been a hit in 14 countries, selling over seven million copies. The song is about a teenager called Tommy killed in a car race while trying to win the prize money for a wedding ring for the eponymous Laura.

Financially Hammered

Rapper MC Hammer spent a reported $20 million on a 40,000-square-foot mansion in the USA complete with Italian marble floors and solid-gold toilet. But the hip-hop artist, once worth an estimated £33 million from sales of albums such as *Too Legit to Quit*, lost millions on it when it was sold a few years later as he filed for bankruptcy.

Help from the other side

Carmit Bachar and Ashley Roberts consulted a spiritual healer to get over their devastation at the 2008 break-up of girl band the Pussycat Dolls. Worldwide hits for the song and dance band whose personnel changed many times have included 'When I Grow Up' and 'I Hate This Part'.

US clean-up

Because of the more puritanical sensibilities of American TV audiences the Rolling Stones had to clean up the more raunchy lyrics of 'Let's Spend the Night Together' to appear on the *Ed Sullivan Show* in 1967. Realizing what an important publicity conduit to the record-buying public the show was, Mick Jagger and co. agreed to sing it as 'Let's Spend Some Time Together'.

Maria's trouble continued

Maria Alyokhina's troubles continued to pile up behind prison bars in 2012. The Pussy Riot punk band member jailed in August 2012 for a raucous protest against President Vladimir Putin had to be separated from other prisoners. The protest in a cathedral offended many members of the Russian Orthodox Church and even behind bars her actions have been said to have attracted death threats. By the end of the year Maria, 24, was moved to a single-person cell in the prison in the Ural Mountains.

Busting the budget

Madonna's raunchy stage gear has been among the most sought-after memorabilia in pop history. The conical corset unveiled during her 1990s *Blond Ambition* tour has sold for £32,450 ($51,920) – a 116% increase on the £15,000 ($24,358) valuation. Madonna first revealed the Jean Paul Gaultier corset when she removed her long black gown to show the shimmering piece made from green silk with the renowned conical cups that are synonymous with the icon's style. Another of Madonna's Gaultier corsets, from the 1987 *Who's That Girl?* tour, had sold for £44,337 ($72,000) in late 2011 when its estimated value was (£4,926) $8,000. Another stage costume from the *Blond Ambition* tour, a two-piece black satin bustier and lycra shorts, had earlier sold for £16,250 ($26,000), 35% above estimate.

Little by little for a big bill

Over-running a London gig cost the Rolling Stones an incredible £5,600 a minute in 2012. To cheering crowds they played 35 minutes too long at the O2 Arena and left them open to a £200,000 fine for breaking council rules. It wasn't a huge chunk out of the Stones' pockets as they were paid a reported £15.6 million for the four-night run, and a fifth night was added.

Bee Gee home gutted

The childhood home of the Bee Gees was destroyed by fire. Although by 2012 it was only a dilapidated wooden house near Brisbane, Australia it had been home to the Gibb brothers – Barry, Maurice and Robin – for 10 years of the late 1950s, early 1960s after the British-born Gibb family emigrated Down Under. Together the brothers, of whom in 2012 only Barry remained alive, produced hits such as 'Stayin' Alive', 'Jive Talkin'' and 'Night Fever'.

Life's a blur for Ronnie

Ronnie Wood, formerly of the Faces, has admitted that more often than not the audience is a blur to him. The guitarist gradually became short-sighted and when he appears with the Rolling Stones refuses to wear his glasses on stage, which means he can't see the adoring crowds.

Sofa so bad

Beach Boy Brian Wilson has admitted that his cocaine habit of the 1980s became so bad that he fished behind the sofa for any stray royalty cheque that might finance his next hit. In his autobiography *Wouldn't It be Nice* he said he rarely left his home and his weight ballooned to 150kg (approx. 330lbs/24 stone).

Pop murder witnesses

Two witnesses to the murder of Los Angeles R&B producer John Dolphin in 1958 later became stars in their own right. Dolphin, who was notorious for not sharing the income from hits with artists, was gunned down by a disgruntled songwriter seen by Bruce Johnston, later of the Beach Boys, and Sandy Nelson, a drummer who had solo hits such as 'Teen Beat' and 'Let There Be Drums'.

Drive to disaster

British drummer Cozy Powell was an accident waiting to happen in 1994. He was driving in bad weather at over 100mph (160kph); was over the alcohol limit; not wearing a seatbelt; and talking to a girlfriend on a mobile phone. The final piece of the fatal jigsaw was a slow puncture in a rear tyre which led to the crash on the M4 motorway in western England that killed the drummer, who was in demand as a session musician and had a solo hit with 'Dance with the Devil' in 1974.

Playful

Looking through the keyhole revealed more than usual in 2013; it laid bare a pop star's sex life. Former Atomic Kitten singer Kerry Katona's home was the subject of the UK TV show *Through the Keyhole* in which a panel had to guess from items in a house to which celebrity it belongs. Katona's house was the pilot for the series and host Keith Lemon probed too deeply into Kerry's drawers – finding a big sex toy and other kinky paraphernalia.

Out of the groove

American singer Lesley Gore was dissuaded by her record label in 1965 from recording any song with the word 'groovy' in it. Presumably the word had a sexual connotation for the executives at Mercury Records but it proved disastrous because she rejected 'A Groovy Kind Of Love' which rocketed British band The Mindbenders to number two in the American charts and was later a massive hit for former Genesis singer Phil Collins in the 1980s.

Van surprise

Big-selling musician Van Morrison had a shock at the age of 64 to be named as the father of a son in the USA. Although he denied paternity of the boy born to employee Gigi Lee the matter was never fully settled because the boy, who was named after Van, died of diabetes-related complications in January 2011 and his mother of throat cancer in the following October.

She bluffed you, yeah, yeah, yeah!

More than 45 years after Beatlemania raged across the world, it was revealed that some Beatles autographs of the time were forged – by John Lennon's aunt. It took a 2012 antique valuation show to reveal that auntie Mimi Smith used to sign photographs of the band if fans turned up at the home she shared with John. It was revealed by an expert on the BBC television programme *The Antiques Roadshow* that Mimi would go to her pantry and forge the signatures of not only nephew John, but also Paul, George and Ringo. A genuinely signed photograph would fetch £2,000 ($3,200) at 2013 prices but the dud Mimi version would be worth £20 ($32).

Storm in a yoghurt pot

In the history of rock and pop's bad boys, R.E.M. didn't figure greatly – so imagine the shock when guitarist Peter Buck was accused of 'air rage' and arrested at the end of a British Airways flight from Seattle to London. It was alleged Buck attempted to play a CD in a drinks trolley, and got into a scuffle over a pot of yoghurt which exploded in the fracas. He was charged with two charges of common assault on cabin crew, one charge of being drunk on an aircraft and one of damaging property. Buck later returned from his US base to appear before a UK court and, after claiming his sleeping pills had reacted badly with a mid-flight glass of wine, he was acquitted.

Ronnie weds again

Guitarist Ronnie Wood married third wife Sally Humphreys, 31 years his junior, in December 2012. Wood was 65 at the time.

My word

R&B singer and record producer R Kelly admitted 20 years into his successful career that he was barely able to read. He said the only reason he made it through elementary and middle school in Chicago was because he "had a great jump shot" on the basketball court.

Dirty trick

L7, a punk band that graduated through grunge to heavy metal between 1985 and 2001, were subject to more than mud-slinging during a US tour in 1992. While their dressing room was empty someone defecated into the band's hairdryer as a practical joke. No one formally admitted to the dirty deed but a leading member of a headlining band was suspected.

Medical bungle

Faith No More and Mr Bungle frontman Mike Patton's right hand is permanently numb yet he is able to excel on a number of instruments including drums, guitar, bass and keyboards. While on stage in the 1980s with Faith No More, he accidentally cut himself on a broken bottle, severing tendons and nerves in his hand. Despite medical opinion to the contrary Patton remained with no feeling in the right hand.

Still shaking them up

Elvis Presley, who was panned for his sexual pelvis movements on TV in the 1950s, still had the ability to shock 36 years after his death. American teenagers were barred in 2013 from singing the 1957 hit 'All Shook Up' in their school play. The Salt Lake City school in the Mormon-dominated state of Utah ruled the lyrics were 'suggestive'.

Up in smoke

Acid house music leaders the KLF burned £1 million in cash in 1994. They had withdrawn the last of the money they had made as the KLF – the K Foundation – and set fire to it in a boathouse on the Scottish island of Jura in 1994. The result was filmed and taken around Britain on tour. KLF founders Billy Drummond and Jimmy Cauty maintain it was not a stunt and, although they had agreed in 1995 not to talk about the burned money for another 23 years, Drummond broke his silence in a BBC interview to say he regretted burning the cash. The ashes were made into a single house brick.

Off his Face?

Ronnie Wood, once of the Faces, reportedly used to spend £12,000 a week on cocaine. The toll on his health included part of his nose collapsing.

Bowling over Beyonce

Fans were offered the chance to appear with Beyoncé Knowles for the famous and prestigious half-time music session at the 2013 Super Bowl in New Orleans. But the lucky winner had to bowl over the singer first by submitting photos.

Katy's a record breaker

The moment 'Last Friday Night (T.G.I.F)' topped the US charts in August 2011 US-born singer Katy Perry went into pop history. She became the first woman to have five number-one singles from her debut album *Teenage Dream*. 'California Gurls', 'Teenage Dream', 'Firework' and 'ET' had reached the summit before 'Last Friday Night (T.G.I.F)'. Katy was also the first artist to achieve five four-million-selling digital tracks in the USA.

Heading for a fall

Rolling Stone Keith Richards vowed to kick his cocaine habit after he fell from a tree, which resulted in brain surgery. He toppled out of a coconut tree while on a break on the South Pacific island of Fiji during a 2006 world tour and fractured his skull. He had to be flown to New Zealand for treatment, where he decided to quit coke. 2010 saw him reportedly giving up his legendary heavy drinking sessions as well.

Lucky teeth

Aerosmith frontman Steve Tyler wore a good-luck necklace of four sharp teeth. One of the teeth is from a raccoon he caught as a boy growing up in Yonkers, New York.

Chauffeur run over

Trouble at a pub opening left a chauffeur dead under the wheels of Keith Moon's luxury car in 1970. The Who drummer had annoyed locals at Hatfield in Hertfordshire by turning up in his Bentley for the opening of a friend's pub and only drinking expensive brandy. A rowdy crowd gathered as he tried to leave the car park, rocking the car and throwing coins. Driver and bodyguard Neil Boland got out to confront the mob and Moon, who didn't drive even when sober, tried to drive to safety but Boland wound up underneath the car and was dragged down the road. Moon was charged with Boland's death, as well as drink-driving and driving without a licence or insurance but later Boland's death was ruled as an accident, clearing Moon, although he pleaded guilty to the driving charges.

Whitney's legacy

Two weeks after her death, American singer Whitney Houston was still breaking world records. She was found dead in a hotel bath on 11 February 2012 and on February 25 she was heading for the *Guinness World Records* for having the most simultaneous hits for a female solo artist in the UK charts. She had 12 tracks in the top 75 and three of them were top 40. 'I Will Always Love You' was at 14; 'I Wanna Dance with Somebody (Who Loves Me)' at 20; and 'One Moment in Time' at 40.

Macho make-up

Elvis Presley from the very macho Deep South had worn eye shadow since high school. It made an even bigger impact on female fans when he made his first TV appearance in *The Dorsey Show* in 1956.

Leonard's long wait

Forty-one years passed between the appearances of two Leonard Cohen albums in the UK albums top 10, a record time gap. Canadian singer Cohen was in the charts with *Songs of Love and Hate* in 1971 and didn't return until February 2012 when *Old Ideas* went in at number two. This incredible gap won Cohen a mention in the 2013 *Guinness World Records*.

U2 cash in

As of 2012 the highest-grossing tour by a rock band was the marathon 25-month world tour by U2. It grossed £465 million ($736 million) from June 2009 to July 2011. More than seven million fans watched the 110 shows as the band, whose hit albums had included *Joshua Tree* and *Rattle and Hum*, circled the globe.

Paying for success

One of the first disc jockeys to feature rock 'n' roll on radio was not totally altruistic about promoting the genre in early 1950s America. Alan Freed, who appeared on several stations during his career but made his biggest impact in New York, was involved in payola – taking kickbacks to promote an artist. Although not illegal at the time, Freed actually took songwriting credits with Harvey Fuqua on the Maguire Sisters' 'Sincerely' and with Chuck Berry on 'Maybellene' among others in exchange for airing them. Payola was later investigated by the US government and declared illegal. Freed died in 1965 from alcoholism.

Making up a song title

A discarded mascara box led to the renaming of a Chuck Berry song that was to become a rock 'n' roll classic. In 1955 Berry had adapted the country song 'Ida Red' to the up-and-coming rock style and renamed it 'Ida May' but the Chess record company did not like either of these titles and, the story goes, it was changed when boss Leonard Chess saw a Maybelline mascara box. The spelling was also slightly altered to 'Maybellene' to avoid a possible lawsuit from the cosmetics firm.

Rock rocks them

American teenagers in the 1950s got the wrong message from the classic 'Rock Around the Clock' by Bill Haley and the Comets. Featured in the film *Blackboard Jungle*, it was a commentary on youth violence in a New York school. But instead of identifying with the embattled teacher in the films, the rebellious youth of the time intensified the anarchy by dancing in cinema aisles, rioting, ripping up seats and fighting among themselves.

Duelling guitars

Two of the world's greatest guitarists are said to have fallen out over a riff and have barely spoken since 1969. The source of the feud was said to be the distinctive riff in the Rolling Stones 'Honky Tonk Women'. Top slide guitarist Ry Cooder is said to have accused the Stones' Keith Richards of stealing the classic riff. Richards denied this but later admitted 'borrowing' Cooder's trademark five-string tuning.

Big spend end

US rapper MC Hammer, once said to be worth $30 million, filed for bankruptcy in 1996 when his debts mounted to $13 million.

Jay's a scream

Rock 'n' roller Screamin' Jay Hawkins' stage persona was a turbaned man with a bone through his nose dressed in either shocking pink or chartreuse suits. The performer, whose biggest recording success was 'I Put a Spell on You', travelled in a zebra-striped car. Originally from Cleveland Ohio, birth name Jalacy Hawkins, he planned to be an opera singer but later self-deprecatingly called himself a 'destroyer of songs'.

Name calling

Elvis Presley happily accepted the fan title of 'The King' but he was nicknamed many other things during his career. Emerging as a 21-year-old he was called 'The Memphis Flash', the 'Hillbilly Cat' and the 'Atomic Powered Singer' yet the one he hated most was 'Elvis the Pelvis' given to him by the media for his groin gyrations on stage and TV during the 1950s.

Great pianos of fire

The legend of Jerry Lee Lewis' allegedly setting fire to his piano remains a mystery. Although an Alan Freed book and a film biopic of Lewis highlight it, Lewis has never commented on it. It was said that after losing the toss and having to go on stage in the 1950s before Chuck Berry, piano man Lewis wanted to make himself a hard act to follow. He went through his usual manic routine of hair tossing, shirt tearing and stomping on the keyboard and was then said to have tossed a bundle of paper into the piano and lit it, much to the chagrin of the theatre owner who presumably was not insured for that sort of artist behaviour. No one in the audience has ever come forward to confirm the fire or Lewis' alleged jibe to Berry as they passed backstage of "Follow that, killer!".

Money saver was a life saver

Doo-wop star Dion inadvertently saved his own life when he wouldn't stump up $36 for an aeroplane flight. His decision on a 1959 multi-band tour of the northern USA meant he went by road. The plane went without Dion who was touring with the Belmonts and crashed killing Buddy Holly, Richie Valens and the Big Bopper (JP Richardson).

Young love

Bill Wyman caused a 'Jerry Lee Lewis'-type media frenzy in 1983 when, at the age of 50, he started dating 13-year-old British girl Mandy Smith – with the consent of her mother. Six years later at the age of 19 she married the Rolling Stones' bass player but it didn't last and she was divorced at 21. In a 2010 interview, however, she confessed to being 14 when she started a sexual relationship with Wyman.

Making his point with an amp

One-hit wonder Link Wray needed a different sort of 'fuzzy' guitar effect when he recorded the instrumental 'Rumble' in 1958 – so he poked a hole in the amplifier speaker with a pencil. 'Rumble' was a huge hit in the USA and the UK.

Distorted view

The Who's experiments with feedback and guitar distortion were not always appreciated. With the band's recording of 'Anyway, Anyhow, Anywhere' – their second chart entry – the pressing plant staff had returned the master tape asking for sound engineers to remove the 'funny squeaking sounds' which were in fact the artful use of distortion, and Pete Townshend giving the guitar hell as usual.

Burnette's freak death

After just three top 20 hit singles American singer Johnny Burnette was killed in a freak boating accident. On 14 August 1964, Burnette's unlit fishing boat was struck by a cabin cruiser on Clear Lake, California. The impact threw Burnette, who had major hits with 'Dreamin'' and 'You're Sixteen', off the boat and he drowned aged just 30.

Boy! What confusion?

Blues music had two Sonny Boy Williamsons and there remains an on-going dispute, which may never be resolved, about who was the originator of the name. Sonny Boy Williamson I was said to be singer and harp player John Lee Williamson, born in 1914, who recorded 'Good Morning Little Schoolgirl' and died in 1948. Sonny Boy Williamson II was Aleck Miller, probably born in 1912, who in the 1940s impersonated Sonny Boy Williamson I on a radio gig and then made personal appearances when Sonny Boy Williamson I was not available. When Sonny Boy Williamson I died aged 34, Miller, who became known by music historians as Sonny Boy Williamson II, was experienced enough to fill the vacuum and was in place to take full advantage of the 1960s blues revival before his own death from a heart attack in 1965.

A bad name

Singer-songwriter Ray Davies was reported as saying that he never liked the name of his band – the Kinks – even though the multi-million-selling group is one of the most influential band brands to have come out of the 1960s pop music boom and lasted as a band until 1996.

Knights win the battle

Irish group Them lost a battle for a place in the US top 10 because they had recorded what were deemed to be suggestive lyrics to the song 'Gloria'. The line "she comes up to my room and makes me feel all right" was deemed too suggestive for teenage radio audiences in the US so it didn't get air play. However, Chicago-based Shadows of Knight saw the advantage of recording it without the offending lyrics and shot to number 10. Six months on in 1965 Van Morrison's Them version had faltered at 71. However Morrison had the last laugh, having a six-decade-long career while the Shadows of Knight disappeared into the music shade with only a few low-charting follow-up singles.

Charting young

British singers such as Laurie London and Helen Shapiro charted aged 13 and 14 respectively in the 1950s and 1960s, but now it seems the record for the youngest chart entrant will only be broken by someone still in the womb. Blue Ivy Carter became the youngest chart entrant in January 2012 at just two weeks old. She already had a musical heritage in her mum being singer Beyoncé Knowles and her dad rapper Jay-Z. Blue's cries, coos and breathing were recorded in the days after her birth and added to dad's track 'Glory' which was into the American charts inside two weeks. The track was officially billed as 'featuring B.I.C.', an abbreviation of Blue Ivy Carter, and it created a world record.

Family trouble

Beach Boy Brian Wilson claimed that his father Murry not only beat him as a child but also forced him to defecate on a newspaper as a punishment. Wilson got some retaliation for his childhood torments by firing his overbearing dad from involvement with the band. Murry had been an effective promoter for the Beach Boys' records but claimed much of the credit for the band's phenomenal success and his overbearing interference was often resented by Brian and others.

Manson revenge theory

The notorious mass murders of actress Sharon Tate and four other people by the Charles Manson group may have been motivated by a thwarted recording career. The horrific murders in 1969 came at 10050 Cielo Drive, Los Angeles which had been the home of record producer Terry Melcher. After Melcher and Beach Boy Dennis Wilson rejected working with budding songwriter and hippy Manson, Melcher left the address. It is believed that the Manson group may have wreaked revenge in such a bloody and violent way for not getting the film and recording contract they expected from Melcher.

AIDS kills Freddie

Freddie Mercury became the first high-profile AIDS victim in rock to die from the disease. He passed away in November 1991 after a long illness the diagnosis of which wasn't confirmed by his band Queen for some time when the flamboyant singer, who reportedly had a promiscuous lifestyle, made fewer and fewer appearances before his death.

Almost dead man's curve

In one of the great pop music ironies musician Jan Berry almost died in the manner of one of his hit songs. Berry was one half of the Californian Jan and Dean duo which pioneered the surfing sound. They charted at number eight in the USA with 'Dead Man's Curve' in 1964 – a song about a teenage street car race that ended in tragedy. Two years later Berry was not far from the eponymous curve in Beverly Hills, California when his Corvette hit a truck. Head injuries and brain damage put Berry in a coma for months and although by 1970 he was walking and talking again he never fully recovered. He did, however, battle back and remained in the music industry writing and performing until his death in 2004.

Doris is a bad girl

Eternal film goody-goody Doris Day actually had a song banned by the BBC. The title song of her 'screwball' film *Move Over Darling* offended the censors at the BBC for being too suggestive. But the British record-buying public didn't agree that it was too saucy and helped it to reach number eight in the singles chart in 1964.

No love lost

Grateful Dead drummer Mickey Hart's last act for his father was to spit on his coffin. Hart, whose father Lenny was absent during his childhood, couldn't forgive him because as the Grateful Dead became successful Lenny re-entered Mickey's life and, after offering to handle the band finances, was alleged to have stolen the lot.

Williams death mystery

Songwriter and singer Larry Williams seemingly had everything to live for when he was found shot in the head in 1980. He was a successful recording artist, had written 'Bony Moronie' and 'Dizzy Miss Lizzy' and had sold material to John Lennon, the Beatles and the Rolling Stones, but his death was ruled as suicide. There were also mutterings about some of Williams' underworld associates in Los Angeles and their possible involvement in his death.

Baker teeth disaster

Despite his terms in prison and his heroin addiction, one of the most devastating things to happen to jazz trumpeter Chet Baker was losing his front teeth. They were demolished in a savage beating he took after a gig in San Francisco in 1968. With his teeth went the embouchure (shaping of the lips) that horn players need. Baker, a heroin addict, was forced to work at petrol stations before he got dentures and had to rework his embouchure in order to restart his music career. He died aged 58 in 1988 when he fell from a hotel balcony in Amsterdam.

Britney Speared

Luxury goods company Louis Vuitton objected in 2007 to being in a Britney Spears video – and sued. The company won a lawsuit that alleged a Spears video seen by millions of viewers of music station MTV violated counterfeiting laws. A Paris civil court halted Sony BMG and MTV Online broadcasting or marketing the video for 'Do Something' in any form and fined them €80,000 ($117,000/£77,000). In the the video, Spears was driving a pink Hummer floating on make-believe clouds but one shot showed fingers drumming on a dashboard covered with what looked like Vuitton's 'Cherry Blossoms' design: dark pink blossoms on a pale pink, weblike background and embossed with the 'LV' logo.

Grave concerns

The body of blues musician Robert Johnson lies in several places and nobody can confirm which is his genuine grave. There are memorials marking likely sites at Mount Zion Missionary Baptist Church near Morgan City, Mississippi and in the cemetery of Payne Chapel, Quito, Mississippi. Record label Sony Music believes he lies under a big pecan tree in the cemetery of the Little Zion Church near Greenwood, Mississippi and has a memorial there, but many believe the blues legend, who died aged 27 in 1938, was so poor that he is in an unmarked pauper's grave close to where he died in Greenwood.

Beyonce rebound

The people of a small market town in Essex, England were overjoyed when it was announced in 2013 that R&B superstar Beyoncé was coming to the annual carnival. Organizers at Maldon, population 14,000, were aiming stratospherically high by inviting her and had received an encouraging message that Beyoncé was available. But joy for the little town turned to horror when the singer's management demanded £50,000 ($75,000).

Upfront Tony

Tony Burrows was a serial lead singer who performed in the role for a number of bands at the same time during the 1970s. A regular in the charts both sides of the Atlantic, session singer Burrows has been accredited as the lead singer on hit pop singles for more groups than any other artist in recording industry history, including a total of five top charted one-hit wonders. His musical achievements include chart appearances with the Ivy League and the Flowerpot Men in the 1960s but his most prolific period was the early 1970s. He was a one-hit wonder with Edison Lighthouse's 'Love Grows (Where My Rosemary Goes)'; the Pipkins' novelty song 'Gimme Dat Ding'; White Plains' 'My Baby Loves Lovin''; and First Class' 'Beach Baby'.

Vile Savile

A British DJ who scaled the heights of the establishment was posthumously unmasked as a paedophile and serial sex offender. Sir Jimmy Savile was a presenter of BBC's long-running music show *Top of the Pops* and had been knighted as well as holding the OBE for his charity work over five decades, in which it was estimated he raised £40 million ($65 million). But a year after his death at 84 in 2011 allegations of sex abuse on children and teenagers poured in in their hundreds. It led the police to believe that Savile may have been one of Britain's most prolific sex offenders. In 2013 allegations were still coming in, this time that he abused staff and patients at a hospice for the terminally ill. Cigar-smoking, marathon-running Roman Catholic Savile never married and at first his family denied the allegations but quickly removed a large and elaborate memorial from his grave site in his beloved county of Yorkshire, England.

Hooked on drumming

Having a hook for a hand didn't stop Victor Moulton enjoying success with 1960's American band the Barbarians. 'Moulty', as he was known, lost his hand at 14 in an explosion but had a specially modified prosthesis to enable him to hold a drumstick.

Pork talk

The giant inflatable pig covered with slogans that has been such a part of former Pink Floyd member Roger Waters' gigs went political in 2008. At a show in President George W. Bush's heartland of Dallas, Texas the pig's penis had "Cheney" (meaning current Vice-President Dick) written on it and its anus was adorned with the words "Impeach Bush Now".

No Monkee business

Stephen Stills fell at the last hurdle to become one of the Monkees. He auditioned in 1965 for a role in the manufactured group to star in a zany pop series and was in the final shakeout but was let down by his crooked teeth and thinning hair. He was friends with Peter Tork who did become a Monkee along with Mike Nesmith, Davy Jones and Micky Dolenz and the series was a four-year TV hit between 1966 and 1970. Stills, a singer-songwriter and multi-instrumentalist, went on to form Buffalo Springfield and become a member of the highly successful Crosby, Stills and Nash combination.

Wyman walks out

Bass player Bill Wyman quit the Rolling Stones just two years short of the band's 30th anniversary. He left after their 1989–90 world tour amid rumours of bad blood between him and the other Stones, although he didn't specify which. This was unusually reticent for Wyman because he was never slow in hitting out at things that annoyed him within the band. He expressed his anger that he didn't get enough credit as a songwriter, saying: "I got a bit disheartened that they weren't generous enough to share, like many other bands do. Like the way the Beatles gave room for Ringo and George to do their thing, and how the Who gave John Entwistle a chance to write stuff." Wyman slammed the decision to airbrush his image from archive photographs on the sleeve of the Stones' 2005 album *Rarities*.

Reverse psychology

Bruce Palmer was never seen facing the camera when Buffalo Springfield made TV appearances. He would always turn his back to avoid being recognized. The reason was that he was a Canadian national without legal papers for the USA unlike his fellow countryman and band member Neil Young. He was later caught by immigration authorities and deported. His place as Buffalo Springfield bass player was taken by Jim Messina.

Tragedy for Eric

Conor, the four-year-old son of blues guitar legend Eric Clapton's died in a horrific fall from the 53rd-floor window of a New York City apartment at 117 East 57th Street on 20 March 1991. Conor was Clapton's son with girlfriend Italian model Lory Del Santo. After the tragedy Clapton wrote the song 'Tears in Heaven' with Will Jennings, a slow tear-jerker and worldwide hit which reflected the pain and loss Clapton felt for his young son. Suddenly in 2004 he announced he would stop playing it.

Fight fright for Aretha

Soul singer Aretha Franklin got a memorable start to her Atlantic label recording career – for all the wrong reasons. She travelled from her native Detroit in 1967 to the famous Fame Studios at Muscle Shoals, Alabama to get a specific 'feel' for the debut album *Aretha's Gold's* according to her producer Jerry Wexler. But with just a song and a half in the can some drinking was done and a massive fight erupted which initially involved Aretha's husband Ted White and a member of the horn section before others got involved. Fists and instruments flew, according to eye witnesses. Feelings were so rancorous afterwards that the rest of the session was scrapped and recording finished in New York. Nevertheless *Aretha's Gold* soared to number one in the American rhythm and blues charts in 1969.

No tribute after all

Keith Richards took several decades to confirm that the 1973 Rolling Stones song 'Angie' was not a tribute to anyone in particular even though his own daughter was called Angela. It was also speculated it was written by himself and Mick Jagger with Angie, David Bowie's wife at the time, in mind. But many years later Keith said neither was right and that the name merely came to him during the composing process.

Doo-wop death

Doo-wop and rock 'n' roll singer Frankie Lymon died of a heroin overdose at the age of just 25. After finding success as the leader of the Teenagers in 1956 with the top 10 song 'Why Do Fools Fall in Love' that was to be the zenith of his chart career. He became addicted to heroin and was found dead in his grandmother's bathroom in his native Harlem, New York in 1968. His short life and career inspired the 1998 film *Why Do Fools Fall in Love*.

Dion confesses

Clean-cut, all-American boy Dion Di Mucci came clean later in his life about his drug habit. In the days before the mid-1960s when drugs, rock and pop went hand in hand, the teen idol admitted he was often high on heroin. This was unbeknown to his adoring fan base, when he and his band the Belmonts were riding high with such hits of the late-1950s–early-1960s period as 'Runaround Sue', 'The Wanderer' and 'Teenager in Love'. He kicked it for a while and then succumbed before declaring himself clean once again.

No to George

Boy George, then known as Lieutenant Lush, was rejected as the joint lead singer with Annabella Lwin of British New Romantic band Bow Wow Wow – for being too wild.

Unloved Spoonful

Skewed fan power may have contributed to 1960s California band Lovin' Spoonful's hit machine coming to a grinding halt. In the super-heated drug culture of the flower power era a member of the band is said to have grassed up his drug dealer to avoid a police prosecution for drug possession. With the dealer out of the way, a shortage of the drugs for the California youth culture was created. An underground network swung into action and, by word of mouth and even a full-page advertisement in a Los Angeles newspaper, record buyers were urged to avenge the dealer by boycotting Lovin' Spoonful records such as 'What a Day for a Daydream'. It is hard to say for sure if the boycott worked but it seems strange that after seven consecutive top 10 hits in the US Hot 100, chart success dried up for leader John Sebastian and the Spoonful.

Maiden in safe hands

Lead singer Bruce Dickinson had no chance of missing any of Iron Maiden's *Final Frontier* tour in 2010–11 because he was also the band's pilot. The heavy metal legends completed the 30,000-mile world tour which covered Russia, Australia and several South American countries, with Dickinson spending many hours in the cockpit of a specially adapted Boeing 757.

End of the line for Lynott

Considering his drug and alcohol dependencies it was surprising that Phil Lynott's untimely death was not due to an overdose. The Thin Lizzy leader and songwriter was found collapsed on Christmas Day 1985 by his mother Philomena at his home in Kew, London. Because of his drug history, which his mum was not aware of, friends took Lynott, 36, to a drug clinic. His condition worsened and he was transferred to a hospital with septicaemia and died of heart failure and pneumonia on 4 January 1986.

Get out of town, Mitt

2012 US presidential candidate Mitt Romney lost not only to Barack Obama but also to the late singer-songwriter Phil Lynott. Romney used Lynott's Thin Lizzy anthem 'The Boys are Back in Town' to whip up the crowds at the Republican convention in Florida until the Irishman's estate ordered him to stop using the iconic track. Lynott's widow Caroline Lynott-Taraskevics said a cease and desist order was issued because there was no way the singer would have supported the Republican candidate's campaign. She and Lynott's mother Philomena were angered by the tune's usage because Phil, who died in 1986, would have rejected any association with the Republicans, particularly the Christian right wing of the party with its anti-gay and pro-rich policies.

Cop that!

In the early days of the 1960s drug counter-culture in California police had a special way of dealing with players of trumpets and other brass instruments they caught in drug raids. There have been many accounts of cops bent on 'teaching' musicians a lesson by deliberately striking them in the mouth – damaging their teeth and lips – so that they couldn't work.

Sly's a riot

Sly Stone of Sly and the Family Stone fame drove many of his fans to violence by his habit of not turning up for gigs. Several times when Stone, who had huge global successes with 'Dance to the Music' and 'Family Affair', failed to appear at sell-out concerts, disappointed and disgruntled fans left in near-riot mood. One was a well-publicized time when things turned ugly in Grant Park, Chicago in 1970 and two later occasions in Washington DC when police had to be called to quieten things down. Stone had a well-documented record of drug abuse and police busts but he was not the only one to let his fans down. Some of his fellow band members had reputations for no-shows, refusing to play or passing out from drugs use.

Damon re-cycles

Green-minded Damon Albarn has been a keen cyclist for years but thieves seemed hell-bent on putting the brakes on him. By 2013 the Blur and Gorillaz frontman, a fan of old-style racing bikes, had had 30 stolen in just a few years, but he remained unperturbed. He is said to usually spend about £600 on a bike, loses it and then buys a replacement from his favourite west London bike shop. Apparently the staff there have failed to persuade him to invest in a padlock.

Inquest re-run

Amy Winehouse had to have two inquests in London because of a legal hitch. After the first inquest following her death in July 2011 it was found that the coroner was underqualified so a rerun had to take place in 2013 – all to come to the same ruling that Amy's death at 27 was misadventure following a vodka binge lasting several days.

Nothing can stop Curtis

When R&B legend Curtis Mayfield wrote 'Nothing Can Stop Me' for Gene Chandler in the 1960s, he had no idea how relevant those words might turn out to be for him. Tragedy struck in 1990 when a lighting rig crashed down at an open-air concert in Brooklyn, trapping the singer of hits such as 'Superfly' and 'Move On Up' under its weight. Curtis' injuries were so severe that he was paralysed from the neck down and although unable to play guitar, he wrote, sang and directed the recording of his last album, *New World Order*. Mayfield's vocals were painstakingly recorded, usually line by line while lying on his back. The long-time effects of his injuries – including a leg amputation in 1998 – led to his death aged 57 in 1999.

Beer inspiration

The two sets of metal umlauts in the band name Mötley Crüe were supposedly inspired by the German beer Lowenbräu that the band was drinking at the time.

Frank's classical finale

Frank Zappa's final performance was as a classical music conductor. Despite being desperately ill from terminal prostate cancer Zappa agreed to work in Frankfurt, Germany in September 1992, with the Ensemble Modern chamber music group which wanted to feature some of his compositions. Wild man Zappa, who had produced such bizarre albums as *Weasels Ripped My Flesh*, could only appear at two performances due to illness but he conducted the opening 'Overture' and the final 'G-Spot Tornado' as well as the theatrical 'Food Gathering in Post-Industrial America, 1992' and 'Welcome to the United States'. Eight weeks later Zappa was dead, aged 52.

Bob's hidden talent

Against all music promotion and marketing rules, Bob Dylan hid his 2013 album from public sight. The legend produced just 100 copies of the four-CD album *The 50th Anniversary Collection* and hid them across a select few specialist record shops in the UK, Europe and Scandinavia. In shades of *Charlie and the Chocolate Factory*'s 'Golden Ticket', Dylan fans who unearthed the most exclusive album ever produced would hit the jackpot. Within days of the announcement in January 2013 copies that had been found were going on eBay for £1,000 ($1,600) with prices expected to soar even higher. The 86-track live album was produced as a super-limited edition so that Dylan would not lose control of the songs under European Union copyright laws.

Tammi's tragedy

Tammi Terell collapsed into the arms of fellow singer Marvin Gaye as the two performed in a Virginia college concert in 1967. It led to her being diagnosed with a brain tumour but eight operations were not able to save her and she died in 1970 at the age of 24. She had charted with her 'It Takes Two' duet with Gaye.

Death stalked guitarist

Ill luck seemed to follow Stone the Crows' guitarist and co-founder Les Harvey. Les was touring with Scottish band the Blues Council in March 1965 when their tour van crashed, killing vocalist Fraser Calder and bassist James Giffen. In 1972 Les was electrocuted at a concert in Swansea, South Wales, by touching a microphone that was not properly earthed with wet hands. Then in 1982 Les' brother and fellow blues rocker Alex, of the Sensational Alex Harvey Band, died, a day short of his 47th birthday, from a massive heart attack suffered while on a cross-Channel ferry from the UK to Belgium.

It's an ill wind . . .

As Buddy Holly's life crashed in flames, another aspiring pop star's career took off in 1959. Holly's plane crashed as he was heading for a gig at Moorhead, Minnesota and his death meant the show couldn't go on until a hastily formed teen band called the Shadows from Fargo, North Dakota volunteered to take Holly's spot. They did so well it launched their 16-year-old singer Robert Velline into a pop career. As Bobby Vee he had a string of 1960s chart hits such 'The Night Has a Thousand Eyes' and 'Rubber Ball'.

Dick dies on stage

Country Dick Montana shocked his audience by dying in front of them. The drummer and singer with the Beat Farmers suffered a fatal heart attack while playing to a packed audience at Whistler, British Columbia, Canada in 1995. He was just 40.

Coma death for Jackie

Jackie Wilson, one of the most dynamic and influential singers and performers in R&B and rock history, spent nine years in a coma. The energetic showman, who was said to have inspired the stage acts of James Brown, Elvis Presley and Michael Jackson, had hits such as 'Reet Petite' and 'Your Love Keeps Lifting Me Higher and Higher'. But in 1975 while on stage at a New Jersey casino he suffered a heart attack, ironically in the middle of the line: "My heart is crying". Jackie had stopped breathing and slipped into a coma. Although he briefly emerged from it, in 1984 at the age of 49, he died from complications of pneumonia.

Torture horror

One of Bob Marley's Wailers, Peter Tosh, was horrifically tortured and murdered in 1987. A gang broke into his Jamaica home demanding money then tortured him because he said he had no cash. As some of the reggae musician's friends arrived, the frustrated gunmen started firing. Tosh was killed by a single shot to the head, disc jockeys Doc Brown and Jeff Dixon also died and several other people were wounded. One of the gang, Dennis "Leppo" Lobban, was sentenced to death but this was commuted to life in jail. The other two gunmen were never identified by name but they were killed in a gang war a few weeks later.

Manson mayhem?

It was alleged in November 30, 1998 that in just a few days the Marilyn Manson rock band band notched up more than $25,000 in backstage and hotel room damages during the New York segment of its Mechanical Animals tour. When things calmed down Manson apologized and offered to make financial restitution.

Suicide mystery

Following his hit 'I Fought The Law' Bobby Fuller of the Bobby Fuller Four was found dead in his car. His body was battered and he died from having petrol poured down his throat until he drowned. The verdict of Los Angeles police? Suicide.

Mean Dean

When the Rolling Stones were just starting out they got no encouragement from one of the (then) giants of the US music industry – Dean Martin. In fact the crooner with a long CV of music and film successes was downright patronizing and insulting to Jagger, Richards and co. on his US TV show in 1964. The Stones were on Martin's *The Hollywood Palace* show after having a couple of minor US chart entries. Martin, also a comedian in his time, used the unsophisticated and unconventional band as the butt of jokes. He said sarcastically: "They haven't got long hair; they have low foreheads and high eyebrows. They're challenging the Beatles to a hair-pulling contest."

Bo diddles Ed Sullivan

When rhythm and blues man Bo Diddley was booked to appear on Ed Sullivan's famous American TV show in 1955, he was forbidden to perform his eponymous song 'Bo Diddley' and ordered to perform the more popular 'Sixteen Tons'. But the master guitarist went ahead with 'Bo Diddley', upset the show host and never performed on a Sullivan show again.

Married in the full glare

Sly Stone married model and actress Kathy Silva on stage during a sell-out 1974 concert at New York's Madison Square Garden but she left him in 1976 after Sly's dog mauled their son Sylvester Junior.

Pity for Pitney

Singer Gene Pitney died just hours after receiving what was to be his last standing ovation. The American singer, songwriter, musician and sound engineer, who had a string of hit singles including 'A Town without Pity' and 'I'm Gonna be Strong', was found dead from heart disease in his hotel room in Cardiff, Wales in 2006. He was 66.

Marriage dilemma

'Godfather of soul' James Brown had a complicated love life even by pop music standards. Officially he had three marriages but the validity of a fourth has always – confusingly – been in dispute. In 2001 Brown went through a marriage ceremony with Tomi Rae Hynie but there were claims that Hynie was married at that time to a Bangladeshi whom she claimed wed her in an immigration scam. Hynie stated that marriage was later annulled, but not until 2004. Brown was angry and, hurt that Hynie had concealed her prior marriage from him, moved to file for annulment even though they might not be married in any case under South Carolina law. In 2003 Brown and Hynie split anyway amid paternity doubts about the son they had together.

Long rap sheet

As a teenager, 1980s rapper Ice T, real name Tracy Marrow, stood out from most of his friends in the gang culture of the Los Angeles school system because he did not drink alcohol, smoke tobacco, or use drugs. His good conduct record went to pieces later when he admitted he was involved in cannabis dealing, stealing car radios, theft of army property, desertion, pimping and a jail break.

Ice loses his cool

Hip hop artist Vanilla Ice was arrested in Los Angeles on 3 June 1991 on firearm charges after threatening a homeless man with a pistol. James Gregory had approached Vanilla Ice, real name Robert Van Winkle, outside a Los Angeles supermarket and attempted to sell him a silver chain. Van Winkle and his bodyguard were charged with three weapons offences. Van Winkle, as part of a plea bargain deal offered no contest, in which he neither admitted nor disputed the charges.

Thrust out of the limelight

In Elvis Presley's third appearance on Ed Sullivan's TV show he was filmed from the waist up in case he used his trademark pelvic thrusts that had previously caused a public outcry.

Split rents career

The British career of American solo act PJ Proby was rent asunder by what today would be described as a 'wardrobe malfunction'. Despite having built up a strong UK fan base with top 10 hits such as 'Hold Me', 'Maria' and 'Somewhere', a notorious trouser-splitting incident at a February 1965 show in Croydon, Surrey led to him being banned by the ABC theatre chain, its sister company ABC TV and BBC TV.

Bum clothes for Gaga

What a difference a generation makes when it comes to 'wardrobe malfunctions'. Split trousers took a chunk out of PJ Proby's 1960s career while a similar incident made Lady Gaga more popular than ever in 2012. She 'accidentally' exposed her bum in front of tens of thousands of fans during her song 'Heavy Metal Lover' while on her *Born This Way Ball* tour in Vancouver, Canada. Her Versace latex pants couldn't cope with her acrobatic choreography and split to expose her curvy bottom. Unabashed, Gaga laughed it off by pulling apart some of the ripped material and joking with fans.

Taken to the cleaners

Chuck Berry claimed that his famous 'duck walk' was all due to an incompetent dry cleaner. Faced with one of his first concerts in New York he took his best suit to a cleaner who managed to shrink it. Berry, who had hits such as 'No Particular Place to Go' and 'My Dinga-ling', had no option but to wear the shrunken suit but it pinched in all sorts of places and he had to adopt the 'duck walk' to avoid his trousers splitting, which would have been disastrous in conservative 1955 America. Fans loved the walk and it became the Berry trademark.

New member of the Doors

An additional band 'member' led to the Doors being barred from many concert bookings. It has been alleged that leader Jim Morrison had more than the microphone in his hand at a show in Miami in 1969. Fellow Doors have both confirmed and denied that Morrison slipped his penis from his trousers but promoters weren't taking any chances on further over-exposure and slammed the door. The Doors' fan base was troublesome anyway with concerts often ending in riots.

Disappearing Dylan

Mystery still surrounds the disappearance of singer-songwriter Bob Dylan in 1966. He became a recluse after a motorcycle accident in New York State and was once thought to have been at death's door from his injuries. It would appear Dylan, whose mammoth output has included singles such as 'Subterranean Homesick Blues' and 'Lay Lady Lay' and albums such as *Blood on the Tracks* and *John Wesley Harding*, had used the crash as a much-needed chance to escape from the pressures that had built up around him. Certainly he damaged neck vertebrae and he admitted: "I had been in a motorcycle accident and I'd been hurt, but I recovered. Truth was that I wanted to get out of the rat race." Apart from a few select appearances, the legendary Dylan did not tour again for almost eight years.

Rita boobs

Underwear is something that is hard to forget to put on but that was the excuse singer Rita Ora gave for her boob being revealed to fans. The 'How We Do' hit maker blamed her wardrobe malfunction at a London gig in 2012 on the fact she had two performances on the same night and was so busy rushing around London on the back of a motorbike to realize she wasn't wearing her bra.

Catholic rips into the Pope

Sinead O'Connor caused world outrage when she ripped a portrait of the Pope to shreds on an American TV show watched by millions. Irish-born O'Connor, a Roman Catholic herself, was a guest on *Saturday Night Live* in 1992 when she followed up her song with her protest against what she called the Church's intransigence on women's and children's issues. She was campaigning about a rape victim being denied an abortion in her home country because of the Government's close ties with the Catholic Church and its rules forbidding it. The outcry from fellow Catholics was swift and savage; she was booed off stage at a concert a week later and her career, which had included the number-one album *I Do Not Want What I Haven't Got*, nosedived with many radios stations ignoring her music.

Otis dies in air crash

Soul singer Otis Redding might have had a longer life than just 26 years if his pilot had heeded weather warnings. Otis and his band the Bar-Kays took off in a Beechcraft aircraft from Nashville, Tennessee to the next leg of their 1967 tour but the December weather was poor, with heavy rain and fog. The plane crashed into a lake near Madison, Wisconsin killing Redding and six other people. The only survivor was Bar-Kays trumpet player Ben Cauley who got ashore on a seat cushion.

Bowie sets things straight

David Bowie's quotes about his sexual orientation swung both ways. If the magazine articles are to be believed he was quoted as saying in 1973: "It's true – I am a bisexual. But I can't deny that I've used that fact very well. I suppose it's the best thing that ever happened to me." Ten years later in a 1983 interview with *Rolling Stone* magazine he was quoted as saying his public declaration of bisexuality was "the biggest mistake I ever made". He added: "I was always a closet heterosexual".

Jimi's farewell

Guitar pioneer Jimi Hendrix died of an accidental drug overdose aged 27. Although some of the details of his death are disputed, he was found in his room at a London hotel on 17 September 1970. Ambulance crews said he was found already dead but friend Monika Danneman, who had been driving the guitar legend around the night before, said that she found him in a collapsed state and accompanied him to hospital, where he died. As a result of a lack of clear evidence about Hendrix's last hours an open verdict was brought on the basis of an accidental overdose. Danneman said she thought Hendrix had taken some of her sleeping tablets to counteract the amphetamines he had been taking and misjudged the dosage.

Puppy love, at a cost

Heavy metal singer Ozzy Osbourne was said to have paid $10,000 for a Yorkshire terrier at an auction in Los Angeles California. With adult Yorkies weighing about seven pounds (3.5kgs), the present for wife Sharon cost him about $1,500 per pound.

Super Bowl boob

Janet Jackson caused an uproar by exposing her right breast in one of the most watched TV programmes in the US She and former *NSYNC member Justin Timberlake were the prestigious half-time entertainment at 2004's Super Bowl XXXVIII. Singing the line "gonna have ya nekkid by the end of this song" from his hit 'Rock Your Body', Timberlake reached over, snatched some fabric from Jackson's bodice, and exposed her right breast complete with nipple ring. The incident sparked a public outcry and hefty fines from the US government's Federal Communications Commission. Timberlake apologized and claimed a 'wardrobe malfunction'.

Sam Cooke shot

The dying words of Sam Cooke, whose singing work spanned gospel, rhythm and blues, soul and pop during the 1950s and 1960s, were "Lady, you shot me!" and set in motion a shooting mystery that has never been fully resolved. Cooke, whose chart hits had included 'Wonderful World', 'Chain Gang' and 'Cupid', was shot on 11 December 1964, at the Hacienda Motel in Los Angeles. The motel's manager Bertha Franklin said that she shot Cooke in self-defence after he broke into her office home and attacked her. It appeared Cooke was drunk and was demanding to know where a woman he had checked in with had gone. Police found Cooke's body clad only in a sports jacket and shoes, but no shirt, trousers or underwear. Later the mystery woman came forward saying she spent the evening with Cooke at a nightclub and back at the motel he forced her onto the bed and she thought she would be raped. She also said she fled, scooping up most of Cooke's clothing by mistake. There were further conflicts of evidence in the court case but the jury accepted Franklin's explanation, and returned a verdict of justifiable homicide. Franklin also said in evidence she beat Cooke with a broom while he was lying mortally wounded. Cooke's family disputed much of the two women's evidence and claimed a conspiracy and that Cooke was so badly beaten that he was almost decapitated.

Bob blows it?

It would appear that Bob Geldof talked his way out of an American chart success with 'I Don't Like Mondays'. With the Boomtown Rats British hit ready to take the US charts by storm in 1980, it is said that, at an American radio programmers' convention, he was heard to say: "I've heard how you programme American radio and it sounds like shit!" Needless to say 'I Don't Like Mondays' disappeared from the US air waves.

Close shave

Californian band the Pyramids tried a different tack as the hair of musicians grew longer and shaggier in the 1960s. In 1964 at the height of the surfing sound they shaved their heads for the publicity it engendered and entered the US Hot 100 with their instrumental 'Penetration'. Despite further recordings they didn't have huge success and, starting with saxophone player Ron Stender, gave up the bald look and grew their hair fashionably long.

Good morning to you both

Male American viewers had a very good morning when eccentric rapper Nicki Minaj briefly bounced out of her top as she stepped on stage in New York's Central Park for *Good Morning America*'s 2011 Summer Concert series.

Johnson death mystery

There is nothing but conjecture about the death of blues guitarist Robert Johnson in August 1938. He was performing at Greenwood, Mississippi when he was said to have died from strychnine poisoning after drinking from a bottle handed to him by the jealous husband of a woman he had flirted with. There were several stories disputing that and also that it was even strychnine because Johnson took three days to die, aged 27, and strychnine is said to work fatally faster.

FBI probe song

Among the most attentive listeners to the Kingsmen's 1963 hit 'Louie Louie' were two American government agencies – the Federal Bureau of Investigation and the Federal Communications Commission. The 'suspect' was the song's indecipherable lyrics which led to suspicions that they were obscene. Even the mostly teenage buying public was so mystified by the slurred lyrics they made up their own, often obscene, lyrics. Such was 'Louie Louie's' popularity it went to number two in the US charts with the Seattle -based band staying in the top-selling list for 16 weeks. The FBI inquiry faltered as the G-men concluded composer Richard Berry's lyrics were unintelligible 'at any speed'. If they had thought to ask, the investigators could have saved a lot of time and money by checking the Old Northwest recording studio in Seattle which was not equipped with the microphones for rock music. This meant Kingsmen leader singer Jack Ely had to stand on tiptoe and strain his voice to reach the ceiling mikes.

Berry goes to jail

Rock 'n' roll pioneer Chuck Berry ended up in jail for breaking a white slavery law. In January 1962, Berry was sentenced to three years in prison for transporting a 14-year-old girl across state lines. Berry, who was prosecuted under the Mann Act preventing human trafficking, was at the height of his career at the time after a series of hits and a reputation for terrific live performances.

Sour Cream

Cream duo Jack Bruce and Ginger Baker had a long history of quarrelling but they continued to work together despite coming to blows. Bass player and singer Bruce and drummer Baker had a volatile relationship previously when they were with the Graham Bond Organization, a blues outfit in the early 1960s. This is said to have included on-stage fights and the sabotage of one another's instruments. After Baker fired Bruce from the band, Bruce continued to arrive for gigs but was ultimately driven away, allegedly at knifepoint. It seemed incredible that, given their prolonged enmity, the two protagonists linked up with guitarist Eric Clapton in 1966 in the short-lived but hugely successful super-group Cream. Continued arguments between the two precipitated the break-up of Cream in 1968 after ground-breaking albums such as *Disraeli Gears* and *Fresh Cream*.

Breakfast banger

Breakfast with Keith Richards can be a blast, according to a fellow musician. Rolling Stones saxophone player Bobby Keys revealed in his 2013 biography that the pistol-packing guitarist once shot his own breakfast. During the 1990s the band was staying at a hotel when Keys' golf ball landed in Richards' breakfast. As quick as he can strum the chords for 'Brown Sugar' Keith whipped out a gun and blasted the ball off his plate. According to Keys, Richards said: 'That's a 10-stroke fucking penalty. You ruined my fucking breakfast.'

Kelly's double whammy

Former Destiny's Child singer Kelly Rowland achieved a bit of one-upmanship on Janet Jackson's infamous Super Bowl breast slip when her latticed top slid up during a 2011 New Jersey concert and offered her fans a view, albeit fleeting, of both boobs.

Cash pay trips Berry

Chuck Berry got his second taste of the inside of an American jail because of his insistence on being paid in cash. He was sentenced in 1979 to four months and community service for tax evasion.

Frank's spank threat

Frank Sinatra is said to have threatened to "kick the ass" of Sinead O'Connor after she ripped up a portrait of the Pope on a US television show. Sinatra, whose Italian heritage gave him a Catholic upbringing, is said to have made the threat in a letter to a newspaper in 1992 but it stated it was because of "her lack of respect for America".

On the run

A high-speed car chase across two states cost funk pioneer James Brown almost three years of his life behind bars. In 1988 he is alleged to have pulled a shotgun on someone he argued with. Atlanta police were called and Brown, whose hits have included 'Livin' in America' and 'It's a Man's World', took off in his truck. The attempt to outrun a posse of police cars took him from Georgia to South Carolina and back again and ended with Brown dragged in handcuffs from his bullet-ridden vehicle. The sentence for reckless driving, resisting arrest, failing to stop for police, aggravated assault and drug and firearms possession was six and a half years but he was out in 30 months.

Speedy reaction

America's National Association for Stock Car Auto Racing (NASCAR) aces rallied around Lisa Lopes after her death in 2002. Many people were horrified that the autopsy photographs of Lopes had been made public and NASCAR driver Dale Earnhardt Jnr led the protests because the same had happened over his father's death a year previously. Earnhardt's team and others painted a symbolic black stripe under their left headlights.

Kiss of failure

In a decision akin to Decca rejecting the Beatles, American heavy rockers Van Halen suffered a similar knockback. In 1976 Gene Simmons of fellow rockers Kiss had produced a demonstration disc for Van Halen and taken it to Kiss' management only to be told they would not sign them, adding that Van Halen had no chance of making it. Van Halen went elsewhere and became one of only five rock bands that have had two albums sell more than 10 million copies in the USA and the most number ones in the history of Billboard's mainstream rock charts.

Hubert was no soul mate

'Godfather of Soul' James Brown had friends in high places – or so he thought. Brown was, surprisingly for the racial climate of the time, consulted by US Vice-President Hubert Humphrey on his 1968 presidential election bid and was so pleased that he said if Brown ever needed help he should just call the politician. Some years later Brown, when hit by income tax problems, tried to call in Humphrey's promise but nobody would return his call. Humphrey never made it to the White House either.

Devil of a story

Legend has it that musician Robert Johnson sold his soul to the Devil to follow his passion for the blues. Johnson was said to have been a struggling musician before the Devil 'tuned his guitar' when they met at the crossroads at Clarksdale, Mississippi and after that Johnson became famous for his music if not wealthy. The alleged crossroads are a pilgrimage point for blues fans more than 70 years later. Johnson appeared to have paid a high price for the deal in the end because he died aged only 27 in 1938, but his recordings continued to sell into the 21st century.

Passing the M&M test

Demanding a bowl of M&Ms in their dressing room with the brown ones removed at the venues they played was a big media story surrounding rockers Van Halen. But there was a method to their apparent madness, it was revealed. The band was one of the first to insist on contract riders (special contractual requests) in order to get the technical side of the show correct at every concert. Lead singer David Lee Roth denied it was the band making capricious demands but a test of whether the venue owners had actually read and properly honoured the terms of the contract small print. He said the riders contained other requirements involving legitimate safety concerns as in the past several members of their road crew had almost been electrocuted. The way it worked was that if the bowl was present as requested, the band members could safely assume the other, legitimate, items were also being taken care of. No bowl, or a bowl with brown M&Ms still present, suggested other, more vital, safety and technical aspects might have been similarly overlooked.

Getting in the spirit

The name for shock rockers Alice Cooper came from a session with an ouija spirit board. At odds with their heavy metal act which incorporates snakes, electric chairs and guillotines, Alice Cooper was a dichotomy because it sounded innocuous and wholesome.

Rolling around

The Rolling Stones demonstrated their flexibility in the 1975 concert performances of the song 'Fingerprint File'. Mick Jagger, who rarely plays an instrument on stage, took Ron Wood's rhythm guitar role while Wood manned Bill Wyman's bass and Wyman played synthesizer as the Stones broke into a rare electronic piece.

Fraternal split

Multi-million-selling country rock duo the Everly Brothers split acrimoniously in 1973. The family animosity was so great it was reported that the only time they met over the next decade was at their father's funeral. Despite a string of successful singles such as 'Wake Up Little Suzy', 'Cathy's Clown' and 'Ferris Wheel' which made them millionaires, Phil and Don Everly pursued solo careers. Don found some success on the US country charts while Phil was a backing singer with several artists. The brothers reunited as an act in the early 1980s after patching things up.

Hell finally froze over

One of the most acrimonious break-ups in a rock act was the Eagles in 1980. After band members Glenn Frey and Don Felder spent part of a California concert threatening each other with violence, the band began to disintegrate. Don Henley was famously quoted as saying that the group would get back together "when hell freezes over" so when the band did re-form after a '14-year vacation' in 1994 their comeback album was called *Hell Freezes Over*.

Crash kills Jenni

Mexican-American singer Jenni Rivera died with six other people when the private jet in which she was a passenger crashed in December 2012. The cause of the crash in the Nuevo Leon province of Mexico has not been explained but it was alleged the singer had connections to a powerful drug cartel for whom Rivera, who was 43 when she died, was sometimes booked to perform.

Pop porn is born

The success of New Wave band Devo was not huge in terms of sales but it was in the forefront of bringing pornography to pop. It had initial visibility with suggestive tracks such as 'Whip It' and 'Jerkin' Back 'n' Forth' then Devo caused a real uproar with its 1979 song 'Penetration in the Centerfold'. Devo's 1990 compilation album *Devo's Greatest Misses* needed a parental guidance warning on the cover about its content.

Christina's foxed

Passionate campaigner against animal cruelty Christina Aguilera once mistakenly wore a real fox fur stole on tour. Her designer had given her the stole in 2007 and she said she was genuinely shocked when members of the campaign group People for the Ethical Treatment of Animals (PeTA) pointed it out. She had thought it was fake fur.

Green goes missing

Eccentric guitarist and songwriter Peter Green left Fleetwood Mac without telling the rest of the band. Police and private detectives were called in 1970 when Green disappeared after a big hit with the instrumental 'Albatross' and the band had to cancel appearances. When Green was found in seclusion he explained his sudden departure was based on personal and religious qualms about the rock 'n' roll business and fame.

Albarn war on war

Blur frontman Damian Albarn's much-publicized anti-war stance was shared by other members of his family, including his grandfather Edward who had died after going on a protest hunger strike in 2002.

Fighting force

Air Force drummer Ginger Baker proved the idiom 'If at first you don't succeed, try, try again' very true as he battled with addiction to an assortment of substances over several decades. He claims to have come off drugs 28 times, each time being drawn back in. The 29th, and to date the last, was 1981, when he moved to Italy, and kicked heroin for good. He remembers: "I moved to a little village in the middle of nowhere, where nobody spoke English. I got into olive farming. It was very rewarding, very hard work but very good therapy."

Witch way to turn

Singer Stevie Nicks was furious that she had constantly been associated with witchcraft. The myth was exacerbated by the fact that Nicks' songs were copyrighted under the name Welsh Witch Music and that the song 'Rhiannon' she did with Fleetwood Mac was about a Welsh witch. Nicks denied she was involved with Wicca worship and said she had to discard many black clothes because some of her weirder fans reckoned they were also a sign of being a witch.

Brown's drug dilemma

James Brown was so strict with his anti-drug policy that for the first 25 years of his professional career he would immediately sack any of his band or backing singers for taking drugs or alcohol. Brown only held out against using drugs himself until the late 1970s and from then on he used marijuana, cocaine, prescription drugs and PCP (angel dust).

Home for Priscilla

The future Mrs Elvis Presley was just 14 when she moved into the rock star's Graceland home under his 'guardianship'. Priscilla, who was to marry Presley at 21, said their sex life before the wedding was "everything but penetration" although she has never revealed a timeline for when the physical contact started.

Booty-ful

It is not just music stars who have a tendency to bizarre behaviour; their fans do too. In 2007 a British fan of Jennifer Lopez was just 15 when her mother paid £10,000 for cosmetic surgery to make her boobs and bum look like those of her idol J-Lo.

Who's this about?

It seems the Who sneaked a masturbation song past the relatively conservative British record-buying public in 1967. Without mentioning masturbation explicitly, 'Pictures of Lily' was written from the point of view of a teenager whose dad gives him certain questionable pictures to aid his insomnia. Songwriter Pete Townshend has hinted the lyrics pertain to Lillie Langtry, the sultry English vaudeville star of the Edwardian era.

Sonny's ski death

Singer and politician Sonny Bono was killed in 1998 after skiing into a tree. Bono, who had chart hits such as 'I Got You Babe', died of injuries sustained from the collision at the Heavenly ski area which bridges California and Nevada. He was 62 and had been elected to the US House of Representatives after his singing career fizzled out. The memorial to Bono in Cathedral City, California reads 'The beat goes on' after the 1960s hit he shared with his former wife Cher.

Porn producer

American producer Huey Meaux, who was behind the Sir Douglas Quintet's 'She's About a Mover', was jailed for 15 years for possessing child pornography. In 1996, a police raid of his office revealed thousands of photos and videos of under-age girls in sexual situations. Meaux pleaded guilty to two counts of sexual assault of a child, drug possession, possession of child pornography and jumping bail. He was released in 2007 and died aged 82 in 2011.

Turner turns on her tormentor

Singer Tina Turner walked out on an abusive marriage with just 36 cents in cash and massive debts to her name. In the late 1970s Tina's marriage to husband Ike and their touring show the Ike and Tina Turner Revue were tailing off in tandem, partly due to Ike's increasing use of cocaine. Things came to a head in 1976 with a violent row on a journey between gigs that resulted in Turner quitting her husband and the tour – fleeing with nothing but the 36 cents and a fuel credit card. She spent months in hiding and filed for divorce after 14 years of marriage. With the 1978 divorce went the Ike and Tina Turner Revue but she retained her stage name, and assumed responsibility for the debts incurred from the cancelled tour as well as a significant tax burden. She went on to become a top female rock artist, win eight Grammys and sell more concert tickets than any other solo performer.

Laced with LSD

Two of the Beatles got their first taste of the drug LSD without knowing it. John Lennon and then wife Cynthia had been to a party in 1965 with fellow Beatle George Harrison and his girlfriend, later to be wife, Patti Boyd when their coffees were laced without their knowledge with the hallucinogen by a so-called friend. Patti became so agitated she had to be restrained from smashing a shop window. Later on their way to a London nightclub they believed, wrongly, the lift they were in was on fire.

Dubious double

Guitarist Jeremy Spencer left the band Fleetwood Mac in the lurch when he suddenly quit in 1971. His departure, said to be because he became convinced by the words of a religious street band called the Children of God, jeopardized the band's 1971 US tour. Spencer's departure in Los Angeles was a touch of déjà vu because just a year before he had replaced Peter Green, who had also gone missing with religious qualms about the rock business.

Crash kills 'Gentleman Jim'

Country singer Jim Reeves, who made the big crossover to success in the pop charts, died in an aircraft crash in July 1964. Reeves was at the controls of his Beechcraft Debonair light aeroplane when it crashed in appalling weather near Brentwood, Tennessee. The impact was so huge that the plane's engine and nose were buried in the ground and it took 42 hours to find the bodies of Reeves, who was known as 'Gentleman Jim', and manager Dean Manuel who was also Reeves' pianist in his backing group, the Blue Boys. In a remarkable touch of morbid irony Reeves' last recording session before his death aged 40 for the RCA Victor label included the tracks 'Make the World Go Away' and 'Is It Really Over?'.

Epstein bows out

The man who built the Beatles never lived to see how big his work would become. The 'Fab Four' manager Brian Epstein died in August 1967 just after the success of the band's *Sgt. Pepper* album. Epstein was found in his pyjamas in a locked bedroom by his butler and housekeeper. His death, aged 32, was officially ruled an accident caused by a gradual build-up of the barbiturate Carbitral in his system, combined with alcohol.

Taste of things to come

Guns N' Roses became legendary for rock 'n' roll shock and excess stories and obviously started as they meant to go on. They shocked with their first album in 1987. The cover of *Appetite for Destruction* was a Robert Williams painting of a recently raped woman.

Ice T's banking career

Rapper Ice T claimed in 2012 that he had been a bank robber. He admitted that after being discharged from the army, he began a career raiding banks using combat skills allegedly acquired in the US Army Ranger School. This criminal part of his 'career' was said to have been in the mid-1970s and his confession came in the 21st century – when the statute of limitations on that sort of crime had expired.

Another Dylan myth?

Bob Dylan was booed and catcalled when he appeared at the 1965 Newport Folk Festival but the legend that his playing of an electric guitar had outraged folk fans may not have been the reason. Alternative accounts by Dylan's keyboard player Al Kooper and one of the festival directors, supported by a recently unearthed audio recording, make the claim that the only boos were in reaction to the MC's announcement that there was only enough time for a short set, which meant Dylan left the stage after just three songs.

Howl of protest

Christina Aguilera tried in 2008 to get a country to change its culture. She headlined the animal rights organization, People for the Ethical Treatment of Animals (PeTA), in its campaign to stop South Korea killing dogs for food and wrote a personal plea to the Seoul government.

Slumber number

Rolling Stone Keith Richards admitted that playing 'Fool to Cry' so often meant he knew it so well that he fell asleep during the number at a 1976 concert.

D's DVT death

A 10-hour flight was blamed for the sudden death of rapper Heavy D in November 2011. After six weeks in Britain he took the long flight back to Los Angeles where a pulmonary embolism, caused by deep vein thrombosis (DVT), led to his death. The blood clot that probably formed in his leg during the flight made its way fatally to his lung. The 344lb (156kg) rapper, whose 'Now That We Found Love' was an international hit, was found collapsed outside his LA home but died later in hospital.

Public death

The video cameras were still running during the car crash which led to the death of rapper Lisa 'Left Eye' Lopes. She was best known as one third of the American rap group TLC and penned many of their hits including 'Ain't 2 Proud 2 Beg'. While on a charity mission in Honduras at the age of 30 in April 2002, she lost control of her Mitsubishi Montero Sport, which rolled several times and hit two trees, throwing Lopes and three passengers out of the windows. She died of neck injuries and severe head trauma. An assistant in the front passenger seat was videotaping at the time, so the last seconds leading up to the fatal accident were recorded. A documentary film on the final 26 days of Lopes' life, entitled *Last Days of Left Eye* premiered five years later at the Atlanta film festival.

Feat of endurance

Lowell George left Frank Zappa's Mothers of Invention because he was fired for playing a 15-minute guitar solo – with his amplifier off. George went on to success with Little Feat

Spicing up the debate

Something that many non-Spice Girls fans have been saying for years was confirmed by member Melanie Chisholm (Sporty Spice) in 2013. She told a BBC chat show that the multi-million-selling line-up with Melanie Brown (Scary Spice), Victoria Beckham (Posh Spice), Emma Bunton (Baby Spice) and Geri Halliwell (Ginger Spice) were auditioned for their looks. She said singing ability was a secondary consideration.

Killer lyrics

Jailed killer Charles Manson wrote, and even recorded, many songs but the man behind the 1969 Sharon Tate massacre attracted his biggest attention musically with his 'Look at Your Game Girl'. It was a track on the Guns N' Roses 1993 album *The Spaghetti Incident* but Manson was not listed as the creator and not mentioned on the album cover. The use of the track, which ends with singer Axl Rose whispering 'Thanks Chas', didn't sit well with all the band members and only Rose and percussionist Dizzy Reed played on the track. Public and record buyer fury was tremendous despite backpedalling by the band's management. Guns N' Roses didn't formally break up as a result but members did go off and do their own things for a few years.

Pilot was high

The pilot of an aircraft which crashed killing America's 'Queen of Urban Pop' Aaliyah did not have a licence to fly. Crash investigators also found cocaine and alcohol in the pilot's body. Aaliyah was 22 when she was killed in the crash in the Bahamas in 2001 along with seven other people. A wrongful death suit against the airline was settled out of court.

Milli Vanilli unmasked

Milli Vanilli has been probably the only act in chart history to have been sued by the disgruntled public. Fabrice Morvan and Rob Pilatus roared to success as the pop and dance duo in 1989 with the Grammy-winning 'Girl You It's True' before it was revealed that the duo had not sung a note on it. The track and others marketed under the Milli Vanilli name were actually created in a German recording studio using then-anonymous singers. Morvan and Pilatus were a good-looking pair and hired to take the act on the road until the real voices – Charles Shaw, John Davis and Brad Howe – stepped forward to tell the truth and claim their due credit. Arista Records disowned the stooge Milli Vanilli and record-buying consumers, claiming they were hoodwinked, also successfully sued. Morvan and Pilatus, who had been out-of-work models and actors, admitted to the masquerade but later failed to register hits with their own records as they tried to substantiate their claim that they had singing talent.

No Cashing in

A US company making haemorrhoid cream was refused permission to use arguably Johnny Cash's most famous song, 'Ring of Fire', in an advertisement. The family of pop and country legend Cash, who died in 2003, were horrified at the idea even though one of the co-writers – Merle Kilgore – had given permission. The other writer had been Cash's wife June but Cash himself often saw the funny side of the song title and in his concert introductions he was reported as saying: "Ladies and gentlemen, I want to give credit where credit is due. I dedicate this song to the makers of Preparation H [a globally-known haemorrhoid cream]."

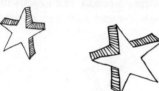

Lady gun gun

Lady Gaga caused outrage in 2013 when she wore a gun bra just weeks after schoolchildren were massacred in the USA. She was slammed for insensitivity for wearing two plastic sub-machine guns at a Canadian concert in January. Despite being a leading campaigner for more gun control in America she wore the controversial bra after 20 children and six teachers were murdered by a crazed gunman at Sandy Hook, Connecticut in December 2012.

Hutchence says goodbye

Michael Hutchence's last words to his personal manager were: "Marth, Michael here. I've fucking had enough." Hours after these words were left on Martha Troup's voice mail on 6 February 1998, INXS lead singer and lyric writer Hutchence was found hanged in a hotel room in Sydney, Australia. The inquest ruled his death as suicide while depressed and under the influence of drugs and alcohol. Police found Hutchence, 37 at the time, was in a kneeling position facing the door after using his snakeskin belt to tie a knot on the automatic door closer. He had strained his head forward into the loop so hard that the buckle had broken. Australia-based rockers INXS enjoyed global success with a number of hit singles and albums such as *X* and *Kick*.

So high for solo career

Big-voiced singer Alison Moyet had album sales of 2.3 million and more than a million singles sold. In 30 years all seven of her studio albums and three compilations have charted in the top 30 in Britain, with two reaching number one. She also achieved nine top 30 singles and five top 10 hits. Not bad for a singer who admitted in a 2010 interview that she never wanted to be a solo artist.

Fleeting stop

There was a short period in the 1970s when promoters got a somewhat different line-up to the one expected when they booked Fleetwood Mac. From late 1973 until 1975 the real band disintegrated when guitarist/singer Bob Weston was fired over a personal matter with drummer and band leader Mick Fleetwood and the group couldn't function. To the humiliation of the real Fleetwood Mac line-up, the group's management put a completely new set of musicians out in their name. Business fell away because gig promoters and bookers became wary about which 'Fleetwood Mac' they were getting. By 1975 the real Mac got back on track to a period of massive global success.

Blanket coverage

Michael Jackson lived fully up to his nickname of 'Wacko Jacko' in 2002 when, in the full glare of the world's media, he dangled his newest baby Prince Michael II, nicknamed 'Blanket', over the balcony of his fourth-storey hotel room in Berlin. The baby, whose mother was a surrogate, was unharmed, but the world condemned the singer's irresponsible behaviour. Jackson admitted he'd made a "terrible mistake" saying that he got caught up in the excitement of the moment. He added: "I would never intentionally endanger the lives of my children."

Marley rejects treatment

A malignant cancer found on his toe was to ultimately be the death of reggae legend Bob Marley. The Jamaican-born front man of the Wailers cited his Rastafarian religious beliefs as the reason for rejecting early intervention through toe amputation. By 1981, aged 36, the cancer had spread to his lungs and brain and, with global hits such as 'One Love' and 'Jamming' behind him, he died in a Miami hospital after a European tour where his condition had worsened.

Mexican Madonna murdered

Selena Quintanilla-Pérez, better known as Latin singer Selena, was gunned down in February 1995 during a row with the head of her fan club. The beautiful Texan Tejano singer was poised to break into mainstream pop when, at 23, she was shot by Yolanda Saldivar who was facing allegations of embezzling club funds. Selena had confronted her former friend over the lost money at a Corpus Christi motel in Texas and was shot in the shoulder. However the bullet had severed an artery and Selena died later as a result of blood loss. Saldivar was later jailed for life with 30 years before she could be eligible for parole. Selena, dubbed 'The Mexican Madonna', had 14 top 10 Latin chart hits and seven number ones. Jennifer Lopez played Selena in a later biopic.

Obsessed fan shoots Lennon

One of the great ironies of pop history is that ex-Beatle John Lennon, pacifist and peace campaigner, should die violently in 1980. Still revered as one of the most gifted songwriters of all time, Lennon was fatally shot aged 40 by an obsessed fan. The man behind such peace-themed chart songs as 'Imagine' and 'Happy Xmas, War is Over' was shot four times in the back by Mark Chapman, for whom Lennon had earlier autographed a copy of the *Double Fantasy* album. The murder was outside New York's exclusive Dakota building where Lennon and wife Yoko Ono lived. There were conflicting accounts as to whether Lennon reached hospital alive but surgeons' efforts, including open-heart massage, failed to save John.

No to Noel

Irish singer Sinead O'Connor let slip in 2013 that Oasis guitarist Noel Gallagher once proposed to her. But she said that he wouldn't remember the incident at an Amsterdam festival because "he was off his face".

Karen's shock death

Velvet-voiced Karen Carpenter died in 1983 aged 32 just as she had turned her life around. After struggling with eating disorders for most of her adult life, Carpenter died of heart failure. Ironically Karen, who was a talented drummer as well as having a distinctive contralto voice, had just seemed to gain some control of her anorexia nervosa and was putting on weight when the tragedy happened.

Harry loves mum's style

Alert online fans pointed out that One Direction's Harry Styles was seen at his 19th birthday party wearing – his mum's shirt. In 2013 hawk-eyed fans compared the party pictures with that of mum Anne Cox, 44, who they said was wearing the same shirt.

Canned Heat death

Alan Wilson seemed determined to involve fellow Canned Heat founder Bob Hite in his suicide attempts. Wilson, nicknamed 'Blind Owl', was known for his depression and eccentric behaviour. In 1969, soon after recording the *Hooker 'n Heat* album, Wilson tried to commit suicide by driving a van off the road near Hite's home in Topanga Canyon, Los Angeles. He failed to kill himself on that occasion but on 3 September 1970 he succeeded with a barbiturate overdose and his body was discovered on the hillside behind Hite's home. Ironically Canned Heat's bear-like front man Hite did die in a van – from a heart attack in 1981 at the age of 38.

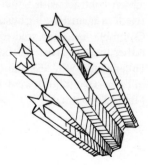

Considerate in death

Boston vocalist Brad Delp was known to be a caring and charitable man. Given the method of his carefully planned suicide in 2007 he remained caring. He lit two barbecue grills in the sealed bedroom of his New Hampshire home but was considerate about whoever would find him. As it turns out, it was his fiancée and the police who were first on the death scene and were greeted with warning notices about their risk of carbon monoxide poisoning. Delp, 55 at the time of his death, also asked in a note that someone ensure that 'Floppy' his cat was unaffected by the noxious fumes.

Alice says knickers to authority

As a publicity stunt it was in a class of its own until ever-controversial Alice Cooper came up against the bureaucrats of America's Federal Trade Commission (FTC). Cooper and his record label Warner Bros planned to wrap his 1972 album *School's Out* in disposable panties, which were popular at the time. Enter the FTC which said it could not be done because the knickers were not 'non-flammable' and thus against the authority's code. The publicity was huge and went on and on. Cooper said the panties were made of the same material as surgical masks and offered to promise that the panties would only be worn on faces. In the end helicopters dumped thousands of panties on to the audience at Cooper's Hollywood Bowl concert.

George fights his label

George Michael fought a losing battle to be released from an eight-album contract with Sony in 1992. Seen as an artist's battle for freedom against the big business ethic, he claimed that after his label Columbia had been sold to Sony he was treated as a component rather than an artist. Michael's lawsuit failed but it cost new label Dreamworks SKG $52 million (£40 million) to sign George. Twelve million (£8 million) went to the artist and the rest to Sony for Michael's contract.

No resting in peace for Brown

James Brown's randy lifestyle came back to haunt him in death. His body was subjected to DNA testing in 2007 following several paternity claims after his death the previous year at the age of 73. Three proved to be children the soul singer had not known about. Brown had also left instructions that a paternity DNA test be carried out after his death with regard to James Brown II, a baby he had from a relationship with his former backing singer Tomi Rae Hynie. That proved positive too and James II was confirmed as a son although not mentioned in the soul singer's will.

Competitive Verve

It was no secret in the rock world that Frank Zappa and Lou Reed had a frosty relationship for years but ironically Reed of Velvet Underground fame was called upon to make the speech when Zappa of the Mothers of Invention was posthumously inducted in the US Rock and Roll Hall of Fame. Animosity was said to date back to 1966 when Reed felt the Verve Records label, to which they were both signed, was not being even-handed and had favoured Zappa's album *Freak Out!* while Reed's efforts remained unreleased. Despite the perceived bad blood, of which the Hall of Fame organizers seemed blissfully unaware, Reed was magnanimous in 1994 and said: "I admired Frank and Frank admired me."

Fever led to Boon death

The circumstances leading to the death of D. Boon, of American punk trio the Minutemen, were bizarre. Sick with a fever, he was lying in the back of a van which crashed in the Arizona desert in December 1985. Boon, 27, whose real name was Dennes, was thrown by the impact out of the back doors and broke his neck. The Minutemen, who were rated as one of the top up-and-coming underground US rock bands of the time, had already released their critically acclaimed double album *Double Nickels on the Dime*.

Truly pissed off

Disgruntled Inger Lorre of the Nymphs showed just what she thought of her record label. She hopped up on the desk of a Geffen Records executive, lifted up her skirt and urinated. For extra effect she chanted each band member's name while casting flower petals into the stream. The glam punk band was annoyed that it had not been allowed to tour for two years and that their producer had suddenly been switched from a Nymphs session to a Guns N' Roses' album.

Crash wrecks Teddy's career

A car crash effectively ended soul singer Teddy Pendergrass' career in 1982. He was left paralysed from the waist down after his Rolls-Royce smashed through the central reservation and hit two trees in East Falls, Philadelphia. His spinal cord was severely damaged and although he restarted his career he failed to chart seriously again. The former member of Harold Melville and the Blue Notes who went solo, died from respiratory failure aged 59 in 2009.

Jackson in child trouble again

A fly-on-the-wall TV documentary ran Michael Jackson into child abuse allegations for a second time in 2003. Millions saw Jacko in his home discussing sleeping arrangements with a 13-year-old boy, which sparked a Santa Barbara county attorney's criminal investigation. Jackson was charged with seven counts of child molestation and two counts of administering an intoxicating agent. Jackson denied the allegations, saying the sleepovers were not sexual in nature, but it took a five-month trial to clear his name.

A Blur in space

British indie band Blur produced the call sign for the ill-fated Beagle 2 Mars probe project in 2003. Bass player Alex James was also part of the campaign to get the British project funded.

Age problem

The sex lives of touring British New Wave leaders Duran Duran were so prolific that they had to have written reminders about the age of consent for each American state they played in. Bassist John Taylor said in his autobiography that they bedded so many groupies and fans that organizers of the 1981 tour feared they would be arrested for under-age sex. Each of the band members was given sheets of paper with the age of consent written in the corner. He also said the band, whose hits included 'Hungry Like the Wolf' and 'Girls on Film', were on such a hectic schedule of US cities that they had to be reminded of where they were.

Ringo stars

Veteran cowboy actor Lorne Greene was one of the most unusual people to have a number-one hit in the USA. His spoken-word single 'Ringo' rocketed to the top in 1964 at the height of Beatlemania, bought by fans unaware that it was a country and western cowboy ballad, not about the Beatles' drummer.

Zappa Monkees around

Frank Zappa replaced the unavailable Mike Nesmith for the final TV episode of *The Monkees*.

Circle of death

Guitarist Jon Andreas Nödtveidt of Swedish black metal band Dissection was found dead in a circle of candles. Often alleged to be a Satanist, Nödtveidt was believed to have shot himself in a Stockholm apartment on 13 August 2006 when he was 31. Reports of an open Satanic bible lying near the body were dismissed.

Bumping up the charity cash

Singer Shakira's baby was helping Third World children before it was born. In early 2013 Colombian-born Shakira revealed her 'bump' when she posed naked with her Barcelona footballer partner Gerard Pique to promote her charity plan. She had organized a 'virtual' baby shower via the Internet so anyone wishing to give her baby gifts should instead donate money to the United Nations Children's Fund (Unicef) for vital polio vaccines and food.

Novice Alice gets them running

A huge leap of faith and some instinctive reverse psychology led manager Shep Gordon into a long-time relationship with shock rockers Alice Cooper. He was reported as saying he signed them after seeing a whole audience run out of one of their early gigs. Shep's reasoning was quoted to be: "Any band this bad must have some merit."

Musical farewell to John

In an eerie coincidence, just as surgeons at New York's Roosevelt Hospital pronounced John Lennon dead on the operating table on 8 December 1980, the Beatles' 1963 recording of 'All My Loving' came over the sound system.

Spiced-up session

British singer Geri Halliwell spiced up a London recording session by stripping down to her bra and panties. The former Spice Girl was recording her new album in January 2013.

Tangled love life

Texan country rock singer-songwriter Steve Earle has been married seven times since 1973, when he was just 18. He married one of them, Lou-Anne Gill, twice.

Hair-raising row

Rapper Vanilla Ice faced a Florida court in 2001 accused of assaulting his wife Laura. While arguing as they drove he claimed he only pulled some of her hair out in order to prevent her from jumping out of his truck's window. He pleaded guilty to disorderly conduct and was sentenced to probation and ordered to attend family therapy sessions.

Marriage quickie

Singer Britney Spears had one of the shortest show business marriages on record – less than two and a half days. Spears, who was riding high on hits such as 'Baby Hit Me One More Time', married childhood friend Jason Alexander at the Little White Wedding Chapel in Las Vegas in January 2004. Fifty-five hours later, stating that 22-year-old Spears "lacked understanding of her actions", the marriage was annulled.

Cross-dressing gets US cross

Queen's cross-dressing video for their single 'I Want to Break Free' left the American record-buying public cold – even in liberal 1984. Instead of increasing the band's popularity as hoped, Queen's US sales plummeted after the promotional video featured singer Freddie Mercury in a miniskirt, guitarist Brian May as a woman in curlers, bassist John Deacon as an old lady and drummer Roger Taylor as a tarty schoolgirl. As a result Queen did not tour their extravagant stage show in the US after 1980 but did take it worldwide.

Huey's a winner

Huey Lewis, of 1980s chart band the News, won an out-of-court settlement with the makers of hit film Ghostbusters because the theme tune which charted with Ray Parker Junior closely resembled Lewis' earlier composition 'I Want a New Drug'.

Blondie session crashed

Two unexpected people turned up at a recording session by American punk band Blondie. In 1980 as lead singer Debbie Harry went through her paces, a car carrying two mystery people called Suzy and Jeff hurtled through the wall of the Sunset Boulevard studios in Hollywood, California. Jeff was having an argument with his girlfriend when he lost control and crashed through the wall. No one was hurt but the band immortalized the rowing couple in the song 'Suzy and Jeffrey' which was on the *Autoamerican* album of the early 1980s.

Music world's mercy mission

The British rock and pop music industry came together in a massive effort to save millions of Ethiopians from famine in the early 1980s. Almost 40 of Britain's chart acts of the time started the effort in 1984 when they formed a charity supergroup – under the name Band Aid – to record the single 'Do They Know It's Christmas'. It not only sold millions of copies and raised millions of pounds at the time but topped the British charts on several occasions when more money was needed. All costs such as studio time, marketing, packaging and distribution were also waived as the whole industry pulled together to help.

Le Bon sailed into peril

Sailing fanatic and Duran Duran frontman Simon Le Bon had a very close brush with death in the high winds and mountainous seas of an Atlantic Ocean storm. On his 70 foot (21m) racing yacht *Drum* he was taking part in the 1985 Fastnet Race in British and Irish waters when the keel snapped off. *Drum* capsized trapping Le Bon and five other crew members in the upside-down hull for more than 20 minutes before an RAF helicopter came to the rescue. Despite his ordeal Le Bon, who was uninjured in the Fastnet race, continued to sail and even took part later in a Whitbread Round the World event, coming third.

Trickster foiled

Queen were wise to the underhand tricks of a Rio de Janeiro promoter who became known throughout the rock world for reneging on deals with foreign acts. In 1980 Queen had their own aircraft parked next to the stadium where they were playing, then loaded and flew it away after the gig. It meant the Brazilian promoter had to pay up in full because he couldn't hold the guitars and gear as ransom – something he had done before.

David's all dressed up

David Bowie's penchant for dresses in the early part of his career caused quite a stir on more than one occasion but rock historians say it was the start of glam rock. On the cover of his 1970 album he was pictured wearing a Mr Fish 'man dress' but that was not the only time he shocked observers with a dress. As a newcomer to the American rock scene he was shown around Los Angeles by a Mercury Records representative and went to visit the girls at Hollywood High School. But Bowie received no 'girl reaction' as he was wearing a dress.

Tragedy turns Green to God

A horrific event finally turned soul and gospel singer Al Green to God in 1974. He was attacked by a girlfriend at his home in Memphis, Tennessee while in the shower. She threw a saucepan of boiling grits over him, severely scalding his back, stomach and arms. Mary Woodson White then committed suicide with Green's .38 handgun. Mary, who had a history of mental illness, was known to be upset because he would not marry her – one reason being that she was already married and had four children. Ironically two of Green's biggest chart successes were the singles 'Let's Get Married' and 'Let's Stay Together'. Green, who had for some time been conflicted about stardom and his religious beliefs, trained as an ordained minister and, at the time of writing, is pastor of the Full Gospel Tabernacle in Memphis at the age of 66.

Good coverage for Springsteen

Bruce Springsteen's publicity machine hit a rich vein of coverage in 1975 when the singer, songwriter and guitarist appeared on the covers of top US magazines *Time* and *Newsweek*. The success of his single 'Born to Run' had marked 'The Boss' out as a new 'saviour' of rock 'n' roll.

Near miss for hit maker Neil

Singer-songwriter Neil Young had a brush with death after having treatment for a brain aneurism in March 2005. Surgeons had operated successfully on the arterial bulge in his brain but he collapsed two days later in a New York street bleeding from the artery in his groin from which the surgeons had accessed the aneurism. With emergency surgery he was quickly patched up and he recovered from both operations.

Ozzy flare-up

Former Black Sabbath frontman Ozzy Osbourne set his hair ablaze. It happened as he tried to tackle a fire in his Beverly Hills home in January 2012 which had been started by a candle. Ozzy, 64, managed to singe his hair in his efforts to beat out the flames but was hampered by having a hand in a cast following surgery.

Los Angeles firemen arrived in time to douse the fire before the house was badly damaged.

Too sexy for my Van

Some of the lyrics for the Van Morrison song 'Brown Eyed Girl' caused a controversy when it was released in 1967 for allegedly promoting premarital sex. A special radio-friendly version had to be recorded replacing "making love in the green grass" with "laughin' and a-runnin', hey hey".

Digging the Stones

A gardener was said to be the inspiration for the title of the Rolling Stones' mammoth 1968 hit 'Jumpin' Jack Flash'. Jack Dyer was Keith Richards' gardener at his Sussex home of Redlands and had a particular way of stomping around the garden. Mick Jagger, who wrote the lyrics, was awakened by Jack's steps one morning while at the house – and the rest is enduring pop history.

ODB dies

Ol' Dirty Bastard of the Wu-Tang Clan collapsed and died suddenly just two days before his 36th birthday in 2004. Many people in the hip-hop industry had never been sure that the eccentric behaviour of Ol' Dirty Bastard, alias Russell Jones, was as a result of mental instability or excessive drug use. He died at a New York recording studio on 13 November but friends had said he had been complaining of chest pains the day before. The official verdict on his death was accidental but the autopsy revealed both cocaine and the prescription drug Tramadol were found in his body.

Young love?

Justin Timberlake was just 12 when he met his future love Britney Spears. In 1993 they were both cast members of American TV's *The Mickey Mouse Club*, as was Christina Aguilera with whom Timberlake was to tour later. Timberlake and Spears were in a relationship – and the media spotlight – from 1999 to 2002 before splitting.

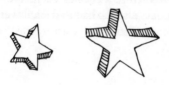

Walmart upset by Sheryl

JUS supermarket chain Wal-Mart refused to sell Sheryl Crow's eponymous second album in 1996. Wal-Mart bosses were unhappy with the lyrics of the song 'Love is a Good Thing', which criticises the company gun policy with the words "Watch our children as they kill each other with a gun they bought at the Wal-Mart discount stores".

Licensed to cheat?

Rob Stewart admitted in 2013 that he cheated his way to a British driving licence four decades previously. Rod said a roadie took his driving test in 1967 after signing in as the rock star – and passed first time. Stewart said he drove illegally in Britain occasionally but eventually made his home in the USA where he passed a legitimate test with flying colours. When his trips have taken him to Britain he has been able to drive on his US licence.

Ill-fated family

The Wilson brothers who formed the Beach Boys in the early 1960s may have had a great professional success but were cursed in personal terms. Brian was left impaired by excessive drug use, Dennis drowned in the Pacific Ocean and youngest brother Carl died from lung cancer in 1998.

Ike predicts death

Singer Ike Turner of the Ike and Tina Turner duo fame was believed to have been plotting his death for some time. On 12 December 2007 he was found dead from a cocaine overdose, aged 71, at his California home just days after he had told friends and relatives he didn't think he would see Christmas.

Kirsty justice move fails

An almost decade-long campaign to get justice for singer Kirsty MacColl collapsed in 2009. MacColl was killed by a speedboat while she was scuba diving in Mexico but the true person to blame was never found. A deckhand who claimed he was at the controls was sentenced to two years and 10 months' imprisonment for culpable homicide but this was immediately transmuted to a £61 fine. He later boasted he was paid to take the 'rap' by a powerful businessman who was allegedly at the wheel. The Mexican government was also criticized for its lack of will to investigate properly why the boat was allegedly speeding in an area from which craft were barred because of diving parties. A minor official was rapped but overall big business and government seemed to have colluded in a cover-up.

Lennon sparks Jesus outrage

The Beatles' reputation literally went up in flames in parts of the USA in what may or may not have been an injudicious comment by John Lennon. Christian fundamentalists across America went berserk and began burning records and Beatles memorabilia when Lennon was quoted as saying in 1966 that the Beatles "are more popular than Jesus right now". Despite his denial that he was rating the band's successes above Christianity and saying that he was merely making what was a sad observation about the times in which he lived, anti-Beatles sentiment swept America. This lasted until the band released *Sgt. Pepper's Lonely Hearts Club Band* and suddenly all was forgiven in America with multi-million sales.

Dylan's name game

Early in his career American heart-throb Bobby Vee hired, and became friends with, a backing musician called Elston Gunn. Gunn's birth name was Robert Zimmerman but to the rock world he became Bob Dylan.

Drummer bashes media

Eagles drummer Don Henley lashed out at the press in his song 'Dirty Laundry' in 1982. The song, critical of media intrusion in the private lives of celebrities, followed his problems when drugs and under-age girls were found in his home by police.

Arrest embarrassment

'Godfather of Soul' James Brown was arrested by police in mid-performance on the stage of a New York theatre in 1978. He had failed to comply with a government order not to leave the USA during a payola investigation of his radio stations.

Love of dad costs a life

Yoko Ono claimed that John Lennon's insistence on going to see his son might have cost him his life. After a recording session in December 1980 she had suggested going for a meal but Lennon was adamant he wanted to go to their New York apartment to see Sean, aged five, saying: "I want to see Sean before he goes to sleep." They were his last words as a moment later he was gunned down and died in hospital.

Not very Slick driving

A member of American rock band Jefferson Airplane was really flying when she crashed her car at 100mph (160kph) in 1971. Singer Grace Slick suffered head injuries when her car slammed into a tunnel wall near San Francisco, California. The incident happened while she was drag racing with fellow band founder Jorma Kaukonen and guitarist Kaukonen claims to have saved her life by pulling her from the wreckage.

High inspiration

A spiritual man all his life, Carl Wilson used to lead prayers before Beach Boys' recording sessions. Appropriately the lead voice on the hit 'God Only Knows', Carl became an ordained minister with the Movement of Spiritual Inner Awareness. His older brother Brian said the pre-recording prayer sessions for albums such as *Pet Sounds* were meant to invoke higher guidance in the music.

Male shame bans records

The male dominated world of the 1950s record business led to a ban on country artist Kitty Wells' song 'It Wasn't God Who Made Honky Tonk Angels' because it was too suggestive and labelled men as an unfaithful bunch. However, the song rocketed her to fame, one of the first women to do so in the country genre.

Death of youngest Gibb brother

The Gibb family of entertainers has always maintained that youngest brother Andy did not die of a drug overdose in 1988. Depressive Andy, who had followed his Bee Gee brothers Robin, Maurice and Barry to chart success but as a solo artist, had been in rehab before his death in England but his previous drug use may have contributed to his demise. The official cause of death was myocarditis –an inflammation of the heart caused by a virus which was exacerbated by his years of cocaine abuse.

A lot at steak for Lady G

Lady Gaga has been no stranger to showing flesh judging by her stage outfits but some animal flesh caused an outcry. She appeared at the MTV Video Music Awards ceremony in 2010 swathed in raw flank steak to the horror of animal rights activists. The meat for the dress, which was designed by Argentine Franc Fernandez, was also Argentinian and came from his local butcher in Los Angeles, California. The flank cut was chosen because it would keep well. Lady Gaga was said to have described it as the most comfortable thing she had ever had made for her.

Alex becomes a big cheese

Many rock and pop stars have second strings to their bow but Alex James might just qualify for the most unusual. The bass player and occasional singer in Britpop band Blur went into cheese making. He bought a 200-acre farm in the fertile Cotswold Hills of southern England and began developing his own cheeses. He marketed three: 'Blue Monday', a creamy blue cheese; 'Farleigh Wallop', a soft goats' milk cheese, washed in cider brandy and wrapped in vine leaves; and 'Little Wallop', a goats' cheese with thyme. A major UK supermarket also signed James to develop some special cheeses with tomato ketchup, salad cream and tikka masala flavours.

A million dollars down the toilet

A Peeping Tom video camera in a women's toilet is estimated to have cost rock 'n' roller Chuck Berry in excess of $1 million in the 1990s when he enraged 59 women. The camera was installed in the women's rest room of his restaurant in Wentzville, Missouri. Despite claiming that it was installed to catch a restaurant worker in the act of theft, Berry, whose 1950s hits included 'Johnny B. Goode', elected for a class action settlement that, with legal fees, cost him more than $1 million. However, Berry's guilt in the case was not proven.

Bloody mistake

Ozzy Osbourne and Alice Cooper might have a distinguished record of 'shock and gore' but the Beatles beat them to it by a few years. In 1966 for the US-only release of their album *Yesterday and Today* the 'Fab Four' were photographed in butcher's coats and holding dismembered dolls and lumps of meat. The American media and public were shocked and chastened record label Capitol was quick to react. It reshot the photo with John, Paul, George and Ringo around a steamer trunk and, to save money, stuck it over the old covers. In the following decades fans who managed to peel off the top cover and reveal the original have made hundreds, even thousands, of dollars for its rarity value.

Bomber Moon

The Who's madcap drummer Keith Moon had a thing about blowing up hotel toilets. His antics of blasting the porcelain to bits started with small fireworks called cherry bombs, then he graduated to large fireworks and even sticks of dynamite. His antics got the band banned from dozens of hotels. Sometimes Moon did it for fun but occasionally there was a revenge motive to his actions. He blew up toilets at one hotel because he couldn't get room service and on another occasion because the hotel management had asked him to turn his music down.

Cola ban hard to swallow

The strictly impartial BBC banned the Kinks' song 'Lola' from its air waves in 1970 because of a line that mentioned a commercial product – Coca-Cola. It was only when composer and Kinks' leader Ray Davies changed the words to 'cherry cola' that the censors of the BBC relented, but the song only made it to 12 in the UK sales' charts.

Richard likes to watch

Rock 'n' roll pioneer Little Richard's propensity for watching others having sex got him into trouble with the law several times. The rocker, whose successes have included 'Good Golly Miss Molly' and 'Tutti Frutti', was first prosecuted under his birth name Richard Penniman in 1955 for watching people making love in their cars, then again seven years later when he was caught masturbating while spying on a couple having sex.

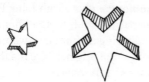

Singer dies in fireball crash

British crooner Dickie Valentine died in a 90mph crash as he drove between gigs. In 1971 a drive in thick fog at 4.20am ended in a huge fireball that also killed Valentine's pianist Sidney Boatman and drummer Dave Pearson. The incident near Crickhowell in South Wales was on a stretch of road Valentine had travelled many times and he was familiar with its hazards. The mystery was why the singer, who had British number ones in 1955 with 'Christmas Alphabet' and 'Finger of Suspicion', had lost control of the car while attempting to take a clearly marked dangerous bend.

Art mirrors reality

Lynyrd Skynyrd were pictured on the cover of their 1977 album *Street Survivors* surrounded by flames and three days after its release several members of the band died in the flames of a plane crash. In view of the tragedy record label MCA had the cover redesigned.

A slice of trouble

Ten-piece hard rockers Mom's Apple Pie became better known globally for their controversial album cover artwork than their music. In the early 1970s the Ohio band released *Mom's Apple Pie I* and *Mom's Apple Pie II*; the first had artwork which showed a matronly woman holding a pie with a slice cut out of it. A closer look at the slice, however, revealed that it resembled a vagina and the album was removed from distribution while an alternative was created. This featured the same picture but the artist saved the woman's blushes by adding a miniature brick wall, topped with razor wire, covering up the vulva in the pie. In an obvious poke at officialdom the artist Nick Caruso painted a policeman looking in the window behind the woman.

Pet takes on the giants

Petula Clark stood up for racial equality against America's right wingers and big business in 1968. She was singing a duet on an NBC prime-time TV special with calypso singer and civil rights campaigner Harry Belafonte when she touched him on the arm, something that was deemed shocking in a country where segregation was still rife. Show sponsor Plymouth Motors wanted the 'touch' edited out but Pet insisted it stayed or she said she would insist the whole show was scrapped. The touch was aired with no outcry from the US public. Plymouth's reputation took a dip when the company's 'racially driven' stance was highlighted by shocked media.

Acid attack

Legend has it that every backstage drink for the rock stars performing at the Woodstock festival was laced with the mind-altering drug LSD. Apparently it could have accounted for some of the strange behaviour by some of the performers over the three-day event in 1969.

Reaching for the stars

Queen's Brian May, voted the 27th greatest guitarist ever in a recent *Rolling Stone* magazine poll, is a star-struck rock star. After reaching the pinnacle of rock success with Queen he became an astrophysicist. May had dropped his studies in the early 1970s to concentrate on Queen's rise to stardom but in October 2007, more than 30 years after he started his research, he completed his PhD thesis in astrophysics entitled 'A Survey of Radial Velocities in the Zodiacal Dust Cloud'.

Ironic farewell to Bobby

The charismatic frontman of Boney M, Bobby Farrell, died in 2010 on the same date as the subject of one of his biggest hits. He was found dead in a St Petersburg hotel after finishing a gig in Russia. Coincidentally, the date of his death, 29 December, was the same as the assassination of Grigori Rasputin, the infamous Russian mystic whose name was taken for the 1978 Boney M hit, which soared to number two in the British charts. In a further instance of life imitating art Farrell, 61, who had complained of heart and stomach problems, died in the city in which Rasputin was poisoned, beaten, shot and drowned in 1916.

Renato's rallying song

A singer who reached the number-one chart spot in the UK once performed to just 20 people in a tiny room. Italian-born Renato Pagliari was one half of the singing duo Renee and Renato with Hilary Lester which achieved the Christmas number-one spot in the 1982 British charts with 'Save Your Love' – but they were one-hit wonders. Renato was a fan of Birmingham-based English-based Premier League football club Aston Villa and one Saturday in 1990 with the team playing badly he was asked at half-time to inspire the team by booming out Puccini's 'Nessun Dorma'. After the performance team manager Ron Atkinson told his players: "Now that is passion! Go and show me some of that in the second half!"

Gun trouble for Jones

Rapper Russell Jones took a few bullets during his short life. In 1994 he recovered after being shot in the stomach in a row with a fellow rap artist. In 1998 he was shot in the back and arm when robbers tried to push their way into his girlfriend's house in Brooklyn, New York. Again he recovered.

Trendsetting trouble

Setting fashion trends in mid-1960's America was not easy – just ask Sonny and Cher Bono. Turning up at a fashionable Hollywood restaurant with long hair and dressed in bell-bottom jeans and flower-patterned shirts, the 'I Got You Babe' hit-making couple were met with howls of derision. The furore in which Sonny was called a "faggot" and Cher a "hooker" was so intense the Bonos, who later divorced, were thrown out of the restaurant in 1965.

Unwanted first for ODB

Rapper Ol' Dirty Bastard managed to be the first person arrested under a California law forbidding a convicted felon to wear a bullet-proof vest. He was wearing it when cops stopped his car in 1999. ODB also did not have a licence to drive. These offences plus arrest for crack cocaine possession and more traffic infringements in New York several weeks later led to him being sent by a court to a drug treatment centre, from which he escaped. When rearrested in Manhattan ODB was jailed for two to four years.

Jail for Earle

His drug use led Texan singer-songwriter Steve Earle to having the prison cell door slammed on him. He fell foul of American law enforcement first in 1993 when he was arrested for possession of heroin then again in 1994, for cocaine and weapons possession. A judge sentenced him to a year in jail after he pleaded guilty but failed to appear in court. Country rocker Earle was released after serving 60 days of his sentence then completed an outpatient drug treatment programme.

Loose talk costs careers

A boy band's drug controversy involved the highest in the land when the British Parliament got involved in January 1997. East 17 singer Brian Harvey was engulfed in a drug-related furore when he was quoted as saying the drug ecstasy "can make you a better person" and stating "it's cool to take drugs". His comments led to them being raised in the House of Commons by former Prime Minister John Major. Harvey was sacked because his comments had damaged the boy band's image. Within months the band had disbanded after scoring 12 top 10 hits in the British charts, a string of top 20 appearances and the number-one album *Walthamstow*, the east London postal district after which the band was named.

Switching arts

World-renowned artist Damien Hirst switched artistic disciplines to music when he linked up with an actor and a chart-topping bass player to form the band Fat Les. Along with actor Keith Allen and Blur's Alex James he recorded 'Vindaloo', which became the unofficial English football anthem at the 1998 World Cup.

Denver's fatal flight

Million-selling country singer John Denver died when the light aircraft he was piloting nosedived into the Pacific Ocean near Monterey, California. Although Denver was a known heavy drinker earlier in his life no trace of alcohol was found in his badly disfigured body recovered from the sea. Denver had just bought the kit plane and was getting the feel of it when he crashed on 12 October 1997. Denver, 53, could only be identified from his fingerprints. Crash investigators revealed that the fuel selector of the kit plane – not built by Denver – had been wrongly placed against manufacturers' specifications in an inaccessible position and it was believed Denver lost control when reaching over his left shoulder to bring in fuel from reserve tanks.

Unwelcome 'voices' for Jim

Jim Gordon was a well-respected session drummer but developed voices in his head as a paranoid schizophrenic. They led him to horrifically murder his own mother, with whom he was living in California in June 1983. Gordon, who had played with such rock and pop luminaries as Eric Clapton, John Lennon, Steely Dan and Jackson Browne, smashed her head with a hammer and then stabbed her repeatedly with a knife. Despite the diagnosis of acute paranoid schizophrenia Gordon was sentenced to 25 years in prison. Gordon co-wrote the Derek and the Dominos hit 'Layla' and although a skilled drummer he played piano on the track.

No Hanks

The Internet was abuzz with talk that the actor Tom Hanks' father was a member of the 1950s Canadian doo-wop group the Diamonds. Certainly someone in the band photograph could pass as the actor's double but it wasn't his father. With hits between 1956 and 1961 such as 'Why Do Fools Fall in Love?' and 'Little Darlin', the vocal quartet's line-up was Dave Somerfield, Ted Kowalski, Phil Levitt and Bill Reed.

Carl perked up for big comeback

Exactly one month after surviving a crash in which he suffered three fractured vertebrae in his neck, a severe concussion, broken collarbone and lacerations all over his body, rockabilly star Carl Perkins was back on stage. Perkins and his band were in a car which hit the back of a pickup truck near Dover, Delaware on 21 March 1956 just as Carl's career was taking off. His car plunged into a ditch and Perkins was lying face down in water when he was saved by his quick-thinking drummer Fluke Holland, who rolled him over. The crash killed Perkins' brother Jay and claimed the life of the pickup truck driver. Carl Perkins, whose 'Blue Suede Shoes' became a rock standard, remained unconscious for an entire day but by 21 April he had battled back to health to resume his career with a gig at Beaumont, Texas.

Dylan lost for words

Although he wrote hundreds, even thousands, of songs, words did not always fly off the page for Bob Dylan. Frustrated by writer's block after the first verse of 'Champaign, Illinois' Dylan ran into Carl Perkins, the creator of the iconic rock 'n' roll song 'Blue Suede Shoes', who offered his help. After Perkins worked out an improved rhythm and improvised the verse-ending lyric, a pleased Dylan told him, "Your song. Take it. Finish it." The pair shared composing rights.

Mötley Crüe court controversy

Mötley Crüe earned the tag 'the most notorious band in the world' within a year of its formation in 1981. By 1982 they had been arrested in Canada and involved in a bomb controversy. Arriving at Edmonton airport in the province of Calgary, Canadian Customs considered the metal spiked stage suits they were wearing offensive weapons and confiscated them. Also destroyed under Canadian obscenity laws were pornographic magazines brought in by lead singer Vince Neil. Later these and a supposed bomb threat against the band in Edmonton were uncovered as publicity stunts. But they worked, as Mötley Crüe became a global name.

Making substitutions

Mental problems are not a rarity in rock and pop music and sometimes bands have to bring on a substitute to maintain their stage performances. The Beach Boys and Pink Floyd had identical problems where they had to bring on a sub. When Brian Wilson suffered mental and drug problems in 1965 they brought in Bruce Johnston on bass and vocals – he led the vocals on 'California Girls' – while Wilson went into seclusion to write songs. Syd Barrett's mental problems revealed themselves when he suddenly stood still on stage during a Pink Floyd gig as if in a world of his own. He was replaced by Dave Gilmour for live shows while Barrett continued his songwriting.

Crash paralysed Phantom

Rockabilly act the Phantom crashed his car 600 feet (200 metres) down a mountainside – and survived. The Phantom, aka Jerry Lott from Mobile, Alabama, was paralysed after the plunge near Spartansburg, South Carolina in 1966. Lott was a one-hit wonder with the high-energy rock 'n' roll song 'Love Me' in 1960 while managed by 1950's teen heart-throb Pat Boone, who was credited with coming up with the bizarre Phantom stage name.

Stars get SWAT-ted

Several top music names of the 21st century were victims of a sick craze by hoaxers. The idea was that the hoaxers try to get police Special Weapons and Tactics (SWAT) teams sent to stars' homes. It started in the exclusive Hollywood area of Los Angeles. Police raced to the home of rapper Chris Brown after a hoax phone call in January 2013 claiming a man was about to shoot a woman. Brown has a reputation for domestic violence after assaulting his girlfriend Rihanna in 2009. Other music business victims of the hoaxers have been singers Miley Cyrus and Justin Bieber and pop impresario Simon Cowell.

Death on camera

Millions of people witnessed the death of Meredith Hunter during a Rolling Stones performance in December 1969. The documentary cameras were rolling when Hunter, 18, was stabbed to death at the Altamont free concert in northern California. As the Stones played their set, which had been interrupted by outbreaks of violence, crystal meth user Hunter pulled a gun before he was disarmed by Hell's Angel Alan Passaro, who inflicted five stab wounds. Passaro was later cleared of murder on grounds of self-defence but the Hell's Angels were criticized for overreaction to crowd trouble which resulted in fights among sections of the 300,000 crowd. The Stones fended off a $500,000 lawsuit by Hunter's relatives with a payment of $10,000.

Kanye's grief

The mother of hip-hop star Kanye West died after cosmetic surgery in 2007. Donda West was 58 when she died after a tummy tuck and breast reduction. One surgeon had declined to carry out the operation because of concerns over her heart. She did not visit the heart specialist as recommended but went ahead with the cosmetic work with a third surgeon. The coroner's report concluded that Donda West died of 'coronary artery disease and multiple post-operative factors due to or as a consequence of liposuction and mammoplasty.' Her death resulted in a California law being passed which made it mandatory for patients to provide medical clearance for elective cosmetic surgery.

Fatwa controversy

Musician and singer Yusuf Islam ran into a media storm when asked to comment on an Islamic censure ruling on British author Salman Rushdie. Yusuf's previous incarnation had been Cat Stevens, a British singer-songwriter with a series of hit singles and albums before he embraced the Islamic faith. Yusuf, who quit the music business in 1977 on his conversion, was asked in 1989 at a student meeting about the Rushdie fatwa and it was interpreted by some that he advocated a death sentence on Rushdie for the perceived offence to Muslims his book *The Satanic Verses* had caused. Despite his denials in a later BBC TV interview it was a subject that would not go away for the creator of singles such as 'I'm Gonna Get Me a Gun' and 'Matthew and Son' and best-selling albums *Teaser and the Firecat* and *Catch Bull at Four*. Yusuf asserted that while he regretted the comments, he was joking and that the BBC show was improperly edited.

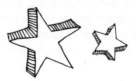

Tit-for-tat songs in rapper feud

New girl on the rap scene Nicki Minaj fell out with veteran rapper Lil' Kim in 2010 after the release of the former's album *Pink Friday*. Kim accused Minaj of copying her image saying, "If you are going to steal my swag, you gonna have to pay." Caribbean-born Minaj and Brooklyn-born Kim became embroiled in an exchange of feuding hip-hop songs and the artwork on the Lil' Kim mix tape *Black Friday* shows her decapitating Minaj with a sword. A disparaging track called 'Tragedy' was released in response by Minaj in 2011 and references in the *Pink Friday Roman Reloaded* track 'Stupid Hoe' were thought to be directed at her rival as well. The row polarized the rap and hip-hop music community.

The wonder of Woodstock

A 600-acre farm in the Catskill Mountains of upstate New York changed the face of music in August 1969. Never before had so many of the biggest names in rock and pop gathered in one place before such a massive audience. Thirty bands performed over three days near the town of Bethel before an estimated 500,000 people. But not everyone was enthused about the exposure to so many avid fans who had walked, hitchhiked, driven and flown to the Woodstock Peace & Music Festival. Among the big names of the time who declined – and possibly regretted refusing – invitations were the Beatles, the Doors, the Moody Blues, the Byrds and Led Zeppelin. Varying reasons included 'not liking hippies', the mud and, in the case of the Beatles, the band was about to split up.

Rock death tragedy

Eleven fans died in a rush to get to the front of the stage for a Who concert in December 1979. They were trampled to death in the race to the front at the Riverfront Coliseum in Cincinnati, Ohio in the early days of festival seating. This type of 'seating', where all the seats are actually removed to get more people into venues, did receive some criticism in the aftermath of the deaths of 11 teenagers.

Inglorious debut

The first thing that happened when up-and-coming rapper 50 Cent signed to Columbia Records in 2000 was to get dropped from the label and 'blacklisted' in the recording industry because of his song 'Ghetto Qur'an'. It mentions drug dealers from his youth of the 1980s in his New York neighbourhood of Queens and got 50 Cent the reputation among feuding rivals in the industry as a snitch. Even though 50 Cent claimed that everybody mentioned in the song appreciated it and it was eventually included on his 2002 compilation *Guess Who's Back,* police believe it was the cause of an assassination attempt on the rapper in 2000.

Riding to the end

Ageing cowboy film and singing star Roy Rogers was the incredible choice to wind up the massive hippy festival at Woodstock in 1969. Organizers wanted Roy, whose TV series had ended 12 years before, to close the three-day event, following acts such as the Who and the Rolling Stones, with a rendition of his song 'Happy Trails'. Probably suspecting how out of time and place he might be, the actor declined.

Lip service to Obama

Beyoncé was accused of letting down one of the biggest audiences she will ever have – by miming. In front of a global TV audience topping millions and a live audience of 700,000 in Washington DC, the pop superstar was accused of lip-synching 'The Star Spangled Banner' at President Barack Obama's inauguration in January 2013. She wowed the crowd with a seemingly flawless performance of the US anthem before it was revealed that she had decided to sing to a pre-recorded track.

Rotten for Apple man Steve

Apple Macintosh founder Steve Wozniak funded the US Festival on Labor Day weekend in 1982 and kissed goodbye to between $10–15 million. He ploughed money into a high-tech set-up and paid top dollar for the big-name bands of the time such as Tom Petty and the Heartbreakers, Santana, Grateful Dead and the B-52s. Marred by blazing weather and dusty conditions at the venue near Los Angeles, Steve's 'party' lost the multi-millionaire a pile of cash. Yet it didn't stop him doing the same again in 1983 with David Bowie, Van Halen and the Pretenders in the line-up.

Bass ace electrocuted

Bass player John Rostill was killed in his home recording studio aged 31. Rostill, who was a talented songwriter as well as a member of the Shadows who backed Britain's Cliff Richard, was electrocuted in 1973.

Festival toll piles up

While the notoriety of a fan's death at the Rolling Stones' Altamont festival in 1969 seems to have become deeply rooted in rock history, another event fared even worse. The US Festival of 1983 near Los Angeles resulted in two deaths – a beating and one drug overdose – 120 major injuries and 145 arrests by police.

Lux lucks out

Lux Interior, leader of the punk-influenced US band the Cramps, died suddenly after being rushed to a California hospital with a burst aortic artery in February 2009. Real name Erick Purkhiser, Lux took his stage name from a car advertisement.

Band's name game

British 1950's band Cliff Richard and the Drifters ran into name trouble the moment they tried to crack the transatlantic charts. The release in America of 'Feelin' Fine' was immediately greeted with a legal threat from the US soul band the Drifters, whose name had been established in the early 1950s, and the record was withdrawn. The British band, desperate for a permanent name, used the temporary handle the Four Jets for their second US single 'Jet Black'. Eventually they settled on the Shadows, presumably unaware that Bobby Vee's backing band had the same name and that Vee was equally unfazed by the Brit newcomers. Of 69 UK singles over three decades, 35 were hits as the Shadows and 34 charted as Cliff Richard and the Shadows.

Changed times

The 25th anniversary celebration in 1994 of Woodstock 1969 showed how the world had changed. Some bands such as Crosby, Stills and Nash returned but new names for the new era were Green Day and Nine Inch Nails. But there was a distinct lack of flower power, as drugs, alcohol, food, cameras and children were barred and the place, staged 10 miles from the original Woodstock site, was well stocked with credit card machines and ATMs.

Numan, new location

Gary Numan, whose electronic hit 'Are Friends Electric?' with Tubeway Army was a British number one, said violence made him quit his homeland to live in the USA. He claimed he was ashamed of Britain after the 2011 riots and cited the harassing of his family as reasons for going to Los Angeles. In September 2011 a fan posed the question "Is it true you now hate England and want to leave?" on his website. Numan replied, "No, that's utter rubbish" but 13 months later he had already emigrated.

Frankie goes to court

The splitting of Frankie Goes to Hollywood in 1987 led to a legal high-water mark in the relationship between performers and their corporate paymasters. Lead singer Holly Johnson left, citing musical estrangement, after a string of single hits such as 'Relax', 'Two Tribes' and 'The Power of Love' and was offered a solo recording agreement with MCA Records. But the record company with whom Frankie Goes to Hollywood had such a run of single and album success, ZTT, claimed Johnson was required to release all solo material through its label until the band's original multiple-album agreement was fulfilled. A subsequent High Court hearing found in Johnson's favour, holding that the highly restrictive terms of the contract constituted an unreasonable restraint of trade. This not only effectively freed the remaining members of Frankie Goes to Hollywood from their ZTT contract but also became famous as an unprecedented victory for the artist over a label.

Bon's highway to Heaven

Just after the album *Highway to Hell* rocketed AC/DC to rock prominence, leader singer Bon Scott died. After a night of heavy drinking Scottish-born Bon was found dead at 33 in a friend's car in Dulwich, south London. Although Bon was asthmatic and the temperature that fateful night in February 1980 was below freezing, his death was caused by inhaling vomit and alcohol poisoning. A coroner ruled his death as misadventure.

A star by any other name

A legal battle between Warner Bros and Prince over the artistic and financial control of the multi-talented singer's work caused him to dump his name. In 1993 he replaced the moniker Prince with a symbol only. He explained in a rather convoluted way: "The first step I have taken toward the ultimate goal of emancipation from the chains that bind me to Warner Bros was to change my name from Prince to the Love Symbol." During the legal row with his record label, the prolific hit maker and songwriter appeared in public with the word 'slave' written on his cheek.

TB strikes the Cat

Cat Stevens almost died as he approached the pinnacle of pop success in 1969. Having achieved acclaim for both his singles and albums, he contracted tuberculosis and was near death for some time. During months in hospital and a year in recuperation he wrote 40 songs in what he said was an experience of spiritual awakening that was to see him ultimately convert to Islam.

Pulling back the Iron Curtain

German-based disco foursome Boney M proved that music can overcome politics as they parted the formidable Russian Iron Curtain in the 1970s. The multi-national band which scored worldwide hits with singles such as 'Rasputin' was allowed by the dour Soviet leader Leonid Brezhnev to perform in the USSR. The only song that was banned from their live sets by the regime was 'Rasputin' – the charismatic priest closely involved with the Russian royal family before the Russian revolution in the early 20th century.

Sobering message

The attempted suicide by two brothers landed British heavy metal band Judas Priest in an American court. The boys' parents alleged that the double suicide bid had been sparked by listening to the band's version of 'Better by You, Better than Me'. They claimed that the song, when played backwards, contained subliminal messages that caused their sons to shoot themselves. The month-long trial in Reno, Nevada ended with exoneration for Priest but lead singer Rob Halford described the court experience as 'sobering'.

Gene's road curse

American rocker Gene Vincent had some unhappy experiences with road accidents. In 1956 his left leg was badly injured in a motorcycle accident which meant he had to use a metal leg brace on stage. Tragedy struck again in 1960 when he was in the car that crashed in England killing his friend and tour partner Eddie Cochran. Again Virginia-born Gene, best known for rockabilly hits such as 'Be-Bop-A-Lula' was injured but recovered enough to carry on a career, although he was in such constant pain from his leg that he took more drugs and alcohol than was good for him. A number of times he rejected surgeons' advice to amputate the leg and he died in 1971 aged 36 from a ruptured stomach ulcer.

Keith's gunpowder plot

Madcap drummer Keith Moon caused a massive explosion at an American TV studio with a gunpowder prank. Moon, always at the forefront of mayhem and practical jokes, was appearing on the Smothers Brothers show in 1967 with the Who and their rendition of 'My Generation' was to end with his drum kit exploding in line with the band's reputation of smashing up their amplifiers and instruments. Having seen the technicians load the explosive pack near the nailed-down drum kit, joker Moon tricked other techies in to adding more, not telling them it had already been done. At the explosive finale Moon was thrown backwards, his drums shot in the air and a blast forward scorched guitarist Pete Townshend's hair.

Bum rap

Rod Stewart confessed in his very frank autobiography of his rock 'n' roll lifestyle that he administered cocaine anally. He admitted in 2012 to buying anti-cold capsules, separating the two halves of the capsules and replacing the contents with a pinch of cocaine before pushing them up his bum, where they would dissolve into his system. He explained that there was a valid reason for it because he was worried snorting the drug through the nose might damage his famous singing voice and put his six-decade-long career at risk.

Kiss of approval

Outrageous rockers Kiss signed their commitment to a book in blood. In 1977 the band, famous for their scary black and white face make-up and extraordinary show effects, donated their real blood to be added to the ink for the first edition of Marvel Comics' *Super Special Kiss Comic Book*.

Ashen confession

The 'did-he, didn't-he' dilemma of Keith Richards' snorting his father's cremated ashes was laid to rest by the guitar ace himself. He made international headlines in 2006 when the story got about that he had mixed his dad's ashes with cocaine and snorted them – something he denied. Later, in his frank autobiography *Life*, the Rolling Stone confirmed that he did snort the last earthly remains of his dear old dad, Bertrand, but not mixed with cocaine. Richards claimed that some of his father's ashes blew on to a table while he was scattering them, and rather than just brush it away he stuck his finger in the residue and snorted it.

Shock death

Former Yardbirds and Medicine Head guitarist Keith Relf's dream of re-forming one of his former bands died with him on 14 May 1976. While practising for the return of his band Renaissance he was killed in a bizarre incident at his London home – electrocuted playing an improperly earthed electric guitar in his basement recording studio.

Showaddywaddy shows how

There are usually losers when bands split or amalgamate but not so with the British rock 'n' roll revival band Showaddywaddy. It formed when two groups, Choise and the Golden Hammers, amalgamated but it didn't slim its line-up. As an eight-member band, with the unusual feature of having two vocalists, two drummers and two bass players, they had a string of 22 UK hits in the 1970s and 1980s reviving rock 'n' roll standards such as Eddie Cochran's 'Three Steps to Heaven'.

Cocktail of death

Stephen Porter probably stands unique in the history of bizarre rock and pop deaths – killed by a cherry. Stephen, who adopted his rock 'n' roll stage name Stephen Peregrin Took from a character in *The Lord of the Rings*, was a founder with Marc Bolan of Tyrannosaurus Rex but died in October 1980 from asphyxiation after choking on a cocktail cherry. Though a post-mortem discovered he had taken both morphine and hallucinogens prior to the choking incident the inquest ruled that neither contributed to his death.

Death tumble

Strawbs and Fairport Convention singer Sandy Denny died several weeks after a fall downstairs. Late in March 1978 Denny, who was known to have drink and drug problems, struck her head on concrete and suffered severe headaches. After being prescribed painkillers that can be fatal with alcohol Denny, birth name Alexandra Denny, collapsed into a coma. Her death on 21 April, aged 31, was blamed on 'mid-brain trauma'.

Cliff rains at Wimbledon

One of the strangest requests for best-selling British singer Cliff Richard was to entertain a restless tennis crowd – for free. Keen tennis fan Cliff, the third top-selling singles artist in UK history with total sales of over 21 million, was a centre court spectator at the 1996 Wimbledon tennis championships when it rained for hours. Richard, who got his start as lead singer of the Shadows in the 1950s, put on an impromptu sing-along to keep the crowds occupied.

It all worked out

Australian songstress Olivia Newton-John's 1981 hit single 'Physical' was banned by a number of US radio stations for being 'too sexy'. The censorship didn't stop the record selling over 2 million copies and going on to become the biggest selling US single of the decade.

Wooden performance

Wooden steps were the most bizarre 'instruments' ever to take a song to number one in the UK. To achieve a heavy stomping beat all members of the British band the Honeycombs stamped their feet on wooden stairs to supplement the drumming of Honey Lantree. 'Have I The Right' stomped all over the chart opposition in 1964 and hit number one in Britain, Australia and across Europe. The stamping in the home studio of producer Joe Meek also meant that microphones had to be clamped in place with bicycle clips.

'Secret' winning combination

Elvis Costello's first broadcast recording was a zany TV advertisement in 1974. His father Ross MacManus, a former big-band singer and musician, wrote and sang the R. White's Lemonade advertising jingle called 'I'm a Secret Lemonade Drinker'. Elvis, real name Declan MacManus, provided backing vocals and between father and son they won a silver award at that year's International Advertising Festival.

Hair-raising rows

The producers of the Monkees TV series had many furious rows because they wanted band members Micky Dolenz, Davy Jones, Mike Nesmith and Peter Tork to have the long hair that was hip for the mid-1960s. They won in the end and the series, and the group, were successes but network TV executives and advertisers, fearing they would be associated with subversion and homosexuality, took some convincing.

Gambling with death

Fooling around with a gun led to the death of Chicago's Terry Kath. At a party in 1978, the guitarist picked up a friend's unloaded .38 revolver, jokingly putting it to his head and pulling the trigger. Kath, who had a history of drug and alcohol problems, then did the same with a 9mm semi-automatic pistol which, unfortunately, was loaded. He died instantly.

Nip slip

British girl band member Kerry Katona had a surprise for the audience at London's Hammersmith Apollo, a sight of a nipple. Her breasts popped out of the well-endowed singer's top during a 2013 reunion gig with Atomic Kitten from which Katona had split in 2001.

Death roll

In 1975 Electric Light Orchestra cellist Mike Edwards quit the hurly-burly of a chart-topping outfit for the simple country life, which killed him. The known eccentric settled in rural Devon, England and died when a huge circular bale of hay, weighing 1,300 pounds (590kg), rolled down a hill and crushed his van in September 2010.

Wells' asphyxiation death

Orleans drummer and keyboard player Wells Kelly collapsed and died on the front step of a London apartment in 1984 after a night's drinking. Death was due to asphyxiation. Kelly, whose hits with Orleans included 'Dance with Me' and 'Still the One', had been on tour in Meat Loaf's backing band.

Randy dies a hero

Spirit guitarist Randy California drowned in the Pacific Ocean in 1997 after heroically saving his son. The singer-songwriter and 12-year-old Quinn had been caught in a riptide while swimming off Molokai in Hawaii. He managed to push the boy to safety but could not save himself.

Mama's weighty problem

The body size of power-voiced singer Cass Elliot was part of her fan appeal and on-stage persona but ultimately it was to cost her her life. Her death in her sleep on 29 July 1974 while in London for a two-week engagement at the Palladium Theatre was from a heart attack brought on by 'fatty myocardial degeneration' due to obesity. She generally weighed 300lbs (136kg). A rumour which had grown up that she had choked on a ham sandwich proved untrue. Her death was ruled as due to natural causes.

Brian Jones' death riddle

Over 40 years after his shock death on 3 July 1969 there remains a mystery over Rolling Stone Brian Jones' last hours and minutes. As late as 2008 a conspiracy theory that he was murdered was investigated without substantiation. At the time of his death he was no longer a Rolling Stone, having been fired a month before because his growing drug problem was disrupting the band's work and progress. Jones was discovered dead at 27 in his swimming pool. A coroner, noting that Jones' alcohol and substance abuse played a role in his death, ruled death by misadventure.

Judge dead

English ska and reggae musician Judge Dread died with a tribute to his backing band on his lips. As he rounded off a live show in Canterbury, England, on 13 March 1998 with the words "let's hear it for the band" he collapsed to his knees. While his fans, who loved his songs for their lurid sexual lyrics, thought it was a joke and part of the act, the Judge (birth name Alexander Minto Hughes) was suffering a fatal heart attack.

Cowboy's last round-up

Dave Rowbotham, a guitarist who played for a number of bands during the booming Manchester music scene in the 1980s, was found bludgeoned to death in 1991. Rowbotham, whose nickname was Cowboy, had been killed with a lathe hammer but no one was ever prosecuted for the murder although it was known that the guitarist had associations with criminals and may have been an informer. Manchester-born Cowboy had played with the Mothmen, Motivation and the post-punk Durutti Column. Manchester band Happy Mondays featured the tribute 'Cowboy Dave', an epic seven-minute final track, on their 1992 album *Yes Please!*

Taxi to Heaven

Stiv Bators, well-known around the 1980s New York punk scene, died in June 1990 after being hit by a taxi in Paris, France. The 40-year-old guitarist was taken to hospital, but he insisted that he was feeling fine and walked out without receiving treatment. He died that night in his sleep. Ironically the Dead Boys was the punk band he was most associated with. Stiv's ashes were scattered across the grave of the Doors' Jim Morrison, who had also died in Paris a decade previously.

Death plunge

Gifted percussionist Jerry Fuchs fell to his death in 2009 when he attempted to escape from a broken elevator. He plunged five flights down the elevator shaft of a dilapidated Brooklyn loft building. Among names he had kept the beat for were Turing Machine, Juan MacLean Maserati and LCD Soundsystem. He was 34 at the time of his death.

Deadly prediction

Social networking site Facebook was the place for a death notice by former Weezer bass player Mikey Welsh. He posted the place and time of his death in advance. On 26 September 2011 he wrote: "dreamt i died in chicago next weekend (heart attack in my sleep). need to write my will today." He followed it with another post that read "correction – the weekend after next." Two weeks later, in a self-fulfilling prophecy, Welsh's body was discovered in a Chicago hotel room, the victim of a heart attack brought on by a drug overdose. Welsh, who was 40 at the time of his death, had quit Weezer in 2001 after a mental breakdown and threw himself into a new art career for which he was critically acclaimed and held 13 exhibitions.

Drug watch failed Shannon

Mammoth efforts to keep Blind Melon frontman Shannon Hoon away from the danger of drugs failed in 1995 – with deadly results. Following a rehab stint, a 'drug sitter' was hired to keep him sober while on tour. Hoon was having none of it and fired the sitter. Although Hoon's band mates remained united about stopping his substance abuse, the singer managed to sneak off the group's tour bus in New Orleans, score some cocaine and slip back into his bunk, where his lifeless body was discovered a few hours later.

Death shocker

The original composer of the song 'My Way' made a fatal error when he meddled with electricity. French pop singer, songwriter and dancer Claude François, who sold 70 million records in his career, was taking a bath in his Paris home when he noticed a light not working properly. When he reached out to fix it, he was electrocuted and died aged 39. He was the 1967 co-writer of 'Comme d'Habitude', a popular French song which Paul Anka adapted for the English language into 'My Way' and became arguably the most-covered song in history by such varied names as Frank Sinatra and Sid Vicious.

Dread-ed hit maker

Even though his lyrics were often lascivious and rude and regularly got his records banned from the radio, Judge Dread was the first white recording artist to have a reggae hit in the genre's home island of Jamaica. Alexander Minto Hughes, born in Kent, England, sounded as though he had real Caribbean roots and when he first travelled there, many of his fans were surprised to discover that he was white. Following a pattern of lewd nursery rhymes set to reggae music, Dread's songs including 'Big Seven', 'Big Eight' and 'Up with the Cock' through the famous ska, bluebeat and reggae record label Trojan.

Ride of death

Drummer Mikel Gius was killed riding his bicycle, which collided with a car in Sacramento in 2005. Sadly, he was the second percussionist with the band !!! (pronounced 'chk, chk, chk') to die. Predecessor Jerry Fuchs had earlier been killed in an elevator accident.

Expensive wake-up call

When a road manager for the Who investigated a $600 phone bill presented to him by a hotel in 1968 he went to drummer Keith Moon's room to find him asleep with a phone still connected to a very expensive transatlantic call to London.

Divine change

After his departure from the Electric Light Orchestra in the mid-1970s, eccentric cellist Mike Edwards changed his name to Deva Pramada, which meant 'divine contentment'. He became a sannyasin (member) of the philosophical discipline of the Indian mystic Osho.

Symbolic name

Prince was not the only musician to replace his name with a symbol. An American dance punk band formed in 1986 under the name '!!!' (pronounced 'chk, chk, chk') which they claimed was inspired by the clicking sound of the African Khoisan language.

SWAT was that?

When an armed New York SWAT team smashed their way into a hotel room in 1968 they emerged not with a cuffed suspect – but autographs. They had been called in after cherry bombs – spherical exploding fireworks – were thrown from a hotel window, but when they burst in they found the Who drummer Keith Moon up to his old tricks with explosives again. Relieved it wasn't a terrorist attack, they released Moon and he obliged with autographs.

On-air censorship

A BBC disc jockey took the unilateral decision in the middle of his own show to ban Frankie Goes to Hollywood's 1984 song 'Relax'. Radio One breakfast show host Mike Read stopped the record in mid-play, describing the lyrics as 'obscene' and refused to play it again. The record-buying public thought differently and the resultant publicity surrounding Read's arbitrary ban sent the languishing 'Relax' soaring to Britain's number-one spot for five weeks.

Seaman semen tale

In his frank autobiography *Rod*, Rod Stewart laughs off a salacious story about him that has done the urban myths rounds for years. It was alleged that as a consequence of an evening spent orally servicing sailors in a gay bar in San Diego, he had to have his stomach pumped in hospital. In his book Stewart was good-humoured about the tale saying: "I have never orally pleasured even a solitary sailor … And I have never had my stomach pumped, either of naval-issue semen or of any other kind of semen." He blamed the bogus slur being put about on a vengeful member of his publicity team whom he had fired.

By-passed by success

Increasing drug use and animosity meant multi-instrumentalist Stephen Porter missed out on the mega-success that was to come with Tyrannosaurus Rex. The band, which became glam rockers T-Rex, started as a duo with Stephen and Marc Bolan. But by 1969 Porter, whose stage name was Steve Peregrin Took, had driven a wedge between the pair and he was fired from the set-up. Starting with the single 'Ride a White Swan', Bolan went on to global success while Stephen went on to a series of short-lived bands and never came close to the success Bolan achieved without him.

True harmony

Against all the rules of rock band infighting and jealousies, German band Rammstein has been incredibly together. Since its formation in 1994, the six-piece industrial metal outfit has had no changes in its line-up.

Riotous comment

With the Northern Ireland peace process still some years away heavy metal band Megadeth managed to inspire an extra slice of unrest in the province's 'Troubles'. Unwittingly band frontman Dave Mustaine dedicated the final song of the gig, 'Anarchy in the UK', to the Irish Republican Army (IRA) with the words 'this one's for the cause!' Protestant Loyalists took offence and fights broke out among the audience in Antrim. The result was that Megadeth had to finish the rest of their tour of Northern Ireland and the Republic of Ireland in a bullet-proof bus. Mustaine, the only constant member of the band which had 20 personnel changes in 30 years, explained that he had been misled by a local about the meaning of 'The Cause'.

Kanye believe this!

Rapper and fashion designer Kanye West sparked controversy among the world's Christians when he appeared on the cover of the January 2006 *Rolling Stone* magazine dressed as Jesus, complete with a crown of thorns.

Tammy's second string

Tammy Wynette, one of the biggest-selling female country singers, continued to renew her cosmetology licence every year for the rest of her life – just in case she ever had to go back to a day job. She trained to be a hairdresser in 1963 but launched a singing career that charted 23 number-one songs during the late 1960s and early 1970s.

Golden future

Schoolboys started the Dutch rock band Golden Earring in 1961 and remain with it at the time of writing. Thirteen-year-old George Kooymans and his neighbour, Rinus Gerritsen, 15, got together in the Dutch city of The Hague. Originally called the Tornados, they had to change their name because a British band of the same name had already had a UK number one. Golden Earring, which became famous for its mega-decibel quadrophonic sound system, had a chain of album and single hits in the Netherlands and Europe but truly hit the world stage with their 1970s single 'Radar Love'. They were once headliners for concerts with Aerosmith and Kiss as support bands.

Hallyday is back

The veteran singer dubbed the French Elvis was back performing in 2011 after a near-death experience two years before. In 2009, at the age of 66, Hallyday was rushed to hospital in Los Angeles, California for emergency surgery on complications from earlier spinal surgery in Paris. He was put into an artificial coma to aid his recovery. Hallyday, a superstar in France who had sold more than 100 million records, had also been treated for colon cancer. He had several times announced retirement but by 2012 was still rocking at live gigs.

No peace for Morrison

The grave of Doors frontman Jim Morrison is one of the most visited places in Paris. And just as irreverent as Morrison was in his short life, so his fans are to his grave. A number of headstones and other memorial items have been stolen, presumably by fans, and defaced headstones have had to be replaced. Fans leave cigarette butts on it, drizzle whisky over it and even burn cannabis in homage to the star who died in 1971.

Driven to drink – slowly

Country star George Jones' songs and videos and those of others about him often feature lawn mowers. Jones has never made a secret of his alcoholism and drug use but has been self-deprecating about the lawn mower incident during the late 1950s when his then wife used to hide all the car keys to stop him heading for bars to feed his habit. Jones was having none of these restrictions and having found the keys to a ride-on lawn mower he once chugged at five miles per hour eight miles to the nearest bar. It took him 90 minutes but he said he did not remember much about the return journey. Another former wife, fellow country star Tammy Wynette, told of seeing George's mower outside a bar 10 miles from their home on a route that involved a major highway.

Is there a surgeon in the house?

Alternative rock band R.E.M. should have added a surgical team to their road crew for their 1995 European tour as almost anything that could go wrong health-wise did. In March drummer Bill Berry had to leave in the middle of the show in Lausanne, Switzerland with a severe headache and ended up in surgery for the repair of two ruptured blood vessels in his brain. Luckily he was taken ill close to one of the most advanced brain surgery centres in the world. Weeks later in Cologne, Germany bass player Mike Mills was gravely ill from complications from an appendix operation and was saved by surgeons. Once the tour had resumed lead singer Michael Stipe developed a hernia and was hurriedly flown back to the band's home state of Georgia for surgery. Amid all this medical mayhem guitarist Peter Buck was . . . fine.

Great Scott

When 19-year-old Scott Halpin bought tickets from a tout for the Who's 1973 San Francisco gig he could not have conceived that he would make rock history. Twice during the concert at the Cow Palace drummer Keith Moon passed out after drinking brandy and animal tranquillizers and the second time he did not return. When a plea went out to the packed audience for a drummer up stepped brave Scott Halpin from Indiana. He was good enough to see the Who through to the end of the show and when he died in 2008 aged 54 from an inoperable brain tumour surviving members of the Who placed a memorial blog on their website. Halpin admitted that the experience gave him a new admiration for rock drummers because after three numbers on Moon's drum kit he was 'shattered'.

Hank says goodbye

Hank Williams, the megastar of 1950's country music, died quietly in the back seat of a car taking him to a performance that had sold the equivalent today of $30,000-worth of tickets. The singer, who was known for his destructive drinking and drug taking, had been unwell after taking sedatives, the hypnotic drug chloral nitrate and alcohol before a doctor administered vitamin B12 and morphine. Williams died from a heart haemorrhage while being driven through West Virginia between shows on New Year's Day 1953. He was 29 and his last single release before his death was packed with irony – it was entitled 'I'll Never Get Out of This World Alive'.

Biting comments

Whichever explanation is put forward for John Lydon's switch to the stage name Johnny Rotten it always comes back to his teeth. One version is it came from a lack of oral hygiene leading to his teeth turning green. Another story says Sex Pistols guitarist Steve Jones saw Lydon's teeth and said "You're rotten, you are!" It was 30 years on in 2008 when Lydon had $22,000-worth of extensive dental work in Los Angeles. The ever socially aware Lydon claimed that it was not done out of vanity. He explained: "It was necessity ... all those rotten teeth were seriously beginning to corrupt my system."

Adam's will power

Hip-hop singer Adam Yauch left a will banning any of his work being used in advertising. The Beastie Boy, who died in May 2012, aged only 47, left his $6.4 million (£4 million) fortune to his wife and daughter but insisted that 'any image or name or any music or any artistic property' created by him was not to be used in adverts.

Great guns of fire

'Great Balls of Fire' piano rocker Jerry Lee Lewis certainly loves his guns but things got a bit dangerous with him on the trigger. In September 1976 Jerry Lee was taking pot shots at his office door when his bass player Norman Owens wandered in to the danger zone and was hit in the chest. He recovered but later sued.

Not Best for the Beatles

Drummer Pete Best was fired from the Beatles as the band stood on the brink of super-stardom. The Liverpool four had just hooked up with producer George Martin when Best was sacked in 1962, a decision that left him shattered and embittered. Some reports said it was Martin who did not rate Best's stick work and wanted Ringo Starr to replace him and there certainly seemed to be a hint of a stab in the back for a loyal old friend in the speed with which George Harrison, John Lennon and Paul McCartney agreed to the change. Best, reckoned to be the handsome one out of the Fab Four and whose attempts at a pop career failed to glitter, later released an album of early band tapes which he called – some said rather pointedly – *The Savage Young Beatles*.

Tammy's mixed messages

Two important, and diametrically opposed, events happened to country singer Tammy Wynette in 1968. She racked up global mega-sales appealing to women in her song 'Stand by Your Man' then didn't take her own advice by annulling her marriage to Don Chapel, whom she had married just a year previously.

Chopper crash kills Vaughan

Guitar ace Stevie Ray Vaughan was killed when a helicopter he was in crashed on a Wisconsin hill in the USA. The Double Trouble band's star was in one of a fleet of helicopters ferrying a touring group, including Eric Clapton, to another venue when it crashed in foggy conditions on 27 August 1990. Also dead in the wreckage were two members of Clapton's road crew and the pilot. Eric denied in his autobiography that he was supposed to be on board the doomed chopper, one of a fleet of four on the day, and had given up his seat to Vaughan.

Clapton's letter heartbreak

Amid the heartbreak of losing his son, rock guitarist Eric Clapton had the added misery of a letter from him from beyond the grave. Four-year-old Conor died in 1990 when he fell from the 53rd floor of a New York skyscraper but had written his first letter to his father days before the accident. The boy and his mother, Clapton's former girlfriend Lory Del Santo, posted the letter to Clapton who was in London but before it was delivered, Conor had died. Lory, an Italian-born model, said: "The baby had learned to write a few words and he said to me he wanted to write a letter to daddy and what should he write? I told him 'Write, I love you'." Eric did not open the letter until after Conor's funeral.

Beatles' ban

The Beatles were not always the darlings of the pop world. The BBC barred the playing of 'A Day in the Life' because it was assumed the line "I'd love to turn you on" was a drug reference. The 1967 track was the last on the Beatles' Sgt. Pepper's Lonely Hearts Club Band album.

Battle of the albums

Feuding rappers Kanye West and 50 Cent clashed in 2007 with album sales as their weapons. The two hip-hop superstars both released albums on 11 September and 50 Cent threw down the gauntlet by saying if West sold more records on the day he would no longer perform music. He was reported as stating he would write music and work with other artists, but not put out any more solo albums. Rather than join the boasting battle, West decided to keep his own counsel and let the record-buying public decide. Things looked good for 50 Cent, real name Curtis Jackson, as at the time he was earning twice as much as West and his previous album had outsold West's almost three to one. But on the big day Kanye sold almost a million copies of *Graduation* in US stores while 50 Cent's *Curtis* only managed 691,000 copies. West won the bragging rights and 50 Cent moderated his media quotes with a conciliatory: "I am very excited to have participated in one of the biggest album release weeks in the last two years. Collectively, we have sold hundreds of thousands of units in our debut week. This marks a great moment for hip-hop music, one that will go down in history." To date he remains a live performer but the real winner of the challenge was label Universal Records – to whom both were signed.

Staying low

R.E.M. frontman Michael Stipe had to moderate his considerable vocal range and avoid high notes on a 1995 European tour because the pain from recent hernia surgery meant he could not hit them.

Perfect timing

David Bowie's debut single 'Space Oddity' could not have been more perfectly timed. Supposed to have been a parody of the failed British space programme, it was released just days before the more successful USA space effort – Neil Armstrong and Buzz Aldrin landing on the moon in July 1969. It rocketed Bowie to stardom with a number-one chart hit in the UK but it took a re-release in 1973 for it to sell in the USA and then it only peaked at number 15.

Technical Hammer

American hip-hop star MC Hammer was a self-confessed 'super geek' where technology is concerned. He was among the first big names of music to sign up to social networking such as Facebook and at the time of writing claims to tweet (on Twitter) 30–40 times a day. Aside from his rapping, song writing and occasional acting his entrepreneurial skills are in technology – consulting for or investing in eight technology companies. In 2012 he was quoted as saying projects in the technology field were taking up to 10–12 hours of his working day.

Tetsu backs out

Tetsu Yamauchi was a rarity in British rock music because he was Japanese. His skills as a bass guitarist were much sought-after and he was part of Free during the early 1970s. He was also a session bassist with the Faces after the departure of Ronnie Lane but in the mid-1990s he retired to a quiet life away from the media glare because he considered it juvenile and vain for people his age – he was in his late 40s – to still be performing rock 'n' roll. Later he even refused invitations to take part in a Faces' reunion.

Musical anarchy in the UK

Punk rock icons the Sex Pistols sailed into trouble when they gate-crashed the Silver Jubilee of Britain's Queen Elizabeth II in 1977. During the public holiday celebration the band's controversial manager Malcolm McLaren was arrested after chartering a boat to cruise down London's River Thames past thousands of spectators with the band belting out their own disrespectful and anarchic version of the national anthem 'God Save the Queen'.

Moving the Van

Marriage solved Van Morrison's attempt to carve out an international solo career which was hampered by bureaucracy in 1967. After the hits 'Here Comes the Night' and 'Baby Please Don't Go' with his band Them, Morrison signed a solo contract with American label Bang Records but, because of visa problems, was threatened with deportation. He managed to stay in the US when his American girlfriend Janet Rigsbee agreed to marry him. The couple had a daughter, Shana, and divorced in 1973.

Lemmy gets fired

The incident that got Ian Kilminster fired from Hawkwind was all due to a mistake. Canadian border guards thought the powder he had in his possession when he crossed from the USA was cocaine and arrested him. Although analysis proved it to be less serious amphetamine, Hawkwind, then promoting their album *Warrior on the Edge*, had cancel to several shows as a result. Ian, better known as bass player Lemmy, was blamed and fired but possibly had the last laugh because he went on to be the star of heavy metal outfit Motörhead.

Ian steps down

A founder of the Rolling Stones was fired from the stage line-up, probably because he didn't fit the band's image. Burly and older than the rest of the band, Ian Stewart, despite his great keyboards skills, was dropped in 1963 but stayed on as road manager and played on many Stones studio recordings. The 'sixth Rolling Stone' died of a heart attack, aged 47, in 1985.

Crazy world of fan worship

1969 was famous for many events but one of the more astonishing was the 'death' of Beatle Paul McCartney. It suddenly became a global debate as to whether Macca had died as long before as 1966 and been replaced by a lookalike. Despite Paul coming forward to say he was alive, some clung on to the story. They claimed clues to McCartney's premature death were:

- Playing part of 'Revolution Number Nine' backwards revealed the words "Turn me on, dead man".
- Playing part of 'I am the Walrus' backwards reveals the words "I buried Paul".
- On the *Sgt. Pepper* album cover the band is standing on Paul's grave.
- On the *White Album* track 'Glass Onion', bearing in mind that walrus might be Greek for corpse, John sings "Here's another clue for you all, the walrus is Paul".
- Symbolically on the *Abbey Road* album cover, Paul is out of step with John, Ringo and George – suggesting he is dead.
- On the *Magical Mystery Tour* cover Paul is the only one wearing a black flower signifying death while the others have red carnations.

Blue Gene

The 'F' word has not always been the province of punk bands and rappers. In a moment of impishness rock 'n' roller Gene Vincent claimed he managed to get a slightly elongated version of the 'F' word on to a 1950s single. The sound quality of 'Woman Love', the B-side to 'Be Bop A Lula', is not great but Vincent is said to have told a producer years later that in the phrase 'huggin' and a kissin' he substituted 'huggin'' with fuckin'. The conservative broadcasters of the day were taking no chances and widely banned it from radio.

State your names

With two Randys in Jimi Hendrix's New York band the Blue Flames something had to change. Randy Texas was already in the line-up so when the young Randy Wolfe teamed up he called himself – Randy California.

A spot of trouble

In 1989 R.E.M. drummer Bill Berry developed Rocky Mountain Spotted Fever, the most lethal and most frequently reported tic-born disease in the United States. Strangely, at the time he was in Munich, Germany just 50 km (31 miles) from the Alps and 8,400km (5,200 miles) from America's Rockies. Berry quickly recovered after treatment.

Agnetha lives in fear

A failed love affair had years of serious consequences for Agnetha Fältskog, the blonde vocalist from Swedish hit makers ABBA. In the late 1990s after the failure of her second marriage, Agnetha was in a relationship with a Dutchman but when they broke up he stalked her. It needed a restraining order and in 2003 a court-imposed ban from entering Sweden to get a temporary respite from her ordeal but that ran out in 2005 and the hassle started again.

Record buyers back the Pistols

Record buyers in 1977 were feeling as anarchic and rebellious as punk pioneers the Sex Pistols. Their new release was a disrespectful version of the national anthem 'God Save the Queen' which was immediately banned by radio stations in Britain. The cover added further insult to Queen Elizabeth's jubilee year by depicting her with the punk emblem – a safety pin –through her nose. Still the public bought the single in millions and accelerated it to number two in the British charts, the highest position for any Sex Pistols single.

Presley's a pay pal

Down on his luck black rockabilly singer Roy Brown discovered that Elvis Presley's signature was pure gold. Brown, who had written R&B hit 'Good Rockin' Tonight', had the US tax authorities threatening to jail him if he did not pay up so he asked Elvis for financial help. The King wrote out a 'cheque' for $1,500 on a paper bag and, because Presley's credit was so good with Memphis banks, one of them cashed it for Brown. Sadly the US Internal Revenue Service (IRS) needed more than that and Brown ended up behind bars anyway.

Malcolm changes his tune

Record producer and band manager Malcolm McLaren changed his allegiances over the years. The rebellious teenager who had a huge interest in the Situationist Revolution movement that resulted in the 1968 student riots in Paris, eventually went 'commercial'. He allowed his co-arrangement of 'The Flower Duet' from Léo Delibe's opera *Lakmé* to be featured in British Airways' global advertising campaign of the 1980s and 1990s.

Plant escapes death

Led Zeppelin singer Robert Plant was involved in a near fatal car accident in 1975 which also injured his wife Maureen. The crash on the Greek island of Rhodes left Plant in a body cast facing months of recovery. Led Zeppelin's tours and recording work on seventh album *Presence* went on hold for months until he was back to fitness.

Primate suspect?

Michael Jackson's pet companion Bubbles the chimpanzee was so famous that he was even listed in the files of the Federal Bureau of Investigation.

Madonna not so anti-war

After seeing the vilification of the Dixie Chicks who criticized the 2003 Iraq war, Madonna backed off from a similar possible confrontation with fans. She postponed the release of – and then re-edited – her anti-war 'American Life' video which originally showed her throwing a hand grenade at a President George W. Bush lookalike.

Chemical reaction

One of the biggest British industrial companies was unwittingly behind the success of the Rolling Stones in the early 1960s. The only member of the early Stones with access to a telephone vital to bookings was keyboard player Ian Stewart and that was his work phone at an Imperial Chemical Industries (ICI) factory. Probably unbeknown to his managers and supervisors, Stewart put his work number on advertisements in the music trade papers as he sought work for the nascent band that would emerge as one of the world's most influential and enduring.

Britney battles for control

Toxic singer Britney Spears thwarted what she claimed was a plot to take control of her affairs. In January 2009, Spears, aided by her father James, won a restraining order against her former manager Sam Lutfi, ex-boyfriend Adnan Ghalib and attorney Jon Eardley who, court documents claimed, had been conspiring to gain control of Spears's affairs. They were barred from getting within 250 yards of Spears or her property.

Wood switches to air guitar

Ronnie Wood played air guitar in a live performance to millions across the world. Playing 'Blowin' in the Wind' with Wood and Mick Jagger at the 1985 Live Aid concert, Bob Dylan's guitar string broke. Anxious to keep things seamless, quick-thinking Wood handed his own guitar to Dylan and strummed the air until a stagehand could bring him a new guitar.

Concert consumer protection

With the great prevalence of lip-synching by artists in the 21st century the Fair Trading Minister of New South Wales in Australia ordered disclaimers be printed on tickets for concerts which contain pre-recorded vocals. Virginia Judge said: "There could have been some instances where people actually purchase a ticket thinking that they're going to have a live performance ... for some people that means that everything is live, it's fresh, it happens instantaneously, it's not something that's been pre-recorded. You want to make sure that they're actually paying for what they think they're getting."

Swarbrick fights back

A double lung transplant saved former Fairport Convention leader Dave Swarbrick's life and career. After the life-saving operation in October 2004 he resumed his career as a solo folk performer and toured again. Prior to the operation emphysema had taken its toll so badly friends raised funds through a charity called SwarbAid because he couldn't work with his extreme breathing problems.

A whiter shade of money

Almost 40 years after their single 'A Whiter Shade of Pale' captivated the world's charts, members of Procol Harum ended up in court. Organist Matthew Fisher won a British court judgment awarding him 40% of the music royalties from 2005 onwards for the 1967 British number one. Fisher contended he was entitled to a share of royalties which had previously gone 50–50 to pianist and singer Gary Brooker for the music and Keith Reid for the lyrics.

Tattoo journey around Rihanna

At the time of writing singer Rihanna had a collection of tattoos around her body. They included:

- a music note on her ankle
- Pisces sign behind her right ear
- a Sanskrit prayer on her hip
- a star in her left ear
- the word 'Love' on her left middle finger
- an Arabic phrase on her ribcage meaning 'Freedom in Messiah'
- an Egyptian falcon shaped in a gun on her right foot
- the goddess Isis above her stomach.

Morrison legacy tangle

Doors frontman Jim Morrison left a problematic legacy when he died in 1969. He bequeathed his estate to live-in girlfriend Pamela Courson who, in turn, died of a heroin overdose five years later leaving Morrison's estate to her own parents. Morrison's parents disputed this but the case hinged on complexities of common law marriages. The Coursons retained the estate, valued at more than $30 million (£20 million) and growing every year.

Skirting decency

British band John's Children had its single 'Desdemona' banned by the BBC because of the lyric "lift up your skirt and fly".

Fans go bananas

In the crazy 'Summer of Love' of 1967 fans chasing a psychedelic high went on a big bender – smoking banana skins. Somehow the word had got about that the linings of bananas had the same qualities as cannabis. In California, in particular, the air was full of the aroma of drying banana skins despite the fact that the psychedelic content was actually zero. As a result banana sales went through the roof but plummeted again as the possibility of a cheap 'high' receded, and parts of the state returned to the familiar aroma of smoking spliffs.

Fogerty battles for credence

John Fogerty, the voice behind country rockers Creedence Clearwater Revival was sued for sounding too much like himself in the late 1980s. His record label Fantasy alleged that the 1984 track 'The Old Man Down the Road' sounded too much like 'Run Through the Jungle' from the 1970s. In short John Fogerty was alleged to sound like – John Fogerty. A judge ruled for John finding that an artist cannot plagiarize himself.

Bolan's shock death

Glam rocker Marc Bolan died in a car crash just two miles from his London home. The Mini in which he was passenger smashed into a tree in Barnes on 16 September 1977, two weeks before his 30th birthday. Ironically Marc, who had big chart hits with 'Metal Guru' and 'Telegram Sam', never learned to drive because of his fear of a premature death. He died instantly and was only in the ill-fated Mini for a night out with his girlfriend because his management had loaned his white Rolls-Royce to Hawkwind.

Jackson child abuse allegation

Child abuse allegations against Michael Jackson by a 13-year-old boy were settled out of court without the singer being formally charged. Police investigating the allegations by Jordan Chandler in August 1993 raided Jackson's home and, according to court documents, found books and photographs in his bedroom featuring young boys naked or partially dressed. With Jackson proclaiming his innocence the investigation was inconclusive and no charges were ever filed. Out of court the Chandlers received $22 million.

Finger loss

Losing part of a finger in a bread slicer did not hamper the chart success of British piano ace Russ Conway. Without the tip of his third finger on his right hand Russ' jaunty and fast-paced piano style saw him achieve 20 UK chart hits between 1957 and 1963. Conway, real name Trevor Stanford, had a cumulative total of 83 weeks on the UK singles charts in 1959 alone.

In the Dogg house with Britain

Snoop Dogg was banned from Britain and its national airline after a near riot at London's Heathrow Airport in 2006. After being barred from British Airways' first-class lounge because his entourage was a mix of first- and economy-class passengers the group vandalized a duty-free shop by throwing bottles of booze around. Seven police officers were injured arresting the group and weeks later Snoop was given an official caution for affray and other offences and barred from entering the UK until 2010.

On-stage rant

The Kinks' frontman Ray Davies quit the band on stage and amid a chorus of expletives in front of an audience of thousands. The band, known for its fractious infighting, was playing at London's White City Stadium in 1973 when Davies blurted out to an incredulous audience that he was "fucking sick of the whole thing" and declared that he was quitting. Onlookers said Ray looked "haggard and ill" and had kissed his fellow Kink and brother Dave, "gently on the cheek" before delivering the "I quit" bombshell. Ray, who was having marital problems at the time, subsequently collapsed with a drug overdose and was critically ill for some time. He recovered from his depression to continue a long musical career, including performing at London's Olympic Games closing ceremony in 2012.

Beatle drug fine

Beatle George Harrison and wife Pattie Boyd pleaded guilty at Esher Magistrates' Court in Surrey, England to possession of cannabis at their London home. They were fined £250 each and given a year's probation.

Transplant fails Rory

A liver transplant failed to save Irish blues and rock guitarist Rory Gallagher. He died aged 47 in 1995 from complications from the transplant operation. Heavy drinking and use of prescription drugs during his rock career had damaged his liver, making the transplant attempt a necessity.

It all in the name

Plain old Brian Warner wanted a suitable name for his shock rock stage act in 1989 and came up with Marilyn Manson. He picked the first name of Marilyn Monroe and the surname of multiple killer Charles Manson because they were conversely loved and loathed by American society.

Loo lewd trap

Former Wham! star George Michael's need for anonymous sex landed him in court in America. He was charged with engaging in lewd behaviour when trapped by an undercover cop at public toilets in Beverly Hills, California in 1998. The sting operation led to Michael pleading no contest and being fined $810 with 80 hours' community service. Rumours about George's sexuality had been circulating for years and the loo incident confirmed he was gay. George reflected afterwards that his actions in going to the toilets in the park might have been a "subconsciously deliberate act".

Enemy at the top

Rapper Tupac angered one of the highest officials in the USA with his hit album *2Pacalypse Now*. Vice-President Dan Quayle attacked the album's content which was strongly themed on police brutality when dealing with the black community. The second highest man in America got involved when a Texas youth's defence lawyer claimed he was influenced by *2Pacalypse Now* in shooting a state trooper. Quayle ranted: "There's no reason for a record like this to be released. It has no place in our society." Tupac's answer to the conservative Quayle may already have been in the gold-selling album's track list: 'I Don't Give a Fuck'.

Home-spun Jon

A large amount of Jon Bon Jovi's charity work has been aimed at ensuring American families get decent housing. In 2006 after Hurricane Katrina devastated the New Orleans and Gulf Coast areas he donated $1 million to building 28 homes in Louisiana in partnership with low-income families. A year later Bon Jovi, who has had rock success with his eponymous band, announced a project to rehabilitate a block of 15 homes in north Philadelphia, Pennsylvania.

Tipped off

Two American rappers got into a tangle over names. Southern US rapper, now known as T.I., originally wanted to be known under the stage name of Tip but had to compromise because of established star and Arista Records label mate Q-Tip. The Q in Q-Tip is said to stand for Queens, the New York borough of his birth, but he argued that he is often referred to as just Tip.

Nuts to airlines

British band Mumford & Sons refused to use British Airways and Virgin Atlantic because they served peanuts. In support of their keyboard player Ben Lovett who had a nut allergy they only used airlines which did not serve peanuts as onboard snacks.

Big business shunned Nat

Velvet-voiced Nat King Cole's attempt to get African-Americans more exposure in US entertainment was defeated by corporate racism. The brilliant jazz musician was given his own show by NBC in 1956 but it lasted only a year because a major corporate sponsor could not be found. In conservative, segregated 1950s America companies were afraid of backing innovation against the bigoted values of the day. The show was pulled even though such top stars as Ella Fitzgerald, Frankie Laine, Mel Tormé, Harry Belafonte and Peggy Lee often appeared for Nat, waiving a fee because they wanted it to be a success.

Kinks banned

The Kinks' reputation for rowdy behaviour on stage led to them being banned from the United States at the vital time when British bands were making real inroads into the American charts. In 1965 at the time of the 'British Invasion' of the American charts the US musicians' union slapped a four-year ban on brothers Ray and Dave Davies, Peter Quaife and Mick Avory crossing the Atlantic Ocean to perform live there.

Holliday hides his fears

British crooner of the late 1950s and early 1960s Michael Holliday hid a massive secret from his audiences. Often billed as the most relaxed man in show business for his cool on-stage demeanour, he hid his crippling stage fright. But after British number-one hits such as 'The Story of My Life' and 'Starry Eyed' the pressure led him to a mental breakdown in 1961. Two years later he committed suicide with a drug overdose.

Nash in swap deal

Contractual problems almost stopped the concept of supergroup Crosby, Stills and Nash in its infancy. With a contract offer from Atlantic Records things looked good until it was discovered that Graham Nash, as a member of British band the Hollies, was technically under contract to the North American arm of Epic Records. In a soccer-style transfer swap, a complex deal struck by CSN's co-manager David Geffen traded Nash to Atlantic with Richie Furay's Poco going the other way.

Wrong Moment

British band Moments fired Steve Marriott in 1964 for being too young to be a lead singer. The 17-year-old had been in show business since he was 13 and had West End musical experience when he got the boot. This was the Steve Marriott who went on to front the highly successful Small Faces and later form the supergroup Humble Pie.

Ritchie's fears come true

Mexican-American rock 'n' roller Ritchie Valens had a morbid fear of aircraft after two collided over his California school killing and injuring several of his friends. When he began his rock career he had bookings all over the USA and was forced to overcome his phobia and fly. In one of the great ironies of music history he died aged 18 in 1959 with Buddy Holly – in a plane crash.

Hell for Havens

Although, as the first act, folk singer Richie Havens was told his Woodstock set would be long he didn't reckon on how long. American Havens ended up occupying the stage for the 1969 festival for three hours because many of the following rock stars had problems getting to the very rural venue. Havens ran out of material and began improvising to see it through until someone took over. The upside was that it brought unknown Havens before a massive TV audience.

Jackson shame

The most humiliating event of Michael Jackson's life was surely the detailed examination of his private parts by police. As part of investigating the Jordan Chandler sex abuse allegations against the singer, police had to examine him intimately for features that the accuser had described. Jordan had correctly claimed Jackson had patchy coloured buttocks, short pubic hair, and pink and brown marked testicles. Reportedly, Jordan had drawn accurate pictures of a dark spot on Jackson's penis only visible when it was lifted. This feature was corroborated by law officers in sworn affidavits.

Room with a spew

Jimmy Osmond threw up on stage with Elvis Presley watching. 'Little Jimmy', as he was known when performing with the Osmond brothers in the 1970s, was at the Las Vegas Hilton when he vomited during his number and sprayed the front row of the audience. The Osmonds were alternating shows with Presley and 'The King' was watching from the lighting booth when Jimmy, who had overdone the free food provided by the hotel for entertainers, let rip. Years later Jimmy, who had been wearing his mini-Elvis jumpsuit for the act, recalled: "I was singing 'I Gotta Woman' and I really did; she was in the front row."

Voice over

Heavy metal frontmen put their voices through hell on stage but Whitesnake's David Coverdale actually seriously injured his. In 2009 Coverdale suffered from severe vocal fold oedema (swelling due to fluid collection) and a left vocal fold vascular lesion (enlarged blood vessels in danger of haemorrhage). The band had to withdraw from the remainder of a planned tour with Judas Priest and Coverdale was months in recovery.

Mad at Madonna

A single advertising video cost Pepsi over $5 million. Madonna's 1989 sexual/religious performance to the song 'Like a Prayer' was so raunchy it was dropped after one showing. Pepsi executives feared a sales backlash from many Catholic buyers of the cola drink around the world. Madonna's fee was $5 million.

Rhythm and rage

Two R&B stars were said to have been involved in a mass brawl in 2013 – over parking. Rapper Chris Brown and pals were alleged to have clashed with Frank Ocean in a parking row at the Los Angeles studio they use where one accused the other of blocking their path. Six men were said to be involved but no arrests were made.

Boxing clever

Chris Martin admits he shadow boxes to work up the adrenaline for a gig. The Coldplay front man said he conjures up images of Sylvester Stallone's Rocky to bring up his excitement level for the band's 90-minute sets.

Santa's lips are sealed

'I Saw Mommy Kissing Santa Claus', Jimmy Boyd's Christmas classic of 1952, was banned in some parts of the USA because it inferred married women were having affairs. Boyd was 13 when he recorded the novelty song, which was actually written from the perspective that Santa is the father of the singer and despite an initial lack of air plays it sold three million copies.

Life expectancy Slash-ed

Guns N' Roses guitarist Slash was given just days to live in 2001, at the age of 35. Alcohol and drug abuse left Slash with a life-threatening legacy of cardiomyopathy, a form of congestive heart failure. Doctors said he had between six days and six weeks to live but he survived through the implanting of a defibrillator, a strict physical therapy regime and massive support from his wife Perla. Slash, who has joint British and American citizenship, says he has been clean and sober since 2006 and gave up his third 'vice' – smoking – in 2009, following his mother's death from lung cancer.

Light-fingered Lennon?

It has been claimed that the harmonica used by John Lennon on the single 'Love Me Do' was stolen. Lennon was said to have lifted it from a shop in the Dutch town of Arnhem before the Beatles' first single was released in 1962. With the subsequent and massive success of the Beatles the shop did not seem to mind either and used the shoplifting line in its future advertising.

Sweet nothings

The BBC forced country singer George Hamilton IV to re-record his 1957 American hit 'Rose and a Baby Ruth' for British listening. A Baby Ruth was a candy bar with peanuts, caramel and chocolate that was popular in the US. The BBC's rigid ban on product placement meant Hamilton had to entitle it 'Rose And A Candy Bar' instead.

Bieber suit dropped

A woman who alleged she had been deafened at a Justin Bieber concert dropped a $9.2 million lawsuit in 2012. Stacey Wilson Betts filed against pop star Bieber alleging she suffered permanent hearing loss at his Portland, Oregon concert but pulled out of the legal action because she said she did not have anyone to represent her.

Pet subject

In 2012 British electronic duo the Pet Shop Boys took up the cause of the 'father of computers' who was vilified for being a homosexual. They worked with the BBC Philharmonic on a piece of music about Alan Turing, the World War II code breaker and computer pioneer who was prosecuted for homosexuality and forced to undertake chemical castration before he committed suicide from cyanide poisoning in 1954. Pet Shop Boy Neil Tennant, openly gay himself, said: "It was a terrible story. Of course the reason they won't pardon Alan Turing is because they'd have to pardon all those homosexual men. Well why don't they? Why don't they pardon them all, actually?"

Getting stage fright?

Music is a high-risk industry, a university study has found. In 2007 scientists at the Liverpool John Moores University in England found that in the first five years following chart success, mortality rates among musicians are three times higher than for the people who buy their recordings. The average death age of musicians was found to be 42 in the USA and just 35 in Europe.

Killer weed killer?

The death of drummer Jeff Porcaro came in curious circumstances. The founding member of American band Toto fell ill and died aged 38 after spraying insecticide on his garden. Although a severe allergic reaction to the weed killer was suspected, the Los Angeles County Coroner found his death in 1992 was more attributed to his rock 'n' roll lifestyle. Porcaro had a heart attack caused by arteries hardened by extensive cocaine use.

Metal massacre

A crazed gunman went berserk at a heavy metal gig in December 2004 and five people died. One of them was lead guitarist 'Dimebag' Darrell Abbott who died instantly with three point-blank shots to the head while performing with heavy metal band Damageplan. The killer, Nathan Gale, went on to shoot six others, killing three people, before being shot dead himself by a police officer. The chilling incident in a Columbus, Ohio music venue was captured on amateur video. Writings found at Gale's home led to the belief that he was a paranoid schizophrenic who believed Damageplan were stealing his thoughts.

Cruel blow

Just before he was crushed by a 300lb hay bale in 2010, former Electric Light Orchestra cellist Michael Edwards was told he had beaten cancer. He had been treated for melanoma.

East v. West

During the mid-1990s US west coast rapper Tupac Shakur and east coast rival the Notorious B.I.G. (aka Biggie Smalls) were involved in a feud. The two artists disrespected one another in song lyrics and their label mates on Death Row Records and Bad Boy Records respectively got in on the act with songs in support of their chosen faction. There was no winner in the hip-hop feud as Shakur was killed in a drive-by shooting in September of 1996 while Biggie was murdered in similar fashion in March 1997.

Star spat was a masterpiece

Madonna and Elton John fell out in 2012 but it was only a war of words. Elton sneered about Madonna's Golden Globe chances when her song 'Masterpiece' was nominated against his 'Hello, Hello'. Elton's partner David Furnish waded in against Madonna on Facebook but Madonna had the last laugh by winning a Golden Globe.

Rock hardmen go head to head

Two ex-husbands of former *Baywatch* babe Pamela Anderson slugged it out at the 2007 *MTV Video Music Awards*. After years of strained relations between heavy metal to hip-hop singer/guitarist Kid Rock and Mötley Crüe drummer Tommy Lee they traded blows which ended with Rock being arrested for assault to which he pleaded guilty.

Girls go to it

When 'California Gurls' singer Katy Perry described herself in 2008 as a "fatter version of Amy Winehouse and the skinnier version of Lily Allen", the feisty Brit singer Lily was not going to let a comment like that pass. Even though Perry claimed it was a joke, Allen knocked Perry for not writing her own songs and threatened to post Perry's phone number on Facebook for the whole world to see.

Grudge race to the top

Britpop's poster-boy bands Blur and Oasis were massive rivals in the mid-1990s and claimed they did not like each other. In 1995 their popularity was put to the test by releasing singles on the same day. The winner was Blur's 'Country House' over Oasis' 'Roll with It'. Oasis' guitarist Noel Gallagher was famously quoted at the time as saying that he hoped Blur singer Damon Albarn and bassist Alex James would "get AIDS and die" but retracted it some years later claiming he was on drugs when he was tricked by an American radio journalist into saying it.

No bed of roses

Axl Rose and guitarist Slash might have been the heart of legendary rock band Guns N' Roses but often the verbal knives were drawn between the two stubborn characters – usually over music and the metal band's direction. The two did not talk for years but traded barbs and insults through the media. Slash quit the group in 1996 but frontman Rose continued on under the Guns N' Roses brand.

King guilty of paedophilia

British singer Jonathan King was convicted in 2001 of sexual assaults on five teenage boys committed in the 1980s. King, who had a 1960's chart hit with 'Everyone's Gone to the Moon' and a 1976 single 'It Only Takes a Minute' under the name of One Hundred Ton and a Feather, protested his innocence but was found guilty of six offences against five boys aged 14 to 16 between 1983 and 1989. He was given a seven-year jail sentence and was released on parole in 2005.

Answering call

Neil Young and Lynyrd Skynyrd had a vocal punch-up in song in the early 1970s. Liberal northern Californian but Canadian-born Neil Young took shots at what he perceived as the continuing racism and segregation of the American South in his songs 'Southern Man' and 'Alabama'. Rising to the cause of the Deep South in a vocal rerun of the American Civil War were Lynyrd Skynyrd from Jacksonville, Florida who recorded the legendary 'Sweet Home Alabama' which takes a swipe at Young in its lyrics.

Hair-raising Spears

Britney Spears shocked her fans in February 2007 by shaving her own head. The bizarre incident came after the singer went into a drug rehabilitation clinic in Los Angeles but walked out after less than a day. The following night, she shaved her head with electric clippers at a hair salon before she admitted herself to another rehab clinic – this time for a few weeks.

Blighted tour

Long-running heavy metal band Anthrax must have thought their tour plans for Europe in 1986 were cursed. In April 1986, the band attempted its first tour of Europe, but it was cancelled after the Chernobyl nuclear power station blast in Ukraine. A few months later Anthrax was due to go to Europe as support for headliners Metallica but that, too, was axed because a bus crash had killed Metallica's Cliff Burton.

Ricky's comes out

Puerto Rican-born singer Ricky Martin eventually gave in to media innuendo and speculation by 'coming out' as gay in 2010. Martin announced that he was a "fortunate homosexual man", ending years of fan speculation on the topic. His twin sons, Matteo and Valentino, were born with a surrogate mother in 2008.

Bitchy fight

The refusal of the Kings of Leon to get involved with a hit TV musical comedy/drama led to a homophobia row. After the band turned down a song placement on *Glee* in 2011, the show's creator and executive producer Ryan Murphy called them "self-centred assholes". Kings of Leon drummer Nathan Followill was accused of homophobia when he retaliated on Twitter telling Murphy to "see a therapist, get a manicure, and buy a new bra". The two sides made up.

Fevered expectations

As the Band prepared to go on stage in the biggest gig of their short career their lead guitarist lay in bed sweating and shaking with fever. Robbie Robertson was diagnosed with psychosomatic fever – a freak form of stage fright – as the Band were to make their world debut at the Winterland, San Francisco in April 1969. Drummer Levon Helms recalled in his book *This Wheel's On Fire* that the immobilized Robertson required a hypnotherapist, a lot of band mates' encouragement and less subtle shouting at by managers to get out of his sickbed. Fans catcalled over the shortened 35 minutes of the first appearance but everything went well for the following two nights the Band had been booked for. Robertson would never be able to forget the incident as the Band's third album was entitled *Stage Fright*.

Nose for trouble

Britney Spears had her fair share of criticism over parenting skills and also as a dog owner. In 2006 she was branded 'worst celebrity dog owner' by both the *Hollywood Dog* and *New York Dog* magazines. Dog-crazy readers of the publications were concerned that the three Chihuahuas she owned at the time were not seen being taken out of her home any more after she had started a family with Kevin Federline.

Bush-whacked by Dixie Chicks

Country music favourites the Dixie Chicks went political in 2003 and even they could not have imagined the backlash from it. Band member Natalie Maines attacked the US President of the time, George W. Bush, with an anti-war message after coalition forces had invaded Saddam Hussein's Iraq. Natalie, who along with band mates Emily Robison and Martie Maguire – and Bush himself – was a Texan chose a London concert to lambast the long war that was to come saying: "Just so you know, we're on the good side with y'all. We do not want this war, this violence, and we're ashamed that the President of the United States is from Texas." It was not just the criticism that caused a storm of controversy but that outspoken Natalie had chosen to coruscate the President from foreign soil, but she remained defiant saying: "I said it there 'cause that's where I was." Not accurately gauging how conservative the country music-buying public in America was meant a sales backlash and a buyers' boycott. Their single 'Landslide' plummeted from 10 in the charts to 43 and a week later was not even in *Billboard*'s top 100. Despite Maines issuing an apology, major sponsors, including tea company Lipton's, withdrew their backing and in one anti-Dixie Chicks display, former fans took the group's CDs to a demonstration at which they would be crushed by a bulldozer. Maines said later: "As a mother, I just want to see every possible alternative exhausted before children's and American soldiers' lives are lost. I love my country. I am a proud American."

Flipping MIA

Rapper MIA chose an audience of 110 million Americans to give the finger. With a world audience of even more millions MIA, birth name Mathangi Arulpragasam, raised her middle finger and 'flipped the bird' to the TV cameras during the highly prestigious half-time entertainment at the 2012 Super Bowl with Madonna. Afterwards MIA (short for Missing In Action), who is generally known for her philanthropy more than controversy, put her action down to "adrenaline and nerves".

Doggone feud

50 Cent got into a row over his music with one of the richest African-American women in the USA The rapper perceived that TV chat show queen Oprah Winfrey was anti-hip-hop and its 'gangsta' image so he named his miniature schnauzer dog Oprah Winfree. He also opened a Twitter account for the dog (@OprahTheDog) which garnered thousands of followers.

Cat shock for Sandi

Scottish pop singer Sandi Thom was shocked to find that her beloved cat was murdered in 2009. Toots, the black and white moggy, had been missing from mother's home in Edzell, Angus in Scotland but Sandi was devastated to be told that she had been shot 'by a local person' and buried in an unknown location. The singer-songwriter and multi-instrumentalist who had a 2006 hit with 'I Wish I was a Punk Rocker' lived in London at the time but Toots was lodging with Sandi's mother.

Caring Kate

Singer Kate Nash took up the cause of a five-year-old girl called Tilly who lost her hands through meningitis. Kate, whose single 'Foundations' made number two in the UK charts of 2007, used her MySpace and Facebook pages in 2009 to help spread the word of the young girl's plight and organized an eBay auction to raise funds for prosthetic hands.

Steve's a busy bee

Guitarist Steve Vai is an avid beekeeper and uses his honey to help good causes. American-Italian Vai, whose legendary style has him rated as one of the best guitar exponents ever, is an honorary member of the British Beekeepers' Association and money generated from selling his honey goes to his Make a Noise foundation, a non-profit organization that raises money for music education.

Boo hoo

Bob Dylan was not the only person to suffer when fans famously decided to boo his 'electric' set at the Isle of Wight Festival. For the whole of 1966 his touring band, the Band, was also given the bird by audiences. It led to drummer Levon Helms quitting after a year because he was sick of the fan abuse.

Bubbly personality

One of the most famous celebrity primates was Michael Jackson's chimp, Bubbles. In 2001 a sculpture of Jacko and Bubbles fetched a massive $5.6 million at auction.

Wedding boos

Only grudging congratulations came from his record label when country rocker Billy Ray Cyrus married in 1993. Bosses at Polygram Mercury Records had strongly advised unmarried Billy Ray – presumably on the basis it might alienate a proportion of his fan base – not to marry Leticia Finley. The couple split in 2010 but a year later divorce proceedings were dropped.

Kelly's a pet

2002 *American Idol* winner Kelly Clarkson puts a lot of time and money into helping animals. She has a ranch sanctuary in her native Texas for more than 80 unwanted animals, which includes amputee goats, blind dogs, and horses with colic. The pop singer-songwriter foots the bills for veterinary care and finds them new and loving homes. One goat she has named Billy Joel but she has not explained why, so it is uncertain if piano-playing Joel should be proud or upset.

Pigs can fly . . .

One missed phone call led to Pink Floyd achieving the biggest publicity coup ever for a newly released album. In 1976 the band featured a giant inflatable pig, called Algie, floating over London's Battersea Power Station on the cover of their album *Animals*. But months before at the photo shoot for the cover innocent-looking Algie was very troublesome. He broke his moorings and floated up to 30,000ft (9,000m) startling airline pilots. Flights to and from London's Heathrow Airport were cancelled as Algie headed towards the coast before crash landing at a farm in Kent. On the first day of the photo shoot a marksman had been employed to deflate Algie with a shot if he broke free but someone had forgotten to book the rifleman for the crucial second day when gusting winds released the pig. Thirty-five years later the scene was recreated to mark the re-release of Pink Floyd's albums but the original Algie was deemed not airworthy and was replaced by a new substitute – who stayed in place this time.

Ozzy behind bars

Black Sabbath frontman Ozzy Osbourne spent six weeks in prison in Birmingham, England during his teens. Years before his wild life in heavy metal bands, Ozzy was locked up because he couldn't pay a fine after a conviction for burglary at a clothes shop.

A little night music

Elvis Presley was not a day person when it came to recording sessions. Many of his songs were recorded at night.

Noelle's a page turner

A homeless bulldog adopted by Latina singer Gloria Estefan inspired a career switch for her. After she took in adorable Noelle, Gloria went on to write children's books *The Magically Mysterious Adventures of Noelle the Bulldog* in 2005 and *Noelle's Treasure Tale* a year later.

Country stars fall out

The start of the Iraq war in 2003 led to a war of words between rival country music stars. Anti-war campaigner Natalie Maines of the Dixie Chicks publicly attacked Toby Keith's pro-war 'Courtesy of the Red, White, & Blue' saying the song made "country music sound ignorant". Keith responded by displaying a doctored photo of Maines with Saddam Hussein on a concert backdrop while Maines retaliated by wearing a t-shirt that read 'FUTK' at that year's Academy of Country Music awards event. The Dixie Chicks had the last word by picking up a Grammy for Album of the Year with *Home*.

Canine witness

A special guest at Sir Elton John's wedding to long-time lover David Furnish was their black and white cocker spaniel Arthur. The couple were among the first people to wed at Windsor Guildhall in England after civil partnerships for same-sex couples became law in the UK in 2005.

Bruce doesn't need job centre

If the work as frontman for Iron Maiden ever dried up, Bruce Dickinson would have a string of other talents to fall back on. As well as holding a commercial airline pilot's licence, he is the band's marketing director, has been a successful screenwriter and is an Olympic-grade fencer.

Singer's cash cache

Singer Jenni Rivera was fined $8,400 after she was arrested by Customs authorities at Mexico City international airport for smuggling cash. In 2009 she failed to declare more than $52,000 that was in her purse. Rivera, who was later alleged to have links with South American drug barons, was fined and released.

Brothers in drugs

For all their clean, all-American boys' image, the Everly Brothers hid drug secrets amid their chart successes. Both Don, the elder sibling, and Phil have been addicted to speed (amphetamines) but Don made matters worse by taking Ritalin when it was an unregulated drug. Don's addiction to the central nervous system stimulant lasted three years and eventually he was hospitalized with a nervous breakdown and got help for overcoming his taste for Ritalin. The drug was used in the treatment of attention deficit disorder (ADD), attention deficit hyperactivity disorder (ADHD) and the sleep disorder narcolepsy.

Eagles duo poles apart

With the personal relationships of the band disintegrating, the Eagles were contracted to produce a live album from their 1980 tour. But by this time band founders guitarist Glenn Frey and percussionist Don Henley were not talking and they mixed *Eagles Live* from studios as far apart as they could get – on the east and west coasts of America. Producer Bill Szymczyk joked ironically that it was the first album where three-part harmonies were fixed by Federal Express.

Bonham's lethal binge

Led Zeppelin drummer John Bonham died in 1980 aged 32 after downing 40 shots of vodka in 24 hours as the band prepared for an American tour. John had fallen asleep and despite being placed on his side by aides he was later found dead. As no other drugs were found in Bonham's body, a verdict of accidental death was returned ruling that he had asphyxiated after inhaling vomit. Led Zeppelin disbanded soon after the tragedy until a one-gig reunion in 2012.

Little Bit bitten

Ozzy Osbourne's tiny Pomeranian dog, Little Bit, weighing 1.9–3.5kg (4.2–7.7lb), was eaten by a coyote, weighing on average 6.8–21kg (15–46lb) near his Los Angeles home in 2009.

Tupac a target

Two years before his violent death, rapper Tupac survived a previous attempt on his life in Manhattan, New York. He discharged himself from hospital just hours after treatment for two gunshots to the head, two in the groin and one that pierced his arm and thigh. He was eventually murdered in a drive-by shooting in Las Vegas in 1996. Police believed both incidents were the result of gang feuds.

Pussy riot?

All-girl punk band L7 never shied away from shocking society. Singer/guitarist Donita Sparks dropped her panties on live television, appearing nude from the waist down, while appearing on British TV show *The Word* in 1992. At a later London gig, the band was also said to have raffled a one-night stand with drummer Dee Plakas. The lucky winner spent a night in the band's tour bus.

Married or not? Jerry's dilemma

Doubts have been cast about how many times Jerry Lee Lewis was married. Officially it was seven but the validity of two of them have been queried because of the timings of the ceremonies. His first marriage, of 20 months, was when he was 14 and his bride Dorothy Barton 17 but his second marriage, to Jane Mitchum, was said to have occurred 23 days before his divorce from Barton was final. For his marriage to wife number three Myra Gale Brown the couple had to go through a second wedding ceremony because his divorce from Jane Mitchum was not complete before the first ceremony took place.

Pink pet tragedy

The beloved dog of singer Pink drowned in the swimming pool of her Los Angeles mansion in 2007. The bulldog she named Elvis had been a gift from Elvis Presley's daughter Lisa Marie and was said to have enjoyed swimming in the pool on many other occasions.

Connie paves the way for success

Connie Francis sang many hit songs in the 1950s without getting her own name in the charts. The aspiring singer was initially a demonstration vocalist on recordings which were to be brought to the attention of established singers who would subsequently choose or decline to record the song. Many of the songs demo-ed by Connie became chart successes but only when more established stars recorded them. Connie's chance was to come in a big way with 35 top 50 chart hits.

Cool venue

Arctic Monkeys' drummer Matt Helders and former bassist Andy Nicholson went back to their roots for a business venture. They opened a pub in their English home city of Sheffield. The Bowery was to be a new bar and gig venue for the area and the band planned to use it for jam sessions for themselves when they are not touring with material from hit albums such as *Humbug* and *Suck It and See*.

Richie drink drive guilt

Bon Jovi lead guitarist Richie Sambora was arrested for drink driving with his ten year old daughter and her friend in the car. Sambora was over the California drink drive limit when pulled over by police who spotted him weaving in 2008. Neither child was hurt but Sambora pleaded no contest, was fined $390, placed on probation for three years, and required to take a driver's education course. Sambora, who shared the songwriting duties with Jon Bon Jovi, had a history of drink problems and the year before had been in a rehab clinic. In 2011 he announced he was returning to rehab.

Spotlight for Joey

Bass players, though vital to a band's backbeat, are not always in the glare of the spotlight but it happened out of the blue to American Joey Page in the early 1980s. Joey was busily playing his part in an Everly Brothers revival tour in the UK when Don Everly was taken ill. Don was unable to complete the tour and returned to the US leaving brother Phil to carry on as frontman. But the success of the Everlys had been based on their harmonies based on parallel thirds. Enter bass player Joey, who successfully took the place of Don to see out the rest of the tour.

Terry's healing hands

Terry Chimes swapped his whirling hands as a drummer with punk band the Clash for helping those in pain. After leaving Joe Strummer and co. he became a qualified chiropractor specializing in neck and back pain.

Joe's purr-fect record

British record producer Joe Meek suffered from mental illness towards the end of his life which led to an occult fixation. As well as recording chart-topping artists such as Lonnie Donegan and the Honeycombs, he taped cats which he claimed were talking to him.

Cope-ing with change

Later in his life the Teardrop Explodes singer Julian Cope became a passionate archaeologist and antiquarian specializing in megaliths. He wrote *The Modern Antiquarian*, a comprehensive full-colour 448-page work detailing stone circles and other British prehistoric monuments, which sold out of its first edition of 20,000 in a month and became a BBC TV documentary.

Heartbroken singer

The beloved brother of Connie Francis was murdered in a gangland hit in 1981. George Franconero Junior was a disbarred lawyer who was co-operating with the federal authorities when he was gunned down by an assassin at his home in North Caldwell, New Jersey. The Mafia was blamed.

Passing the buck

When a huge stash of drugs was found in a police raid on Keith Richards' Chelsea home in 1973 he blamed the previous tenant for leaving marijuana, heroin, methadone and Mandrax tablets in the flat. The only trouble was that the previous tenant was, at the time, a well-respected member of the British establishment and a former Foreign Office minister with no drug involvement.

Pet trouble

Vanilla Ice had his legal troubles over the years and even his pets conspired to land him before a court. His pet wallaroo, Bucky, and goat companion, Pancho, escaped from Ice's in Port St Lucie, Florida home in November 2004 and after a week of wandering the wayward duo were returned to their relieved owner. The police took a dim view of the escape and Vanilla Ice, real name Robert Van Winkle, had to pay a $220 fine for expired pet tags and a further undisclosed amount for allowing the animals' escape.

Peter eyes new business

'In Your Eyes' hit maker Peter Gabriel also had his eyes on being an entrepreneur. The singer was a principal in 2005 with broadcast entrepreneur David Engelke in a joint venture, buying Solid State Logic, one of the world's largest producers of recording studio hardware such as mixing consoles.

Lana retains old job

Million-selling singing success did not stop Lana Del Ray from continuing her old job as a babysitter. The New Yorker admitted in 2012 to still having the same babysitting job twice a week even though her second album *Born to Die* sold around three million copies worldwide.

High is the Moon

The sight of the Who drummer Keith Moon bursting naked through the bedroom window was what Bianca Jagger's wedding night had in store for her. After leaving new husband Mick partying and going to bed alone in 1971, Nicaraguan beauty Bianca awoke to find Moon, a well-known heavy-drinking pop hell-raiser, abseiling through her sixth-floor hotel window. He wore only a pair of women's panties on his head and a pair of novelty glasses from which the eyeballs bounced out on springs.

Diamond geezer

American rapper Akon was a part owner of a diamond mine in South Africa in 2007. He said the mine was dedicated to avoiding use of conflict diamonds while also donating profits to local communities.

Neil's burning ambition

Neil Young has been one of rock music's ambassadors in the forefront of the environmental movement and was one of the first in the USA to use eco-friendly biodiesel in all his touring vehicles. However, the Canadian-born hit maker of albums such as *Harvest* was less successful when he got involved in a hybrid engine project with a 1959 Lincoln car which he called the Lincvolt. The car caught fire in November 2010 in a California warehouse. The 'After the Goldrush' singer said he and his team were committed to rebuilding the car and added: "The wall charging system was not completely tested and had never been left unattended. It was not the fault of the car," he said.

Chasing the King

Bruce Springsteen has admitted to trespassing at Elvis Presley's Graceland home. About 16 months before Presley's death in 1977, a young Bruce, after a concert in Memphis, climbed over a fence into Elvis' property. He was caught by Graceland security guards and ejected despite his up-and-coming profile as an artist. Many years later Springsteen admitted that the one thing he hates about superstardom is – fans scaling the fence of his home.

Who's fishing?

The Who frontman Roger Daltrey winds down from the rock 'n' roll lifestyle by fishing for trout. He loved it so much that he designed and created his own trout fishery. Daltrey was quoted as saying: "When I go fishing. I come away feeling like I've smoked half a dozen joints." Specialist angling magazines have praised Roger's Lakedown Trout Fishery in Dorset, England as one of the prettiest.

Madonna – woman of words

Madonna has at various times switched her words from song lyrics to books. Although she made a controversial literary start in 1992 with her book, *Sex*, at the other end of the scale was her series of children's books. *The English Roses* have been well received and sold millions after the biggest launch in publishing history in 2003. They have been published in more than 100 countries, in 30 languages.

Dictator couldn't silence Gil

The lyrics of politically aware singer Gilberto Gil landed him in jail. But being imprisoned by Brazil's military dictatorship in 1969 followed by exile from his homeland did not stop his political activities so when Brazil regained democracy he returned to became a city councillor, hold a prominent post in the Green Party and, from 2003 to 2008, serve as culture minister. Throughout that time his successful singing and songwriting career spanned rock, Brazilian music, samba, African music and reggae.

Battling to the end

Incurable lung cancer was not going to stop Beach Boys guitarist Carl Wilson from doing the work he loved. Carl, whose distinctive voice was the lead on million-selling hits 'Good Vibrations' and 'God Only Knows', knew he was dying but in the autumn of 1997 he continued touring even though he needed oxygen while on stage. Two months after the tour ended, in February 1998, Carl died aged 51.

Anthrax trash

An avid fan of rockers Anthrax won a competition in 1989, not for gig tickets but to get the band to wreck her home. It was the top prize in an MTV Anthrax competition and the heavy metal heavyweights did not disappoint and trashed her home. Much to her delight.

Starr-ing role

Beatle Ringo Starr became an engine driver as an artistic change of direction. His love of acting won him the job of the narrator for the first two seasons of the animated children's TV series *Thomas the Tank Engine* in 1984. He was then on track for a return to music when he formed Ringo Starr and his All-Starr Band with such rock luminaries as multi-instrumentalists Todd Rundgren and Edgar Winter.

Chuck Berry shame

During a police investigation into a camera found in the ladies' toilets of Chuck Berry's Missouri restaurant, a raid on the rock 'n' roll performer's home found among the resulting toilet videotapes that one of the 'women' was under-age. Because the cops also found 62 grams (approximately 2oz) of marijuana, felony drug and child abuse charges were filed against Berry. Admitting the possession of drugs, Berry avoided the child abuse charges. A court gave him a six-month suspended jail sentence, two years' unsupervised probation and ordered him to donate $5,000 to a local hospital.

Green Peter gets green job

Peter Garrett, avid environmentalist and frontman of alternative rockers Midnight Oil, landed one of Australia's top political jobs in 2007. Garrett, who was head of the Australian Conservation Foundation, sat on the international board of Greenpeace and was a Nuclear Disarmament Party member, became environment minister. As a musician he had performed many impassioned songs, such as 'Beds are Burning' in 1988, on a range of environmental and minority rights' issues.

Verging on anti-Catholic

Singer and piano star Billy Joel saw his song 'Only the Good Die Young' banned for allegedly being anti-Catholic. The 1977 album track song is about a guy trying to convince a Catholic girl to let him take her virginity.

Madonna slip shows

Millions watched – and noticed – in 2012 as Madonna's normally nimble footwork let her down as she performed the prestigious half-time show for the NFL Super Bowl. Strutting her way across a set of bleachers' benches to her song 'Music' Madonna, aged 53 at the time, was unable to step up onto one of them and had to repeat the dance move to hoist herself up. A US TV audience of 100 millions was tuned in.

P Diddy's in fashion

Rapper Sean Combs likes to do things in numbers. Operating over the years with three names – Sean, Puff Daddy and later P Diddy – he has had many strings to his business bow. In addition to performing and acting his interests have included record and film production, a restaurant and fashion design company which saw him nominated for a Council of Fashion Designers of America award in 2004.

Mind over drugs

Former Wild Orchid member Stacy Ferguson credits hypnotherapy with aiding her battle against crystal methamphetamine addiction. She became hooked on crystal meth while touring with the American all-girl band and when she left in 2001 she took her addiction with her to hip-hop band the Black Eyed Peas where she was just called Fergie. After a rehabilitation programme which included hypnotherapy, Fergie recounted: "It was the hardest boyfriend I ever had to break up with."

George moves on

There was life for guitarist George Harrison after the Beatles split in 1970. In 1979, with friend Dennis O'Brien, he established Handmade Films and became a successful movie mogul. Among Handmade's successes were *The Life of Brian*, *The Long Good Friday*, *Time Bandits*, *Mona Lisa* and *Withnail and I*. George even made a cameo appearance as Mr Papadopolous in the controversial *The Life of Brian*.

Pour Syd

Syd Barrett was said to have once dissolved a whole bottle of Nembutal sleeping tablets into milk and poured it over his head before a show. The sad late-1960s incident came as his involvement with rock band Pink Floyd was approaching its end because of the genius guitarist's growing mental instability.

Who dunnit mystery

The Woodstock Peace Festival of 1969 might not have been quite so friendly after all. One incident recalled by some was an activist interrupting the Who's performance with a diatribe about the jailing of a political prisoner in the US. Some say guitarist Pete Townshend used a break in songs to shove protesting Abbie Hoffman off the stage but the guitarist denied it even though he said he was annoyed that the band's set had been interrupted. Hoffman himself was no help in solving the mystery because he said, before his death in 1989 from a drugs and drink overdose, that he had been high on LSD at the time of the Who incident. Coincidentally the incident was not on any film footage with a 'camera change' cited as the reason they weren't rolling at the crucial moment when Townshend was alleged to have shoved his guitar into Hoffman's back.

Grave concerns

Peter Green swapped the adoration of rock fans for jobs as a gravedigger and hospital orderly after quitting Fleetwood Mac in the early 1970s. The talented guitarist and singer-songwriter, whose lyrics included "who is going to carry me to my grave?", drifted aimlessly while being treated for schizophrenia.

Police song 'arrested'

Some radio stations in the 1980s handcuffed their disc jockeys by stopping them playing the Police's 'Can't Stand Losing You' because it was a song about suicide.

Calling out the King

Jerry Lee Lewis was caught with a gun at Elvis Presley's home in Memphis, Tennessee. Armed with a Derringer, which he pointed at security guards in 1960, he demanded Elvis come out of his Graceland mansion. Elvis stayed behind closed doors and Jerry Lee returned to his own in the same city although the purpose of his trip to Graceland was never explained.

Janis' deadly legacy

The death of Janis Joplin in 1970 led to a revenge attack on friends she left behind. Friend Peggy Caserta had in a book after Joplin's death identified the Los Angeles drug dealers who had supplied the singer with heroin. The furious dealers tried to wreak revenge on Peggy but could only find her friend Kim Chappell so they stabbed her instead. Both lungs were punctured yet she still managed to survive the attack.

John's aid for farmers

The figure 40 loomed large for guitarist and singer John Mellencamp. His brand of American Heartlands rock has sold 40 million albums and, as of 2012, he had raised $40 million (£25 million) for the charity Farm Aid, an organization he founded in 1985 to raise awareness about the loss of family farms across the USA.

Hendrix gets fired up

Two virtually unknown acts in the USA in 1967, the Who and Jimi Hendrix, flipped a coin to see who would go on the Monterey festival stage first. The Who won the toss and left the crowd dazzled with their aggressive guitar- and amplifier-smashing finale routine. But what followed is still remembered more than 40 years later as the performance at Monterey with Hendrix playing his blazing guitar to howling feedback. The Who may have won the toss, but not the day's plaudits.

Long tall story?

The legendary rock 'n' roll song 'Long Tall Sally' was destined for the toilet until Little Richard and friends stepped in. They were shown the lyrics by a young girl in 1955 who was trying to raise money for an aunt's hospital treatment – they were written on toilet paper. Little Richard, Enotris Johnson and Robert Blackwell bought the lyrics, added a rock composition and created one of the most covered songs in pop history.

Airport rage

There is something about airports that affects the normal cool of Icelandic singer Björk. Twice she has clashed with the press at airports. In 1996 she scuffled with a female reporter at Bangkok International Airport in Thailand then again with a photographer at Auckland in New Zealand in 2008. Both occasions were after long-haul flights and on neither occasion did the media victims press charges.

Murder rap

Rapper Snoop Dogg, alias Calvin Broadus, was acquitted of being involved in a murder in August 1993. Snoop Dogg was arrested in connection with the death of Phillip Woldermarian, a member of a rival gang in Los Angeles who was shot and killed during an argument. Snoop's bodyguard, Lee McKinley, like Broadus defended by OJ Simpson's lawyer Johnnie Cochran, was acquitted on grounds of self-defence.

Neil or not Neil?

Neil Young was sued by his record company for not sounding like – Neil Young. It came during a stage of the Canadian's career when he was experimenting with different styles and sounds. After massive successes with *After the Goldrush* and *Harvest* in the 1970s Young flopped with the electro-synth *Trans* in 1983 and the country-style *Old Ways*. Geffen Records had also demanded a return to rock 'n' roll and he quickly turned out *Everybody's Rockin'* which still did not suit record label executives, who sued Young for $3.3 million citing records being 'not commercial' and 'musically uncharacteristic of Young's previous recordings'. Because he had been promised no creative interference from the label Young counter-filed a $21 million suit alleging breach of contract. The label owner David Geffen ultimately personally apologizing to Young for the suit and interference with his work.

Rockers smell victory

French cosmetics firm Guerlain was forced to change the name of a perfume after falling foul of one of the world's biggest rock bands. Litigious US rockers Metallica sued after the perfume manufacturer used the same name for a product launched in 2000. Later Guerlain renamed the perfume Metalys.

Phone call hell

In 1977 Robert Plant received the phone call that every touring rock musician with a family at home must dread. He learned that while he was on a Led Zeppelin US tour his five-year-old son Karac had died from a stomach infection.

Kim's flower power

A second career blossomed for New Wave girl singer Kim Wilde. She followed up her 1981 recording of 'Kids In America' and other UK chart hits with at stint a a horticultural college, three series of TV gardening programmes, a Gold award at the Royal Horticultural Society's Chelsea Flower Show and two books on gardening. Although 'Kids in America' reached number two in the UK charts and number one elsewhere in Europe, Kim, the daughter of 1950–60s rocker Marty Wilde, became better known for her green fingers than her music.

Multi-talented Dave

When he wasn't driving the backbeat of British indie band Blur, Dave Rowntree kept busy. Even when touring with the band he kept up his first career as a computer animator with his own company then, after Blur stopped recording in 2003, he trained as a solicitor.

Hangover idea is success

Hangovers don't tend to be the most creative atmospheres, but one was for musician and DJ Moby. During one particularly bad hangover in 2002 he was craving, but not able to get, tea and the ordeal persuaded him to open his own teahouse. The result was the successful TeaNY bistro and tea distributor in New York which eventually opened outlets online and in the UK.

Rocker strikes an academic chord

In his guise as an astrophysicist Queen guitarist Dr Brian May was installed as the Chancellor of John Moores University in Liverpool, England in 2012.

Punk professor?

In honour of their frontman being an academic and nerd, Los Angeles punk band the Descendents entitled their first album in 1982 *Milo Goes to College*. Milo Aukerman had a PhD in biochemistry from the University of Wisconsin-Madison.

Brian D:Reams of the stars

Brian Cox and D:Ream had a huge British chart hit with 'Things Can Only Get Better' – and for Brian they certainly did. While playing keyboards for the 1990s pop rock/synthpop band he got his PhD in physics at the University of Manchester and by 2012 he was voted one of the sexiest men on British TV as the handsome face of astronomy on such programmes as *Wonders of the Solar System* and *Stargazing Live*.

Rage against each other

Tensions within Rage Against the Machine led the metal rappers to implode very quickly. Continuing problems within the Los Angeles band prompted vocalist Zack de la Rocha to quit, which led to its complete break-up in 2000 after nine years together. De la Rocha launched a solo career, while guitarist Tom Morello and other band members formed Audioslave. It took seven years for things to smooth over and Rage to re-form.

Coke cash splash

Public Enemy rapper Flavor Flav admitted in a 2011 radio interview that he was spending $2,600 a day on crack cocaine at the height of his drug addiction.

Fans bite back

Fans of Chicago band Creed sued them over a disastrous 2002 gig. Four Creed fans filed a class-action suit demanding refunds and compensation totalling $2 million claiming frontman Scott Stapp was "so intoxicated and/or medicated that he was unable to sing the lyrics of a single Creed song". The suit also also claimed Stapp "left the stage on several occasions and for long periods of time during songs; rolled around on the stage in apparent pain or distress and appeared to pass out during the performance."

Baker sues from the grave

Jazz trumpeter, flugelhornist and singer Chet Baker may have died in 1988 but by 2009 he was back for revenge against record companies that had conned him. His estate sued Canada's major labels for failing to pay for countless unauthorized reissues of his work over decades. It was estimated that 300,000 Baker tracks had been released on mainly compilation CDs. Co-defendants Warner Music Canada, Sony BMG Music Canada, EMI Music Canada and Universal Music Canada, rather than face a potential CA$6 billion penalty in court, settled for around CA$50 million.

Bum idea

A squidgy backside prevented a 2013 member of boy band One Direction from joining pop music's cool league. Irish-born Niall Horan wanted to celebrate his homeland with 'Made in Ireland' tattooed on a cheek but was told his butt was not tight enough to do the work.

Paparazzi stoop low

Britney Spears caused a media storm in 2006 when a photographer shot the singer getting out of a car wearing no panties. The incident of 'going commando' on a night out in Los Angeles was covered by the world's media. A few other publicity-hungry stars have followed her example since.

Fan death charge

Lamb of God heavy metal singer Randy Blythe was charged with manslaughter in 2012. A 2013 trial was planned over a fan being fatally injured at Prague's Club Abaton in the Czech Republic. It was alleged that Blythe was involved in an incident in which fan Daniel Nosek, 19, suffered serious head injuries after falling off the stage and died a month later.

Mötley pooh

Mötley Crüe's bassist Nikki Sixx had a big reputation for rock 'n' roll debauchery. But was one of his favourite on-tour jokes really seeing how long he could go without washing while still attracting groupies? Rock legend has it that his unwashed record was over two months.

Naked truth?

Although it has not been confirmed by the man himself, it has been claimed that in 1986, when every major label was trying to sign Guns N' Roses, frontman Axl Rose promised a female artist and repertoire (A&R) scout from Chrysalis Records that he would sign with her if she walked naked down Sunset Boulevard in Los Angeles. Not surprisingly, Chrysalis did not sign up the bad boy rockers, who went to Geffen Records.

Have dope will travel

Before he was arrested for drug possession in Japan in 1980, Paul McCartney had twice previously been arrested for having marijuana, once in Sweden and once in Scotland.

Killer rapper

A row over hair left in a sink plughole put British rapper Conscious D behind bars for 10 years. In 2013 he admitted the manslaughter of Korean girlfriend Da In Lee during what was described as a 'petty quarrel' over the plughole. Conscious D, real name Daniel Jones, was sentenced to 10 years for strangling her and attempting to flee to the USA. A jury cleared him of murder.

Door kills two

A falling door at a concert venue killed two members of a sea shanty band in 2013. Trevor Grills, one of 10 singers in the English-based group Fisherman's Friend, and tour manager Paul McMullen died from head and leg injuries respectively during the freak accident at a concert venue in Guildford, Surrey.

Dogg dogged by drug squad

Hip-hop proponent of marijuana Snoop Dogg has been charged with possession of the drug at least eight times – in 1990, 1998, 2001, 2006 (twice!), 2007, and twice again in 2012. The last time was at Kjevic Airport in Kristiansand, southern Norway, where officials discovered eight grams of weed and a large amount of cash. The violation relieved Snoop of some of that cash – NOK12,000 in fines and also an additional NOK38,000 for carrying more cash than allowed. He was released.

Lady steps down

In 2013 Lady Gaga admitted she had been performing through the pain barrier for some time and was temporarily stopping touring. Gaga revealed she had been secretly battling synovitis, a chronic arthritis linked to swelling of the joints which could put a stop to her physically energetic stage career. Left in extreme pain after a Canadian concert in February 2013 she cancelled the rest of the *Born This Way Ball* tour.

Cop's crusade on pop stars

Arresting John Lennon would have been a great talking point for any policeman but British Sergeant Norman Pilcher could add such 1960s hit makers as Donovan, Beatle George Harrison and at least three Rolling Stones to his case tally. It would appear Pilcher had an aversion to pop stars and hippies as they seemed to be his main targets as a drug squad officer. But his methods were not always lawful as it was widely believed that Pilcher was planting the drugs his victims were convicted of possessing. In 1972 Pilcher was jailed for four years after being convicted of perverting the course of justice and perjury in a drug smuggling trial. Harrison had already raised doubts about Pilcher's methods and the planting of evidence when he said that during a raid on his house, police found 120 marijuana cigarettes which were not his. His actual stash was not found by police at all.

James looked killer in the face

A terrifying close encounter with a fan had horrific consequences for James Taylor. In December 1980 the singer was near his home in New York when the 'fan' pinned him to a wall in a maniacal frenzy and began talking in an incomprehensible language. Taylor escaped but the 'fan' was Mark Chapman, who was back just 24 hours later, gunning down John Lennon outside the next building.

Nelson in trouble

Willie Nelson lived up to his 'outlaw' image by being busted several times for drug possession. Variously in 1974, 1994 and 2010 he was fined or put on probation for possessing marijuana or magic mushrooms. He was 75 when he was last arrested for drugs.

Drug dealer saved Lennon

John Lennon was saved from a possible heroin addiction because his dealer was too greedy and sold diluted product. Lennon's widow Yoko Ono claimed that heroin cut with too much baby powder kept her and John from a deadly addiction. In maximizing his profits the dealer probably lost a lucrative customer had the ex-Beatle succumbed to addiction for a long time. Yoko also said that both she and John had a fear of needles so never injected the drug.

Drug clear-out failed

John Lennon had advance knowledge of a police drugs squad raid on his home in 1968 but he still ended up with a criminal record and a £150 fine. Lennon and wife Yoko Ono had been tipped off about the raid and thought they had thoroughly cleaned the London flat, rented from fellow Beatle Ringo Starr, of any drug traces. An extra worry was that previous tenant Jimi Hendrix may have hidden drugs there. Lennon claimed police had planted drugs but pleaded guilty to possession of marijuana and was fined.

Cash taps the Russians

Before he became a successful country singer Johnny Cash was a radio operator at the forefront of the Cold War. As a Morse Code operator in the US Air Force he monitored Soviet Army transmissions and was the first American to hear of the death of dictator Joseph Stalin in 1952.

Just being a dope

Singer Justin Bieber apologized in front of a TV audience of many millions for smoking cannabis. The teen idol's clean-cut image went out the window when he was spotted smoking a joint at a party then he used a comedy sketch on America's popular *Saturday Night Live* in February 2013 to admit his drug shame. He also used Twitter to tweet to fans: "Trying to be better. I never want to let any of you down."

Pink Floyd hell

One of the longest and messiest band break-ups was that of Pink Floyd, drawn out agonizingly from the late 1980s to the mid-1990s. The progressive and psychedelic rock band's main protagonists were songwriter/guitarist Roger Waters and guitarist Dave Gilmour who eventually ended up splitting up and fighting through the courts for the right to use the name Pink Floyd. With 250 million sales behind them from albums such *Dark Side of the Moon*, *The Wall*, *Wish You were Here* and *Animals*, acrimony overwhelmed the band. At one point Gilmour and drummer Nick Mason were touring the USA. as Pink Floyd, followed on a not dissimilar itinerary by Waters with his new band Radio K.A.O.S. with the latter in much smaller venues than those hosting his former band mates' performances.

False report consequences

Singer Boy George invited the police into his home and ended up arrested. Police searched his Manhattan home after the former Culture Club frontman reported a burglary. It was alleged that they found cocaine and former heroin addict George was arrested on charges of drug possession. In court in 2006 the cocaine possession charge was dropped and George pleaded guilty to falsely reporting a burglary. He was sentenced to five days of community service, was fined $1,000, and ordered to attend a drug rehabilitation programme.

George mixes cars and drugs

Singer George Michael got a reputation for driving while under the influence of drugs. In 2007 he was arrested in London after motorists reported a car obstructing the road at traffic lights. He pleaded guilty of driving while unfit through drugs, was banned from driving for two years and sentenced to community service. In 2010, again in London, he crashed his car into a shop front in the early hours of the morning. The 'Careless Whisper' singer was caught on CCTV mounting the kerb in his Range Rover and driving into the shop. Again he admitted driving while unfit through drugs and this time was sentenced to eight weeks in jail, a fine and a five-year driving ban.

Who are we?

They might have been working together for the best part of 50 years but the Who guitarist Pete Townshend and singer Roger Daltrey have not always seen eye to eye. In 2006 the two had a spat over a charity fundraiser. The Who had been offering live webcasts of their European tour performances at $10 a time but Daltrey was said to have had some concerns about the project, and it was stopped. A clearly annoyed Townshend was reported to have said: "Roger seems to think when I provide bandwidth for the Who website, and for live streaming, he is being exploited in some way and wants a piece of the future profit. Don't think there is much chance of profit when it is all aimed at charity."

Gene's open relationships

Kiss frontman Gene Simmons was once quoted on National Public Radio in the US as saying that he had slept with 4,600 women. In 2002, when he was 53, the hard rocker and hard player, famous for his black and white stage make-up, said his chat-up philosophy was: "If you want to welcome me with open arms, I'm afraid you're also going to have to welcome me with open legs."

Coal seam runs out

Nu-metal band Coal Chamber's music career ended up the pits after an on-stage implosion. In May 2002 lead singer Dez Fafara and guitarist Meegs Rascon fought during a show in Phoenix, Arizona. A pre-show argument continued on stage with violence and Rascon allegedly hitting Fafara in the head with the headstock of his guitar. Fafara announced: "This is the last Coal Chamber show ever!" and stormed off. Drummer Mike Cox's finale was to demolish his kit before he also walked off. It was nine years before Cox, Fafara and Rascon patched things up for a short Australian tour.

Moon strikes again

There have been many tales of the destructive antics of Keith Moon but one that has not been verified was that after leaving a hotel he asked his driver to turn around saying: "I forgot something!" Keith ran back to his room and, moments later, a television flew out of a window.

Bad boy image

In the 15 years between 1998 and 2013 hip-hop artist Dark Man X had a total of 37 criminal charges against him. Although he was found not guilty on several occasions and plea bargained others, DMX faced numerous driving and drug convictions, but other charges included weapons possession, car jacking, parole violation, impersonating a federal agent and animal cruelty. Despite this lengthy rap sheet DMX, birth name Earl Simmonds, had to date spent less than two years behind bars but had spent some time in mental institutions.

Watt a punch!

It has been reported that in 1984 Rolling Stones drummer Charlie Watts punched Mick Jagger because he took exception to being called 'his drummer'. During the alleged incident, in Amsterdam, Charlie apparently retorted "You're my fucking singer".

Kings of falling out

Striving for perfection led to a bust-up for the Kings of Leon before a gig in Scotland in 2009. Frontman Caleb Followill was furious with his band mates – his brothers Nathan and Jared and cousin Matthew – over the sound quality for their set at the T in the Park festival in Kinross. Backstage staff pulled the furious factions apart before things got out of hand but at the end of the set the singer trashed his beloved Gibson 325 guitar and threw its broken frame into the crowd.

Poison-ous relationship

Glam metal rockers Poison picked a massive occasion to fall out – the prestigious 1991 MTV Music Awards. Lead singer Bret Michaels brawled backstage with guitarist C.C. DeVille over what was described as DeVille's inept live performance. The band was scheduled to play 'Unskinny Bop' but were delayed by a commercial break. Said to be high and drunk, DeVille missed the cue when they came back live and started playing 'Talk Dirty to Me'. Then to add to his woes his guitar lead became disconnected mid-performance. DeVille was fired but five years later he had patched up his differences and returned to the band.

Taco Bell hits wrong note

Fast food chain Taco Bell's 2008 national promotion for cheap meals did not chime well with 50 Cent. The rapper, whose birth name was Curtis Jackson III, was not consulted before Taco Bell publicized that it was cheekily asking that 50 Cent change his name to '79 Cent', '89 Cent' or '99 Cent' to promote its menu items costing less than a dollar. It reached news outlets before 50 Cent's ears and he sued for $4 million, arguing that Taco Bell used Jackson's name and trademark without his authorization and he also feared being accused of 'selling out' by becoming a paid endorser of products. A Manhattan court ruled in Jackson's favour but the damages arrangements were kept confidential although it was said that both parties in the row were satisfied.

Howling success

Dogs Banana and Louie reached the heady heights of the pop charts in 1966. Their barking at the end of 'Caroline No' helped them to 32 in the US national chart and 16 in Canada. The dogs, a beagle and a dachshund, had a friend in high places in the pop world – they were the pets of former Beach Boy Brian Wilson and were recorded as part of Wilson's appropriately named *Pet Sounds* project.

Shahin shunned

In 2013 Iranian-born hip-hop artist Shahin Najafi could not show his face in his homeland because he is hated for his songs critical of the political regime. He was in hiding in Germany after several Islamic religious leaders ordered his execution for releasing a song that they claimed insulted Shia Islam's 10th Imam. In 2012 a pro-government website posted an online 'Shoot the Apostates' computer game inviting people to shoot and kill Najafi. Forty authors of a religious publishing house upped the stakes even further in 2012 by pledging their book royalties to whoever killed Najafi.

Jail for George

Boy George was jailed for 15 months in 2009 after being convicted of imprisoning a male escort. The former Culture Club singer – real name George O'Dowd – shackled Audun Carlsen to a wall of his London flat and lashed him with a chain while screaming insults. The 29-year-old Norwegian was found in the street begging for help and wearing just his underpants.

Dogged by fame

His Old English sheepdog Martha inspired Paul McCartney to write the song 'Martha My Dear' for the 1968 double album *The Beatles*, also known as *The White Album*.

Jacko's Bubbles gets wacko too

After sharing Michael Jackson's private bathroom, sleeping in his bedroom and watching movies in a private theatre, the star's chimpanzee Bubbles found life tough. He grew up to be an aggressive adult chimp, deemed unsuitable as a companion for humans, and was sent to a Florida animal sanctuary. It was said that Bubbles attempted suicide and had to be treated by a vet. No details of the manner of the suicide bid were released.

Death farce

The tragic death of reggae star Judge Dread in 1998 had some farcical elements. The white reggae singer died on stage in England. An off-duty doctor tried to resuscitate him to no avail then, according to one account, the ambulance carrying the singer to hospital would not start and, when the Judge's fans began pushing it, police stepped in and accused them of trying to steal it.

Mindy found dead

Country singer Mindy McCready was found dead, aged 37, in February 2013. Her body was discovered at her Arkansas home with a gunshot wound just a month after the suicide of her long-time boyfriend David Wilson. McCready's major hit was the anti-male chauvinism single 'Guys Do It All the Time'.

Feathering his nest

DJ Terminator X's career took off when he quit as a Public Enemy rapper in 2003. He retired to breed ostriches on his stud farm in North Carolina.

Taking the pee

Double hell raisers they may have been, but are the two urine-related stories about Mötley Crüe's Nikki Sixx and ex-Black Sabbath frontman Ozzy Osbourne really true? It has gone down in rock folklore that in 1984 the hard drinkers dared each other to lap urine from a pavement. Allegedly Ozzy licked up his own and that of Sixx while the Mötley Crüe bass man was said to have drunk his own.

Reptilian friends

Guns N' Roses guitarist Slash once owned 80 boa constrictor and python snakes. He considered them too dangerous to have around once he became a dad to son London in 2002.

Losing a big one

Geffen Records missed out on signing one of the biggest rock bands of all time – because they they were in the process of suing one of their established artists. Georgia-based R.E.M. were just emerging from the underground scene to major recognition and were on the verge of signing with Geffen in 1988 when the label's management started to interfere in the work of Neil Young and tried to sue him. R.E.M. were put off by the company's action and signed to Warner Bros instead. Led by Michael Stipe, R.E.M. went on to sell more than 100 million albums including *Monster*.

Falling out with fans

Hip-hop artist the Notorious B.I.G. attacked two autograph seekers with a baseball bat. The fans seemed to enrage the gangsta rapper as it was alleged he chased their cab and attacked it and them with a baseball bat in 1996 before he was arrested. Later B.I.G. pleaded guilty to second-degree harassment and was sentenced to 100 hours' community service.

Admirable Nelson

Country singer Willie Nelson saved one vital possession from his burning ranch house in 1970 – his guitar called Trigger. The instrument, named after TV cowboy Roy Rogers' horse, was the only possession he saved from the blaze. The Martin N-20 classical guitar had a hole worn in it over the years as it was meant to be played finger style, instead of with the pick which Nelson favoured.

Free Dappy is happy

N-Dubz rapper Dappy broke down in tears after he escaped a jail sentence in 2013. The singer was given a six-month sentence suspended for 18 months at Guildford Crown Court in England and was ordered to do 150 hours' community service. He was also ordered to pay £4,500 compensation and £2,000 in costs. The 25-year-old had faced a maximum of three years' imprisonment after being convicted of assault and affray. The court heard during a nine-day trial that Dappy became angry and violent after two teenage girls rejected his offer to get into his car to go to a party at his recording studios. It sparked a fight which led to three men being injured. The trial was told that Dappy, charged under his real name of Costadinos Contostavlos, had been drinking on the day of the incident and celebrating the release of his single 'Rockstar' with former Queen guitarist Brian May.

Smiley Kylie

Not content with being an accomplished songwriter, one of Australia's best-known export Kylie Minogue is an author as well. In 2006 she published *The Showgirl Princess* aimed at girls aged six and upwards and based on Minogue's life.

Combs succumbs

Rapper P Diddy diversified his business interests in 1998 with a clothing line called Sean John, but he ran into controversy with accusations that labour laws were being violated at the Honduran factory where the clothes were made. Allegations included workers being subjected to body searches and involuntary pregnancy tests; bathroom access being tightly controlled; and employees forced to work overtime and only paid sweatshop wages. P Diddy, birth name Sean Combs, allowed the formation of a union and installed air conditioning and water purification among other improvements to the workers' conditions.

Johnny's real ring of fire

Country singer Johnny Cash, whose greatest hit was arguably 'Ring of Fire', almost wiped out an endangered bird species singlehandedly. In 1965 an overheated wheel bearing set his truck ablaze and with it 500 acres of Los Padres National Forest in California. In the resulting inferno 49 of the last 53 of an endangered variety of condor perished too and it led to Cash being the first person sued by the US government for starting a forest fire. Cash denied it was his fault but settled the lawsuit by paying around $642,000.

Memories up in flames

A fire in a warehouse destroyed an estimated $850,000 worth of singer-songwriter Neil Young's rock 'n' roll memorabilia collected over decades.

Songs were war casualties

Lulu's 'Boom Bang-A-Bang' and the Cure's 'Killing an Arab' were banned from British radio plays when the Gulf War started in 1991 despite the fact that they had been played thousands of times after they charted in 1969 and 1979 respectively.

Religious change brings trouble

As singer-songwriter Cat Stevens was welcome in the USA of the late 1960s–early 1970s. As singer-songwriter Yusuf Islam after a religious conversion to Islam in 2004 his name was on a terrorism list and he was deported from the USA. His flight to Washington DC was intercepted at Bangor, Maine and Yusuf detained. He denied he had any connection with Islamic terrorism and claimed US Homeland Security had someone else of a similar name on its watch list.

Richard loses it

Rock 'n' roller Little Richard claimed to have lost his virginity to an older woman at the age of 13 in 1945. However he was kicked out of his parent's home at 14 because of his effeminate behaviour and because he would often play with his mother's make-up and wear her clothes. This resulted in beatings from his father. It was said that he had his first homosexual experiences soon after leaving home.

Alien audience for Chuck

Alien life is in for a rocking good time if they find the NASA Voyager 1 or 2 space probes because they will get a 'shot of rhythm and blues' from Chuck Berry. Berry is the only rocker on the Voyager Golden Record of Earth sights and sounds which is on both spacecraft. Chuck will blast them with his already universal rendition of 'Johnny B Goode'.

Festival equality

Death and life came out equal at the Altamont Festival in 1969. One man was stabbed to death, two people were killed in hit-and-run accidents and another drowned in an irrigation canal. Happily the score was evened up with four births among the estimated 500,000 crowd.

Death crash

Mötley Crüe lead singer Vince Neil was jailed for a car crash that killed a friend. In 1984, he was in a head-on collision which killed his passenger, drummer Razzle Dingley of the band Hanoi Rocks. Neil was sentenced to 30 days in jail for driving under the influence of alcohol and vehicular manslaughter. The unrepentant Mötley Crüe would later release two box sets entitled *Music to Crash Your Car By*.

Tammy's suffering

Country singer Tammy Wynette had 26 major surgeries during her lifetime including gall bladder, kidney and throat operations. In 1994, she suffered an abdominal infection that almost killed her then she developed a chronic inflammation of bile ducts and was intermittently hospitalized from 1970 until her death in 1998 aged 55. A clot on the lung was the cause of death.

A bitter price

The Animals' mega-hit of 1964 'The House of the Rising Sun' became a source of contention within the band. The arranging credit for the traditional song went only to keyboard player Alan Price which meant only he received songwriter's royalties for the hit. This caused bitterness ever since, especially with guitarist Hilton Valentine who contended all the band should have benefited. It was explained there was insufficient room to name all five band members on the record label and Alan Price's name went on because he was first alphabetically.

Barred from Israel

Singer Yusuf Islam was deported from Israel in 2000 accused of financially aiding the Islamic organization Hamas. The singer denied any support for militant Islamists.

Self-help song

It took 18 months for singer Cyndi Lauper to concede in an interview that her 1983 hit 'Girls Just Want to Have Fun' was a song about masturbation.

Bad parting

British rocker Graham Parker showed his contempt for Mercury Records after he signed for rival Arista by releasing a single called 'Mercury Poisoning'.

Slick name?

Jefferson Starship's Grace Slick shocked nurses in a US hospital when she said was going to name her new daughter "god" with a lower case g. It may have been just the pethidine talking but she settled for the slightly less bizarre China.

Lennon in the cold

In his poverty stricken days as a Liverpool art student John Lennon once burned the furniture to keep warm in the dingy flat he rented.

Bing's big

In 1948 it was estimated that crooner Bing Crosby's recordings filled more than half of the 80,000 weekly hours allocated to recorded radio music in the USA.

Plane strange

Actress Megan Fox has to listen to Britney Spears on plane flights because she feels that she'll never die listening to the singer.

Hemmed in?

Kanye West asked picture agency Getty Images to delete from its database a photograph of him wearing a leather skirt. West, who wore the skirt for the Hurricane Sandy benefit gig in 2013, took a ribbing from fellow rappers but had in the past been a promoter of men wearing skirts. Other skirt pictures of West were still available at the time of writing. Rival rapper Lord Jamar wrote an unflattering take on West and skirts with an online track called 'Lift Up Your Skirt'.

Bare start to career

Guitar ace Carlos Santana got his first work in the strip clubs of Tijuana in Mexico in the early 1960s, playing sets in between the strippers' acts.

Too religious for Aunty

The BBC banned Don Cornell's 'Hold My Hand' from the radio because of its religious content. It sold a million copies in the UK and shot to number one in the singles charts.

Feet feat

Adoring fans have thrown themselves at the feet of Jon Bon Jovi over the decades but he started at their feet in 1982, working part-time in a women's shoe shop.

Fan ban

Former members of the British band the Smiths have tried to get rid of a VIP fan – British Prime Minister David Cameron. Guitarist Johnny Marr, a former member of the anti-establishment Mancunian band, said he was ashamed to have a Conservative in his 40s as a fan. He added: "He shouldn't like us; we're not his kind of people." The Smiths broke up in 1987 but in 2013 Cameron maintained he loved their music and planned to continue listening.

Eternal kisses

The temple-style memorial of heavy metal guitarist Randy Rhoads at San Bernardino, California has been covered in lipstick kisses by fans.

Unable to face the bald truth

In the late 1960s record producer Phil Spector kept his house dark because he did not want anyone to see his balding head. He was in his early 30s at the time.

Gaga's ga-ga superstition

Lady Gaga once admitted she felt she would be punished if she had a loveless one-night stand. She was quoted as saying: "I have this weird thing that if I sleep with someone they're going to take my creativity from me through my vagina."

Nasty to the Lady Gaga

She may be one of the world's most popular music performers, but Lady Gaga once had the childhood nickname of 'Germ'.

Allergy alert

Singer Gareth Gates, who was runner-up in the first British *Pop Idol* series in 2002, was allergic to cheese, coffee and oranges.

New wave, new word

British band the Vapors had record buyers reaching for their dictionaries when their hit single of 1980 'Turning Japanese' was described as "onanistic". The dictionary told them what they wanted to know – it's about masturbation.

Handy lyrics

Songwriters seemed to slip masturbation-themed songs past a very naïve record-buying public in the 1950s. Rockers Johnny Otis and Gene Vincent had hits with 'Willie and the Hand Jive' and 'Who Slapped John' respectively, seemingly without the public reading any sexual connotations into them.

Single-minded

American singer Don Cornell's 1952 hit 'I' was the UK's only single-letter titled pop chart entry until Xzibit's 'X' in 2000.

Ringing the changes

Rapper 50 Cent widened his business interests when he won a licence to be a boxing promoter in the state of New York in 2012.

Wrong name?

Given the mayhem that Mötley Crüe have created in their rock career, they were originally going to be called the comparatively gentle name of White Horse – until somebody pointed out Tommy Lee and co. were "a motley looking crew."

Impressing Presley

Elvis Presley was said to have climbed a high wall to get into the hotel room of a woman he fancied in the 1950s. He had the added incentive of overcoming the obstacle because stripper Tempest Storm had breasts said to be insured for $1 million.

Fresh start

Coldplay frontman Chris Martin has the pre-concert ritual of always brushing his teeth before he takes the stage.

Glitter fades

A cruise operator took 16 years to remove paedophile pop singer Gary Glitter's recordings from its ships' playlist. Glitter was arrested for his first child-sex offence in 1997; Thomson Holidays removed his songs in 2013.

City ban

Problems on their first tour got the heavy metal band Mötley Crüe barred from the Canadian city of Edmonton, Alberta.

Speedy name

The name of hard rock band Motörhead is a reference to amphetamine users.

Band tribute

One of Iggy Pop's first bands will always be remembered because it was in honour of the now-defunct Iguanas that Iggy, real name James Osterberg, took his enduring stage name.

Going with the Flow

Los Angeles band Tony Flow and the Miraculously Majestic Masters of Mayhem needed a change of name to hit the big time. They became the Red Hot Chilli Peppers.

Sexy Brown

R&B and hip-hop artist Bobby Brown's raunchy stage act often got him into trouble with the law as he was several times arrested for lewd and lascivious content after simulating sex acts on stage with random female audience members.

Janis checks out

Raw-voiced blues singer Janis Joplin was found dead in a Los Angeles hotel room in October 1970 – just 16 days after Jimi Hendrix and at the same age of 27. Joplin's death was attributed to a heroin overdose combined with the effects of alcohol.

Artists turn on art

Acid house duo KLF used profits from their recordings to subvert the art world and in the 1990s staged an award for the worst artist of the year.

Casting off the past

Mötley Crüe's Nikki Sixx said he legally changed his name from Frank Carlton Serafino Feranna Jr because he wanted to get all traces of his errant father out of his life for ever.

Dogg on the run

Snoop Dogg was not going to miss a prestigious TV appearance – even when he was on the run from the police. Cops were rushing to the Universal Amphitheatre as rapper Snoop, a suspect in a murder inquiry, presented an MTV award but he slipped away before they arrived. He handed himself in at a police station a few hours later.

U2 togetherness

Unique amid a rock world of ever-changing line-ups is Irish band U2. The Edge, Bono, Larry Mullen Jnr and Adam Clayton have been together since 1976 and they were all at school together.

US ban

Folk rocker Donovan Leitch found his chances of competing with Bob Dylan on his home turf stalled because of drug charges in the UK. He was refused entry to America until late 1967 and had to drop out of the all-star bill at the Monterey festival.

Rapper death

D12 rap group member Proof was shot and killed during a heated argument over a game of pool at a nightclub in Detroit in 2006. Another man who was shot in the row died a week later.

Mother – in law

Rapper and producer Eminem was sued in 1999 by his own mother. Deborah Mathers-Briggs alleged her son had slandered her in the lyrics of *The Slim Shady LP*. From a claim for $10 million she was awarded about $1,600.

Shocking for Lou

At the age of just 14 Lou Reed, later of the Velvet Underground, underwent electroconvulsive treatment meant to cure him of his bisexuality. He wrote about the horrific experience in his 1974 song 'Kill Your Sons'.

Drug death

But for unusually potent heroin, blues singer Janis Joplin may not have died of an overdose. Several of her dealer's other customers also overdosed that fatal week in October 1970.

Escape plan

It was revealed that if Michael Jackson had been convicted of child abuse offences in 2003 he would have gone on the run. Plans were in place to whisk him to exile in Bahrain. He was acquitted but still went to live in the Gulf kingdom.

Richard mixes it

Little Richard gave up rock 'n' roll debauchery in 1957 to study theology and become a preacher. He was lured back in the 1960s but resumed his ministry again in 1977.

Front men in the background

Bands named after their members do not always take their name from the lead singer. Examples include: Van Halen, Manfred Mann, the Dave Clark Five and the Spencer Davis Group.

Viper attack

Australian singer Jason Donovan collapsed with a drug-induced seizure in the Los Angeles celebrity nightclub the Viper Room in 1995. Eerily it was in the same place that actor River Phoenix had died of a drug overdose two years before. Donovan, who had four British number-one hits, recovered but said he did not fully quit smoking joints and snorting cocaine until 2000 when he became a father.

Revenue men pursue John

His mansion and other effects had to be sold to pay off the British taxman after bass player John Entwistle died in 2002. Ironically Entwistle had worked for the Inland Revenue, as it was then called, in 1962–63 before he joined the Who. Entwistle died aged 57 from a cocaine-induced heart attack in a Las Vegas hotel room where he spent the night with a stripper.

Name taken

Alice Cooper, the solo artist, got his name from his first successful band, before that he was known as Vincent Furnier.

Weddings by the score

As a celebrity preacher, piano-abusing rock 'n' roller Little Richard was in demand to conduct weddings in the 1980s and 1990s. In 2006 he married 20 couples at once who had won the opportunity in a contest.

Wow take a bow

Annabella Lwin was a 14-year-old Saturday girl in a dry cleaner's shop in Liverpool when she was heard singing along to the radio and recruited to front British New Wave band Bow Wow Wow.

Bassey daughter murder fear

Big-voiced ballad singer Shirley Bassey left it almost 25 years to express her murder suspicions over her daughter's death. Samantha Bassey was found aged 21 floating in the River Avon in 1985 after an evening's drinking but her death was recorded as an accident. In a 2009 interview Welsh-born Dane Shirley of 'Goldfinger' and 'I Who have Nothing' hit fame said: "I never believed that [it was suicide]... If she'd jumped off the bridge, all her bones would have been broken. But there was not a bone broken. In fact, she did not have a mark on her. So if anything, I'm suspicious about her death. She didn't have any water in her lungs. If someone's drowning, they gasp, don't they?" As a result of her comments in 2009 a police inquiry was reopened.

Hoax 'kills' Dury

Boomtown Rat Bob Geldof, when he was a guest DJ on a British radio station in 1998, announced the death of fellow musician Ian Dury based on hoax information. Dury was dead within two years after a long fight with cancer.

Cobain's first death

Global news network CNN pronounced Nirvana frontman Kurt Cobain dead in Italy in March 1994 when he was in a drug overdose coma. However they only had weeks to wait to be right as Cobain committed suicide on 5 April that year.

Satire backfire

A mock obituary for Alice Cooper in the early-1970s British music magazine *Melody Maker* had fans believing it. So much so Cooper had to reassure them in a statement saying: "I'm alive, and drunk as usual."

Fats not blown away

Rock 'n' roll piano player Fats Domino was thought to have been a high-profile victim of the devastating Hurricane Katrina in 2005. After the storm, "RIP Fats. You will be missed" was spray painted on his New Orleans home and featured widely in the media. But Fats turned up alive and well, having been rescued by the US Coastguard and taken to safety in Baton Rouge.

Miley still smiling

Web-savvy fiends have twice 'killed' Miley Cyrus online in 2008. In September the *Hannah Montana* star was first reported dead in a false Reuters news report that said she had been in a fatal car accident. Miley performed a concert a day later but in November hackers got into the singer/actress' YouTube account and announced she had been killed by a drunk driver. It was also untrue.

Premature obituary for Houston

Whitney Houston was wrongly reported as dead just a day after the 9/11 destruction of the World Trade Center. On 12 September 2001 she was rumoured dead from a drug overdose but in fact she died in 2012 and, although cocaine use contributed to her death, it was attributed to drowning in a bath.

Led Sandy

The late Sandy Denny was the only guest vocalist ever to appear on a Led Zeppelin studio album. She dueted with Zeppelin frontman Robert Plant on the track 'The Battle for Evermore' on 1971's Led Zeppelin IV. Denny died after a fall in 1978.

Bad news leak

A mystery leak from its online archives had Madonna proclaimed dead by a BBC News video uploaded on YouTube in September 2010.

Internet resurrection

An internet hoax 'killed' guitarist and singer John Cougar Mellencamp in 2012. At the time of writing he was alive and still playing aged 61.

Technical hitch

In a technical error a draft obituary of rock star Ozzy Osbourne's wife Sharon was accidentally published on the ABC News website in the USA in 2004.

Funny 'death' for Dave

Folk musician Dave Swarbrick saw the funny side of being declared dead in 1999 by British newspaper the *Daily Telegraph*. The Fairport Convention violinist had in fact been suffering from a chest infection at the time of the mistake but he quipped: "It's not the first time I have died in Coventry [England]."

Insane visit

California punk band the Cramps were, incredibly, allowed to hold a live concert at a mental hospital in 1978. The band, led by singer Lux Interior and guitarist Poison Ivy, played in the chronic ward of the California State Mental Hospital and the inmates' various – and often overt – reactions were recorded on video.

Kanye alive

Rapper Kanye was the subject of an Internet hoax news report in October 2009 alleging he had been killed in a car crash. It spread like wildfire through all the social networking channels and prompted West's then-girlfriend Amber Rose to quash the rumour by tweeting: "This 'RIP Kanye West' topic is not funny and it's NOT TRUE!"

Sick joke for Kurt fans

After the Nirvana frontman's suicide, sick jokers announced in 1989 they were opening a "Church of Kurt Cobain" in Portland, Oregon. Hundreds of potential followers turned up before they realized they had been duped.

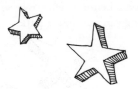

John Lennon crimewave

A spate of crime in 2013 in the Brazilian city of Belo Horizonte revealed how huge the Beatles were in South America in their heyday. It seems thousands of women called their sons after John Lennon. Police caught John Lennon Ribeiro Siqueira on suspicion of robbery; John Lennon Fonseca Ferreira for burglary; and John Lennon Gomes on suspicion of five murders. At the same time the body of John Lennon Sebastiao da Silva was found in a car, apparently the victim of a revenge killing.

Naked truth

The Red Hot Chilli Peppers became almost as famous for their "socks on cocks" pictures as their music. The California band have posed many times naked with just socks hiding their manhoods. It started in 1983 for the cover of their *Abbey Road E.P.* where they mimicked the Beatles on the famous London zebra crossing, only the Chillis were naked with socks preserving their modesty. They have also done the routine many times while performing on stage.

Tulisa humiliation

Hip-hop artist Tulisa Contostavlos found her sex life revealed to the world in 2012. A sex tape of the former N-Dubz singer-songwriter was seen by almost a million on-line viewers before a court injunction stopped it. Tulisa's ex-boyfriend Justin Edwards later admitted responsibility and apologized for the leak of the video.

John's field for ever

Part of New York's Central Park was named Strawberry Fields in memory of John Lennon, who was shot in 1980 outside his apartment building yards from the park.

Being nice to mic

American singer-songwriter Stevie Nicks liked to feel at home when she was performing live. Over the years she decorated her microphone stand with small stuffed toys, scarves, ribbons, chiffon and beads.

Fast friend

Former Velvet Revolver guitarist Slash's real name was Saul Hudson but his nickname was given to him by a friend's father because the young Saul was always on the move.

Honey of a hit

The Honeycombs were the first band to reach the top of the UK charts with a female drummer. Honey Lantree pounded out the beat on 'Have I the Right' in 1964.

Jury is out on the Dolls

American record buyers couldn't make up their minds about the New York Dolls when they first burst on the proto-punk scene. A 1973 *Creem* magazine poll voted them the best, and worst, new group and a reviewer likened their guitar work to the "sound of lawnmowers".

Alive and kicking

In August 2012 US broadcaster NBC announced the death of Neil Young. But the Canadian singer-songwriter was alive and kicking. Astronaut and the first man on the moon Neil ARMSTRONG wasn't.

The talented need not apply

Accomplished guitarist Steve New was rejected by the Sex Pistols because he was technically too good. The Pistols had auditioned him with a view to replacing the less-talented Steve Jones but as the signature raw sound of the band developed it was decided New's adept technical lead guitar work was not required.

Heaven and earth

British band Procol Harum have been remembered high and low. In space an asteroid is named after the creators of 'A Whiter Shade of Pale' and on earth an orchid bears the band name.

Pistols under fire

After fights and damage to other bands' equipment during their early gigs, the Sex Pistols had earned their bad boys reputation – and a ban from several London venues.

Family shocker

Singer Bobby Darin, who found chart success in the late 1950s–early 1960s, was 32 before he discovered the 'parents' who brought him up in New York's Bronx were actually his grandparents and his older 'sister' was really his mother. The shock discovery in 1968 sent him into a period of self-imposed seclusion.

Julian gets the sack

Singer Julian Cope is said to have worn a potato sack for the recording of the Teardop Explodes' final album *Wilder* in 1981.

Mack the surprise

Artists have often been wrong about the prospects of songs they record and Bobby Darin was right off beam in his dislike for 'Mack the Knife' as a single. The 1960 song went to number one in the US, sold two million copies and won the Record of the Year Grammy.

Ooh my song

More than 15 years after the rocker's death Ritchie Valens' estate sued Led Zeppelin. In 1975 Robert Plant et al. released 'Boogie With Stu' on the album *Physical Graffiti* which was heavily based on Valens' 'Ooh, My Head'. Valens' publisher, Kemo Music, filed for copyright infringement and an out-of-court settlement was reached with Ritchie's mother's name added to the credits.

Seeger shocker?

It was reported that backstage there was equal drama to the 1965 Newport Festival when Bob Dylan supposedly upset fans by going 'electric' for the first time. It was reported that folk singer and accoustic purist Pete Seeger was dashing around backstage looking for a way to cut off Dylan's 'heresy'.

Tarnished Glitter

Gary Glitter's glam rock career hit the skids in 1999 when he was jailed for four months for having pornographic images of children on his laptop. The singer, real name Paul Gadd, who had three UK number ones amid his 26 1970–80's chart singles, was also placed on the UK's sex offenders' register. Sales of his recordings collapsed and his part in a Spice Girls' film was cut.

Work mates only

Despite 50 years in each other's company Pete Townshend once made it clear that he and leader singer Roger Daltrey were not buddies. He said in a 2010 interview: "Roger is my partner in the Who. He is not my partner in anything else. We love each other but we are not regular social buddies." In the past Townshend had claimed Daltrey hit him so hard in 1973 during a fight over the recording of the *Quadrophenia* album that he lost his memory for two days.

North Korea goes wacko

Nuclear-mad North Korea used a Michael Jackson peace anthem to promote its hatred for the United States. To the background of Jackson's 1985 number one 'We are the World' communist North Korea's 2013 propaganda film, posted on a government website, depicted a boy dreaming of a long-range attack on the USA with images of skyscrapers being blitzed. North Korea had recently angered the world with an underground nuclear test.

Marriott fire death

A fireman and music fan was shocked when he found the dead body of a pop star in a blazing bedroom – for it was his idol Steve Marriott. The former Small Faces and Humble Pie singer and guitarist died in his blazing thatched cottage in April 1991, yet he should not have even been there. After a flight from a recording stint in the USA he was staying at a friend's home but at some point during the night he took a taxi to his own home in Essex, England where he perished in the blaze. Marriott, 44, who had been drinking heavily and had argued with his wife, also had cocaine and Valium in his body but death was ruled as accidental due to smoke inhalation.

A mother of a diet

Singer Mama Cass Elliot lost a third of her body weight on a six-month-long crash diet before a lucrative Las Vegas run of shows at Caesar's Palace Las Vegas in 1969. She shed 100lbs (45kg) of her 300lbs (135kg).

Mario's deadly addictions

Cross-over artist Mario Lanza loved his food and his drink to the extent that it damaged his health. Tenor Lanza, whose breadth of vocal appeal spanned opera to popular ballads, let his addictions of overeating and drinking seriously affect his health and his relationships with directors, producers and other performers. He died in 1959 from a pulmonary embolism (blood clot) at the height of his appeal and aged only 38.

Passing up a golden chance

British band leader Ted Heath told an auditioning 16-year-old girl that she had a good voice but she was too young and should go home and return in four years. That girl was Alma Cogan, who made her way without big-band exposure to become Britain's highest-paid entertainer of her era. In the 1950–60s Alma had UK chart hits with 'Sugartime' and 'Bell Bottom Blues' but died in 1966 aged only 34 from cancer. Heath said later that rejecting Alma was "the biggest mistake of my life".

Swinging Frank

Frank Sinatra knew how to make a song swing – and his politics swung, too. After campaigning on behalf of two Democrat US Presidents, Franklin D. Roosevelt in 1944 and John Kennedy in 1960, he later switched his allegiances to Republicans Richard Nixon and Ronald Reagan. The reason for the switch was said to be a snub by Kennedy who, although they were friends, refused to visit Sinatra because of his alleged Chicago Mafia connections.

Death ends comeback bid

Johnny Kidd was on the verge of a comeback in 1966 when he was killed in a car crash in Lancashire, England. As Johnny Kidd and the Pirates a new line-up of musicians was about to go on the road to revive the hits from earlier days such as 'Shakin' All Over' and 'I'll Never Get Over You'.

Rapper rapped

Rapper Akon ran into controversy for an on-stage act which included simulated sex with a 15-year-old girl at a club in Trinidad and Tobago. It was filmed and uploaded to the Internet in 2007 and caused a wave of criticism. As a result phone company Verizon Wireless removed Akon's big-selling ringtones from its site and decided against sponsoring a forthcoming tour on which Akon was the opening act.

Marble-ous shrine

French singer-songwriter Serge Gainsbourg's home was kept as it was the day he died in 1991. The Paris house was covered in graffiti from an adoring public but the interior of black and white marble with art works and sculptures remained a shrine to his talent.

Fightback to award win

A folk singer who once lay in a coma for weeks fought back to be crowned Britain's best in 2013. Nic Jones, whose arrangements have been covered by Bob Dylan, had to be 'rebuilt' after a car crash in 1982. Apart from brain, eye and ear damage Nic, who was known for his progressive open tunings on the guitar, broke wrists, elbows and arms. His determination was hailed as he won the BBC Radio 2 Folk Singer of the Year award.

Too sexy Roxy

American record retailers 'dressed up' British art rock band Roxy Music's album *Country Life* before they would display it. The cover of the band's fourth album was deemed too sexual as it pictured two models, actually a couple of German Roxy Music fans, posed in a forest wearing semi-transparent lingerie. Record shops in many areas of the USA put the album in opaque plastic covers.

Damp reception

The then British deputy Prime Minister had iced water poured over him at the 1998 televised Brit Awards. Anarcho-pop British band Chumbawamba's Danbert Nobacon had a bucket of the stuff ready for New Labour's John Prescott.

Animals turn on each other

More than 40 years after the band carved an enduring niche in pop history the ownership of the name was being fought over. Original Animals' drummer John Steel was said to have owned the Animals' name in England, by virtue of a trademark registration he had made. Lead singer, and arguably the best-known face of the Animals, Eric Burdon, objected in 2008 claiming he personally embodied any goodwill associated with the band name. Burdon's argument was rejected partly because he had billed himself as 'Eric Burdon and the Animals' in 1967, thus separating the goodwill associated with his own name from that of the band, which had enjoyed massive UK and American popularity with 'House of the Rising Sun' and 'Don't Let Me Be Misunderstood' in the mid-1960s.

Coming out of the Shadows

An ice cream salesman who had never written a song in his life came up with a hit band and chart song in a weekend. In 1964 Shadow Morton bluffed his way into being given the chance to write song lyrics, but he did more than that. Sitting on a Long Island beach, he came up with the words to 'Remember, Walking in the Sand' and in a weekend he had found girl covers band the Shangri-Las, a studio and a good enough demo disc to convince the Red Bird label he had a hit. He was right – 'Remember (Walking in the Sand)' went on to multi-million international sales. The Shangri-Las, again with Morton, scored big with 'Leader of the Pack' soon after.

Comical Kiss

The bizarre on-stage make-up of hard rockers Kiss depicts comic book characters. Rhythm guitarist Paul Stanley is Starchild, front man Gene Simmons the Demon, lead guitarist Ace Frehley the Spaceman or Space Ace and drummer Peter Criss Catman. Simmons attributes the make-up designs to fans.

Biking horror kills Duane

Tragedy struck twice to cut short the success of the Allman Brothers Band and eerily motorbikes featured in both cases. In 1971 innovative guitarist Duane Allman died horrifically in Macon, Georgia. His bike struck a truck but, although Duane was thrown off, the bike landed on him and he travelled more than 25 metres along the road trapped under it. He died in hospital aged 24 from massive internal injuries. Three blocks away from that crash scene in 1972, and also aged 24, bass guitarist and another band founder Berry Oakley crashed his motorcycle into a bus. Declaring that he was OK after hitting his head, he was taken home but hours later he died from cerebral swelling caused by a skull fracture sustained in the crash.

Man-to-man chat

Kanye West personally settled a legal wrangle with ace stuntman Evel Knievel who sued the rapper for alleged trademark infringement in West's video 'Touch the Sky'. Knievel took issue with West taking on the persona of 'Evel Kanyevel' who attempts flying a rocket over a canyon. In 2006 Knievel also claimed the "vulgar and offensive" images depicted in the video damaged his reputation. Just days before Evel's death in November 2007, he amicably settled the suit following a visit from West. Knievel was quoted as saying: "I thought Kanye was a wonderful guy and quite a gentleman."

Name game

Schoolbook doodlings came to be the name of one of the biggest-selling rock bands in the world. The band was about to become the Hookers at a name brainstorming session in Boston, Massachusetts when drummer Joey Kramer said he used to write the word 'aerosmith' all over his notebooks. To mystified band mates such as lead singer Steve Tyler he explained the name had popped into his head after seeing the jacket art of a circus performer jumping out of a biplane on Harry Nilsson's album *Aerial Ballet*.

Rodriguez reappears

More than 20 years passed between bouts of success for folk artist Rodriguez. A hiatus in his career saw him live on the poverty line for decades before an unexpected comeback. He disappeared so far off the musical radar that many fans believed he was dead. After two poor-selling albums in 1970 he did years of manual labour in his native Detroit in the USA but all the time he was developing a following in South Africa of which he was unaware. Only after a few dedicated fans tracked him down in the 1990s to prove he hadn't, as rumoured, committed suicide did his career take off again. By 2013 he had written 30 new songs and new recording deals were in the offing.

Hairy moment

When Texas rockers ZZ Top met up again in 1978 after a two-year hiatus from performing two of them – guitarist Billy Gibbons and bass player Dusty Hill – were sporting chest-length beards. The only non-bearded member of the blues trio was the inappropriately named drummer Frank Beard. The look stuck as the band soared to the peak of their success in the 1980s and 1990s with best-selling albums such as *Eliminator* and *Afterburner*.

Water tragedies

Water proved a too-frequent cause of tragedy for piano rocker Jerry Lee Lewis. His fourth marriage to Jaren Pate ended in tragedy in 1982 when she drowned in a swimming pool at the home of a friend, just weeks before divorce proceedings would have been finalized. Twenty years earlier his son from an earlier marriage, Steve Allen Lewis, drowned in a swimming pool aged just three.

Like a rock

Kid Rock and Creed frontman Scott Stapp went to court to stop their private sexual moments going global on the Internet in 2006. A sex tape from 1999 in which the two were allegedly seen receiving oral sex from groupies was uncovered. A California-based pornography company planned to release the video in 2006, but both Rock and Stapp went to court successfully to stop distribution.

Electronic shocker

Electronic musician, singer and songwriter Skrillex, birth name Sonny Moore, was wrongly reported as dead from a cocaine overdose in 2012. He continues to perform.

Nowhere to hide for Gary

Following his conviction for child sex offences in the UK British glam rocker Gary Glitter fled on his yacht to Spain. Upon being discovered there he found the world was not big enough to escape the media frenzy that surrounded the pervert. He set sail again to Gibraltar, Cuba, Mexico, South Africa, Zimbabwe, Colombia, Portugal, Brazil, Venezuela, and Thailand, before settling in Cambodia. Even from there he was deported to Vietnam under suspicion of child sex abuse.

Arguments in song

A strange phenomenon developed in pop music where artists jousted in song. The practice of answer songs started in the 1950s with the reply usually having the same tune but different lyrics. Examples include Jim Reeves emotional hit of 'He'll have to Go' countered by Skeeter Davis' 'He'll Have to Stay' and Big Mama Thornton's pre-Elvis version of 'Hound Dog' responded to by Rufus Thomas with 'Bear Cat'.

Anthrax name problem

Having the name of a fatal disease was good for heavy metal rockers Anthrax until 2001. The 9/11 World Trade Center terrorist attack was followed by a massive scare in the USA when anthrax spores sent by post extended the terror campaign and people started surfing the web about anthrax the disease and not Anthrax the band. The band ran into a public relations nightmare and included information about the disease on its own website. This was followed by media stories claiming the band was going to change its name. It was jokingly suggested in a band press release that they might change their name to something more cuddly such as 'Basketful of Puppies' but at a November 2001 9/11 benefit gig Anthrax took the stage wearing boiler suits spelling out: "We're not changing our name."

Brotherly love

New Wave singer Boy George's drug addiction was laid bare in front of millions of TV viewers in the mid-1980s. Fearing for George's life his younger brother David O'Dowd made an appearance on UK national television to highlight George's cocaine and heroin habit, which George had been publicly denying. In 1986, Boy George was arrested for heroin possession but despite his brother's impassioned plea to seek help it was some years before George, the former lead singer of British band Culture Club, declared himself clean of drugs in 2009.

Boxed beat

Michael Clarke joined the Byrds as a drummer in 1964 and did not even own a kit. Lacking experience other than playing congas semi-professionally around California, Clarke initially had to play on a makeshift set-up comprising cardboard boxes and a tambourine. But the folk-rock band went on to huge mid-1960s success with 'Mr Tambourine Man', 'Eight Miles High' and 'Turn, Turn, Turn'.

Sensible blah talking

British alternative pop singer Captain Sensible formed a political party in 2006. The former member of punk band the Damned created the Blah! Party saying: "We want the Blah! Party to be the party of protest; a channel through which the people of the UK can vent their dissatisfaction at nonsensical everyday things, and protest against the government and the current crop of political parties."

Got to get out of this place

Singer Ronny Spector escaped from prison by walking through a closed and locked glass door. But this was not a jailbreak but a final bid for freedom from her marriage to record producer Phil. Despite slashed feet she kept walking away from a domineering husband who kept the former Ronette of 'Be My Baby' fame a virtual prisoner in their Hollywood mansion. The couple were married from 1968 to 1974.

Unearthly interests

Former Troggs leader Reg Presley always had an interest in the unknown. When his own 1960's hit 'Love is All Around' was covered by Wet, Wet, Wet in 1994 he used the royalties bonanza to fund research into crop circles, alien spacecraft and lost civilizations. He died from lung cancer and a series of strokes in 2013.

Fired by inspiration

In music one man's despair can be another's inspiration and so it was for Deep Purple's Ian Gillan. As British heavy metal band Deep Purple were recording at a château overlooking Lake Geneva, Switzerland in 1971, the session was interrupted by the sight of the Montreux Casino concert hall burning down. Fascinated by the sight across the lake, Gillan, Deep Purple's songwriter, was inspired to pen the now legendary 'Smoke on the Water' while American Frank Zappa and his band the Mothers of Invention were running for their lives from the flames which devoured all their equipment.

Savile's angry

British DJ Jimmy Savile did not see the funny side when a "joke" announcement of his death was aired by a fellow broadcaster. Savile took legal advice in 1994 over Chris Morris' joke on BBC Radio 1. Savile died in 2011 before revelations of his decades of being a sex predator came to light.

Tour slump

After the notorious obscene language interview on BBC TV in 1976 only seven of the Sex Pistols' following 20 tour gigs took place.

Kris crossing the skies

Country singer Kris Kristofferson knew the highs and lows of trying to make a music career. He was trained as a helicopter pilot in the US Army where he reached the rank of captain and he needed those flying skills later when he tried to make a living in music. In the 1960s he would earn enough working as a chopper pilot for a petroleum company to allow him time to spend a week in Nashville, Tennessee trying to pitch the songs he had written to the established country stars of the time. Roger Miller, Jerry Lee Lewis and Ray Stevens were among the first to record Kristofferson compositions.

Following the Followills

Kings of Leon brothers Caleb, Jared and Nathan Followill spent much of their childhoods in a car criss-crossing the Deep South of America. Their father Ivan was a travelling preacher so the boys saw the southern United States through the windows of a purple 1988 Oldsmobile car, camping for a week or two wherever Ivan was scheduled to preach.

Jones is a knock-out guest

Singer Grace Jones slapped a British TV chat show host as millions of viewers watched aghast. *The Russell Harty Show* was high in the TV rankings in 1981 and rocketed even higher when Jamaican-born Jones hit Harty across the face after the presenter turned his back on her to speak to the other guests on the programme. Jones claimed she was furious at being ignored.

Doctor phobia kills Zevon

By the time he consulted a doctor rock singer and songwriter Warren Zevon was condemned to death. The artist, known for the dark and bizarre sense of humour in songs such 'Werewolves Of London', had a lifelong phobia of doctors and things medical. So by the time he was diagnosed with a cancer associated with asbestos exposure it was untreatable. He died aged 56 in September 2003.

Randy upsets them

Singer-songwriter Randy Newman's single 'Short People' upset more than a few people because it was thought it was taking the rise out of the vertically challenged. In fact it was a satire on the many prejudices in the world and the persecution of people who are short. It wasn't a personal plea because Newman himself was 6ft (1.83m).

Ronson remembered

One of David Bowie's Spiders from Mars band members has been remembered in a street name in Hull in England. One of the most sought-after session guitarists of the 1970s and 1980s, Mick Ronson is remembered on a housing estate close to where he was brought up. He died aged 46 of liver cancer in 1993.

Party snub

Grammy-winning banjo player Winston Marshall was barred from his record label's own party in 2013. Set to celebrate the award with fellow Mumford & Sons band members, he turned up for the Universal Records' after-party and was not allowed in. It seems the doormen didn't recognize him in jeans, hoodie and bobble hat and without a ticket.

Smiths feud on

Nine years after the demise of the Smiths the band members were still at war. Often gelling musically but not personally, the Smiths self-destructed in 1987 but in 1996, drummer Mike Joyce and bass player Andy Rourke took lead singer Morrissey and guitarist Johnny Marr to court, claiming they had not received fair shares of recording and performance royalties. The High Court and the Court of Appeal both found in favour of Joyce and ordered he be paid over £1 million in back pay and receive 25 per cent thereafter. As the Smiths' royalties had been frozen for two years because of the dispute, Rourke settled for a smaller lump sum to pay off his debts and continued to receive 10 per cent. A judge described Morrissey as "devious, truculent and unreliable". Morrissey, who had fallen out with Marr before the band split said: "The Smiths were a beautiful thing and Johnny [Marr] left it, and Mike [Joyce] has destroyed it." He appealed against the verdict, but was not successful.

Email error

Numerous news outlets reported the drug death of singer Lou Reed in 2001. A hoax email announcing the 'tragedy' purported to come from news organization Reuters.

Nice to meet you

Texas rockers ZZ Top were said to have beefed up their act in the late 1970s by adding a Texas longhorn to their line-up. At a concert in their home state, the band is said to have rocked on with the animal on stage. Strangely, though, none of the audience of several thousand that day appeared to have taken a photograph to immortalize one of the more bizarre rock 'n' roll events.

Slippery character

Snake stories have defined Alice Cooper's rock career. A genuine snake lover, Cooper used them as stage props for many years. One of his originals, Chichita, escaped down a lavatory so he replaced it with a four times larger, 45lb (20kg), boa constrictor named Yvonne. One of Cooper's other boa constrictors, named Kachina, was said to have died from the bite of a rat that was supposed to have been the serpent's lunch.

Family affair

Wolfgang Van Halen made an early start in the heavy rock business. He was just 15 when he replaced bassist Michael Anthony in Van Halen. It made the rock band a truly family affair because Wolf's father was its guitarist Eddie Van Halen and the drummer his uncle Alex.

Fergie's drug and sex confessions

American singer Fergie has been very candid about her wild teen experiences before she joined hit makers the Black Eyed Peas. In a 2007 interview she admitted going on a sex and drugs spree when she turned 18, saying: "I have had lesbian experiences. I won't say how many men I've had sex with – but I am a very sexual person."

Nilsson robbed

Harry Nilsson was bankrupt at the time of his death in 1994. The singer-songwriter's business manager had stolen all his hard-earned fortune running into millions of dollars, yet was only jailed for three years.

Insane for Roky

Roky Erickson, whose lyrics with band 13th Floor Elevators had advocated drug use and brought him to the attention of police in Texas, was arrested in 1969 for possession of a single cannabis joint. Facing a possible 10 years in jail, Erickson pleaded not guilty to an Austin court by reason of insanity and was sent to a state hospital. After several escapes, he was sent to the Rusk State Hospital for the Criminally Insane, where he was subjected to more forced electroconvulsive treatment and thorazine and was not released until 1972.

Song ban

Conversion to Christianity led Megadeth leader Dave Mustaine to announce he would not play certain songs live.

Posh spots

Ex-Spice Girl and footballer WAG Victoria Beckham had the cruel childhood nickname of 'Acne Face'.

B-b-banned by the B-B-BBC

The Who's 1965 anthem of youth 'My Generation' was initially banned from TV and radio. BBC executives felt that lines such "People try to put us d-down" and "Just because we g-g-get around" would offend people with a stutter or speech impediment. The corporation eventually gave in to the record-buying public and the song, written by guitarist Pete Townshend, went to number two in the UK charts and peaked at 74 in the USA.

Song bashed

The Rolling Stones' 'Street Fighting Man' was banned in the USA out of fear that it would incite violence during the National Democratic Convention in Chicago in 1968.

'Colonel' Tom was a deserter

Elvis Presley's manager Tom Parker was a deserter from the US Army during the 1930s. He was caught and punished with a period of solitary confinement that left him psychotic and discharged from his artillery unit on mental health grounds. After finding success with Presley, Parker became known as just 'The Colonel', but whether he deserved the rank is debatable as he was only styled Colonel in the Louisiana State Militia by the state governor – as thanks for his help in a re-election campaign.

Bob's tangled love life

Bob Marley is credited with having 11 children, three with his wife Rita, several by other women and two he adopted. One of the 11 was said to be the daughter resulting from Rita's affair with another man but nonetheless she was acknowledged as Bob's daughter.

Wing and a prayer

Siouxsie and the Banshees were just an untried duo of Siouxsie Sioux and friend Stephen Severin at a festival in 1976. They stepped in when a band pulled out of the Sex Pistols-organized event in London and improvised a 20-minute set based on the Lord's Prayer.

No love for song

American all-girl group The Shirelles 1960s hit 'Will You Love Me Tomorrow?' was too sexually charged for some radio station in the US.

One Count of murder

The leader of the Black Metal music movement in Norway, Varg Vikernes, was jailed in 1994 for murdering a rival. Vikernes, also known as Count Grishnach, was sentenced to 21 years after stabbing Mayhem guitarist Oystein Euronymous Aarseth and being convicted of the arson of three churches. The follower of far-right politics was paroled in 2009 despite absconding from a low-security prison in 2003 and recaptured in possession of guns, knives and other military gear.

Meek shotgun rampage

Depression and mental illness finally got the better of record producer Joe Meek in 1967. At the age of 37 he killed his landlady in her London home before turning the shotgun on himself.

Bessie killed

Blues singer Bessie Smith died aged 43 after receiving horrific injuries in a road accident. She was a passenger in a car which hit a lorry near Clarksdale, Mississippi in 1937 and suffered severe crush injuries with an arm severed at the elbow. She died next day. To make matters worse another car ploughed through the accident scene, narrowly missing Smith as a doctor treated her at the roadside.

Bowie robbed

David Bowie was robbed of being a chart topper at the grand old age of 66. His 2013 single release 'Where are We Now?' went straight to number one in the iTunes downloads chart but because, as well, it was being given away to fans who bought his new album *The Next Day* chart bureaucrats said it would not count in the singles charts. It was Bowie's first new release for 10 years.

Near miss

Geri Halliwell might not have been in the Spice Girls but for belatedly seeing a newspaper advertisement. In 1994 she had seen the original ad but went skiing and missed the audition because her face got sunburnt. However she came across the ad again two months later and applied in time for second auditions and sailed through final selection to become 'Ginger Spice'.

Sour joke

DJs from a Texas radio station were fired and their employers sued in 2001 after announcing, as a 'joke', that Britney Spears and her then-boyfriend Justin Timberlake had died in a car crash.

Mac attack

Personal chaos reigned when Fleetwood Mac's song 'Rhiannon' went platinum in 1976 as all the band's relationships collapsed simultaneously. Drummer Mick Fleetwood split from his wife Jenny and John and Christine McVie, both long-term band members, parted. At the same time new recruits from America Lindsay Buckingham and Stevie Nicks, who had come in on Mac's seventh album *Fleetwood Mac*, ended their personal relationship. However musically the band was still to reach its zenith,with their *Rumours* album selling over 40 million copies worldwide.

Gaga's game

Lady Gaga's *Born This Way* was the first album to debut in a social networking game – 'Gagaville' on Facebook in 2011.

Disappointed Richard

Frustration at the inability of former Bob Dylan backing group the Band to gel is believed to have driven singer and multi-instrumentalist Richard Manuel to suicide. He was found hanging in his Florida hotel room in 1986 aged 42. Known to have struggled with alcohol and drug addiction, Manuel despaired at the Band's dissolution in the late 1970s and the re-formed line-up's inability to blend. A post-mortem revealed Manuel had been drinking heavily and taken cocaine on the day of his death.

High notes to a higher calling

The parishioners of the Anglican Church at Finedon, England had no problem in 2013 if their organist didn't turn up because they had a chart-topping multi-instrumental pop star as their vicar. The Reverend Richard Coles took holy orders after playing saxophone for 1980s band Bronski Beat and then charted at number one with Jimmy Somerville in the Communards.

Jumping Jack cash

Mick Jagger's jumpsuit from the Rolling Stones' 1972 American tour sold at auction for £20,000 ($32,075) in 2012. The flamboyant sequinned outfit, designed by Ossie Clark, was worn by the Stones frontman on the tour hailed as one of the greatest in the group's career.